ROUTLEDGE LIBRARY EDITIONS:
THE GOLD STANDARD

Volume 5

A CRITIQUE OF THE GOLD STANDARD

A CRITIQUE OF THE GOLD STANDARD

H. L. PUXLEY

Routledge
Taylor & Francis Group
LONDON AND NEW YORK

First published in 1933 by George Allen & Unwin Ltd

This edition first published in 2018
by Routledge
2 Park Square, Milton Park, Abingdon, Oxon OX14 4RN

and by Routledge
711 Third Avenue, New York, NY 10017

Routledge is an imprint of the Taylor & Francis Group, an informa business

British Library Cataloguing in Publication Data
A catalogue record for this book is available from the British Library

ISBN: 978-1-138-56184-7 (Set)
ISBN: 978-1-351-24702-3 (Set) (ebk)
ISBN: 978-0-8153-6627-0 (Volume 5) (hbk)
ISBN: 978-1-351-25896-8 (Volume 5) (ebk)

A CRITIQUE
of the
GOLD STANDARD

by

H. L. PUXLEY
B.A. (OXON), M.A. (YALE)

LONDON
GEORGE ALLEN & UNWIN LTD
MUSEUM STREET

FIRST PUBLISHED IN 1933

PRINTED IN GREAT BRITAIN BY
UNWIN BROTHERS LTD., WOKING

Preface

This book is the result of three years' work at Yale University. Its composition was only rendered possible by the Commonwealth Fund of New York City, through whose generosity I was enabled to give my whole time to research during this period. My debt of gratitude to the Fund, on this and other scores, is great indeed.

Professor J. H. Rogers of Yale University not only first encouraged me to embark upon writing this book, but also inspired the majority of the ideas expressed in it, though, needless to say, no direct responsibility must be imputed to him for anything that I have written. His never-failing capacity for finding time, in the midst of the great pressure of his own work, to discuss my difficulties with me, alone made it possible to eliminate many of the imperfections of the book. Undoubtedly, if I had never been privileged to "sit at his feet," this book could never have been written.

AGRA
July 1933

Contents

CHAPTER PAGE

I. THE ORTHODOX THEORY OF THE GOLD STANDARD 11

§ 1. Introductory; purpose of book
§ 2. Purpose of Gold Standard; stable foreign exchanges
§ 3. Reasons for confidence in perpetuation of Gold Standard (i) automatic self-distribution of gold
§ 4. (ii) Use of Bank rate;
§ 5. (iii) and of open-market operations
§ 6. The breakdown of the unregulated Gold Standard

II. GOLD MOVEMENTS AND THE PRICE-LEVEL 29

§ 1. Recent phenomena which modify orthodox gold-standard theory; (i) disappearance of gold from circulation
§ 2. (ii) Power of member banks to create credit *ex nihilo*
§ 3. Volume of currency no longer related to gold holdings
§ 4. Volume of currency is, however, related to member bank reserve balances; these may in turn be influenced by Central Bank policy
§ 5. Summary of chapter. Value of currency no longer related to gold holdings

III. CENTRAL BANK POLICIES AND THE QUANTITY OF MONEY 54

§ 1. Central Banks now determine total volume of currency, (i) as issuers of currency notes
§ 2. (ii) As keepers of member banks' reserve balances, volume of which may be affected by open-market operations
§ 3. New philosophy of Central Bank management; determination of credit policies in interest of internal stability in preference to steady foreign exchanges. Consequent divorce of gold flows from influence on volume of currency

CHAPTER PAGE

§ 4. In any case, changes in price-level due to inflow or outflow of gold may not be dispersed through unsheltered industries as well as sheltered

§ 5. Summary of chapter. Final destruction of automatic self-distribution of gold

IV. CENTRAL BANK POLICIES AND INTERNATIONAL CAPITAL MOVEMENTS 72

§ 1. Importance of exchange transactions on capital account to workings of Gold Standard

§ 2. Sane regulation of international lending may go far to restrain gold movements

§ 3. Recent phenomena which have disrupted normal international capital movements

§ 4. (i.) Breakdown of confidence in solvency of debtor countries

§ 5. (ii) Distrust and uncertainty of conditions in creditor countries themselves

§ 6. (iii) Non-commercial gold movements

§ 7. Summary. Bank rates have lost much of their influence over international capital movements

V. WAR DEBTS, REPARATIONS, AND TARIFFS 104

§ 1. War debts differ from pre-War international indebtedness (i) by being unproductive

§ 2. (ii) In that they were contracted by governments, not by individuals or corporations

§ 3. (iii) In that they are owed to inexperienced creditors, who take no steps to aid capital or interest repayments from overseas

§ 4. Debtor countries have been forced to redress balances by exporting gold

§ 5. To protect their gold reserves, debtor countries have resorted to new expedient of exchange control

§ 6. Summary. The endeavour to meet the "transfer problem" threatens to strangle international trade

CONTENTS

CHAPTER PAGE

VI. THE DILEMMA 136

§ 1. The case for abandonment of the international standard in favour of pursuit of internal stability

§ 2. Argument of champions of internal stability is divisible into three steps

§ 3. (i) Central Bank may control "interest rates." This ignores complex variety of interest rates, many of which are only remotely influenced by the Central Bank

§ 4. (ii) Interest rates determine volume of borrowings. This ignores factor of demand in the determination of volume of credit which will be raised

§ 5. (iii) Volume of currency determines the price-level. This under-emphasizes importance of velocity of circulation and other factors

§ 6. Positive disadvantages of the managed fiduciary standard

§ 7. Summary. An amended international gold standard the solution of the dilemma

VII. TOWARDS A WORKABLE GOLD STANDARD 167

§ 1. Necessity for international co-operation

§ 2. Legal gold requirements of Central Banks should be reduced by international agreement

§ 3. Further recommendations for economy in use of gold

§ 4. Co-ordination of credit policies of Central Banks for avoidance of gold movements

§ 5. For reinforcement of equipment of Central Banks in their pursuit of internal stability, (i) public works programmes should be added to their regular armoury

§ 6. (ii) Member bank reserve balances should be controlled by law

VIII. THE THREE EVIL GENII AGAIN 205

§ 1. Unanimity of aim may overcome political difficulties in way of international co-operation on problems of War debts, reparation, and tariffs

§ 2. The case for a reduction of tariffs. International barter the alternative

§ 3. The case for a scaling-down of War obligations

CHAPTER PAGE

IX. THE WORLD BANK 213

§ 1. The utility of a Central Bank of Central Banks
§ 2. Advantages of establishment of a World Bank. Pooling of gold reserves, obviation of gold movements, fixing of gold points
§ 3. Co-ordination of national credit policies (i) for stabilization of long-time value of the standard
§ 4. (ii) For dampening of short-time credit cycles
§ 5. Revival of international lending
§ 6. Conclusion

APPENDIX—A STATISTICAL EXAMINATION OF THE DEGREE TO WHICH CENTRAL BANKS MAY ACHIEVE INTERNAL STABILITY 235

§ 1. Value of statistical examination of history of Federal Reserve System
§ 2. Federal Reserve Banks' control of open-market short-term interest rates considerable; of customers' loan rates slight
§ 3. Central Banks' influence over long-term interest rates dependent on "bearishness" of public
§ 4. Volume of loans outstanding not completely responsive to height of interest rates
§ 5. Price-level only varies roughly with quantity of currency
§ 6. Summary. Possibility of Central Banks' attaining anything approaching stability remote

INDEX 267

A CRITIQUE OF THE GOLD STANDARD

CHAPTER I

THE ORTHODOX THEORY OF THE GOLD STANDARD

§ 1. Social institutions, like human beings, change as they grow older. John Smith, respected president of a society for the prevention of cruelty to animals, may be an entirely different character from Johnny Smith, the schoolboy who delighted in pulling the wings off flies, and may be accorded very different treatment by his contemporaries. Yet, because of the continuity of his life history, he will still be called John Smith, and friends who have grown up with him will regard him instinctively, if unintelligently, as the same individual whom they knew at the age of ten. Some of them, indeed, while making some adjustments in their attitude in accordance with his present respected status, will still be so obsessed with his essential sameness with past stages in the development of his character that they will mete out to him fundamentally the same treatment as they were wont to offer to Johnny Smith, the schoolboy.

So it is with many of the man-made institutions of Society. To the Constitution of the United States, drawn up to safeguard the rights of citizens of a nation of settlers and pioneers struggling with Nature in an unknown continent, amendments, official and unofficial, have been added to adapt it to the needs of a powerful and numerous people dwelling securely in a vast country of wellnigh limitless resources. Yet, in spite of these adaptations which have changed its character with changes in the situation of the country, citizens still speak of it as the same old Constitution. More curious still, they acquiesce in, or actively support, the persistence of certain of its anomalies, such as the existence of a single President, whose duty it is not only to keep his finger upon the activities of all State Departments but also to discharge the social functions which are elsewhere delegated to Kings or Presidents divorced from political life.

So it is also with the gold standard. Conditions have changed rapidly during the century in which this hoary institution has been deemed essential for the successful development of international trade and commerce. Admittedly changes have been achieved in its workings which have helped to modify it towards conformity with the needs of a changing world. Despite these changes, however, the gold standard is not operating as successfully as it has done during much of its career, and still less successfully when judged by the present higher standard of efficiency. This seeming failure is due to the appearance of a number of new political and economic phenomena, the reactions of which upon the workings of the gold standard have not been adequately realized. Even when fully understood, these phenomena present a problem of discouraging magnitude to economic champions of gold; but at least it is wiser to expose the worst, discouraging though it be, than to continue blindly to trust in the automatic self-regulation, which has commonly been attributed to the gold standard in orthodox theory, in the light of recent events which have palpably destroyed what self-regulation ever existed. So long as older economists continue to write and to argue as if the gold standard of the present day were the same, and operating under the same conditions, as that which they knew and studied and became accustomed to before the Great War, little of constructive value can be expected of them.

It will be the purpose of this book to consider the new phenomena which appear to be interfering with the smooth operation of the gold standard and to suggest possible measures for combating their evil influence. First, however, in order that our objective may be made clear, it will be necessary to examine the end, for the attainment of which the gold standard is employed, and the means by which, according to orthodox theory, it attains that end.

§ 2. The historical reasons for the adoption of the precious metals as a medium of exchange by civilized countries bear a dry academic flavour in view of modern conditions. Indiscriminate barter of goods against goods, of shoes against dentists' fees, of toothpicks against movie shows, of natural gas against the service of Senators, is no longer conceivable. Some standard had to be found in terms of which the exchange value of every commodity on the market might be measured. Just as articles which are to be compared in length are reduced to feet or metres, so as to be immediately comparable with any other article measured in the same units, so commodities whose exchange values are to be compared must in modern times be reduced to some common denominator. The alternative would be interminable haggling in each individual transaction over the ratio in which two groups of commodities were to be exchanged. Instead of the simple calculation, 1 Senator = \$1,000 a month, 1,000 cubic feet of natural gas = 60 c., one movie show = 50 c., therefore 1 Senator = 10,000 cubic feet of natural gas per month + four movie shows, etc., the Senator would be forced to haggle with every tradesman who supplied his daily wants according as the tradesman deemed that his commodities had recently appreciated in terms of Senators' services, and so on.

In the search for a common denominator for the measurement of exchange values, gold gradually won wide favour, its only serious rival being silver. Into the long story of bimetallism it is unnecessary to go. Suffice it to say that one after another the important nations of the world found that the adoption of a single standard involved fewer complications in their internal currencies than bimetallism, and that, largely on account of its smaller bulk, gold was preferable to silver for the purpose.

A standard of value having been fixed inside each country, however, the problem still remained of fixing an international standard. Each nation in the course of its history adopted its own "unit of account," the dollar in the United States, the pound sterling in England, the franc in France, the mark in Germany, and so on. All these units were well understood, and their value easily appraised, inside their respective countries, but when a French trader wished to sell his wine in England he did not wish to be paid in pounds which had no circulation in his own country. If, however, the pound sterling consisted always of a given weight of gold of known purity, he would be able to count on buying an equivalent number of gold francs upon his return to his own country provided the franc were also legally defined as a certain weight of gold, i.e. provided France were also "on the gold standard." Thus an important corollary of the establishment of gold as the internal standard for the measurement of exchange values or prices, a corollary which has since far surpassed the utility of that standard for internal purposes, was the simplification of international trade to which it gave rise through the stabilization of the rates of exchange of the currencies of gold-standard countries.[1] When the pound and the franc were simply names for a certain weight of gold, the French trader was not only perfectly satisfied in accepting pounds for his wine but could also calculate beforehand the sterling price at which he would be prepared to offer his wares.[2]

[1] "The primary object of the international gold standard is to maintain the parity of foreign exchanges within narrow limits."—*Report of Macmillan Committee on Finance and Industry*, London, 1931, p. 19.

[2] "From the point of view of business and commerce, the great advantage of the international gold standard is precisely that it eliminates fluctuating rates of exchange."—T. E. Gregory, *The Gold Standard and its Future*, London, 1932, p. 9. With stable exchange rates, an American trader can deal in goods priced in sterling as simply as in goods priced in dollars.

A further advantage accrued from thus making a gold pound, a gold dollar, or a gold franc the standard of value and unit of account. On account of its universal acceptability and relatively stable supply, a supply that is small in proportion to the already existing stock, the value of gold itself might be expected to fluctuate but little in terms of other commodities. Had a wheat pound been chosen, a poor harvest in any year would seriously dislocate the price structure. Again an international wheat standard might become quite unmanageable if a year of bumper crops in the United States coincided with a severe drought in Europe.

Thus the object of the gold standard was and is to furnish a measuring-rod, whose value in terms of other commodities shall not fluctuate over short periods, and in terms of which the exchange value or price of any commodity in any country may be compared with that of any other commodity "that trade and commerce may flourish and abound."

Now, according to orthodox theory, the total amount of currency which might be issued in any country was linked by a more or less constant ratio to the amount of gold held in that country.[1] With the adoption of gold as the standard, therefore, it was reasonable to hope that the supply of the medium of exchange would increase with approximately the same steadiness as the volume of trade. Gold production is not subject to seasonal or other short-period fluctuations, since even the development of new mines takes time, so that gold prices would enjoy greater stability than prices of commodities measured in terms of any other standard. This being so, the only condition necessary for the attainment of the object of the international gold standard was that there should be a free market for gold in each country in which gold could be

[1] "The quantity of circulating credit tends to hold a definite relation to the quantity of money in circulation."—Irving Fisher, *Purchasing Power of Money*, p. 50. The quantity of money in circulation, in turn, was supposed to be closely linked to the size of the country's gold holdings.

exchanged for any other forms of the money of that country at a fixed rate of so many units of account per ounce of gold, with the provision, of course, that gold could be freely imported into or exported from any country. Where these provisions were made by law, the gold standard would, according to the orthodox theory, attain its end provided that each country retained just enough gold (and practically no more) to meet the requirements of internal trade at the current price-level, and to redress any temporary disturbance which might occur in the international balance of trade with its neighbours.

The means by which exactly, or almost exactly, this amount of gold was to be retained by each country will be considered in the next three sections of this chapter.

§ 3. From the earliest days of the emergence of a real international gold (or bimetallic) standard, it has been assumed that there exists an automatic tendency towards a proper distribution of the metal between countries using it as their standard. Thus Ricardo, the father of the orthodox theory of the gold standard, asserts: "Gold and silver having been chosen for the general medium of circulation, they are by the competition of commerce distributed in such proportions amongst the different countries of the world as to accommodate themselves to the natural traffic which would take place if no such metals existed, and trade between countries were purely a trade of barter."

This assumption is based on the following argument:

The value of the currency of any country is determined by its supply relative to the number of transactions which it is required to facilitate. Thus if the trade of the United States is expanding without a corresponding increase in the volume of currency, the value of the currency unit will rise, i.e. prices will fall. But if the United States is on the gold standard, the currency unit will be synonymous with a certain weight of gold. A rise in the value of the currency will then be equivalent to a rise in the value of gold in the United States. If no simultaneous expansion of trade is taking place to raise the value of gold in France, gold will now be in greater demand in the United States than in France and will flow from the latter to the former. But even as it flows it will rectify the disequilibrium, for as it reaches the United States it will increase the supply of currency there and so check the rise in the value of currency relative to the commodities, i.e. check the fall in prices, while, as it leaves France, it will decrease the supply of currency there and therefore raise the value of currency and gold towards the higher value placed on the latter in the United States. By this process gold will always tend to flow whither it is most needed, and by so doing will tend to equalize gold prices throughout the world.[1]

Perhaps a simpler way of explaining the stimulus which is supposed to cause gold to flow between countries is to consider the effect of a so-called "rise in the value of gold" in any country upon international traders. These are, after all, the agents who are likely to transfer the gold from one country to another, for gold will not flow of its own volition. Now a rise in the value of gold in any gold-standard country is, according to orthodox theory, synonymous with a fall in prices in that country. The country in question will therefore become a bad country in which to sell commodities but a good country from which to buy them. Foreign buyers will exceed foreign

[1] "Any fall in the value of gold in one country (indicated by a rise in prices in that country) relative to the value of gold in other gold-standard countries would generate a movement of gold out of that country into those other countries where its values are greater. Inflow to those countries would tend to lower its value there, i.e. to raise prices; and the efflux from the country which lost some of its gold would tend to raise its value in that country, i.e. to lower prices. And these two sets of forces would continue to be effective until equilibrium was restored. . . . In short, the operation of the gold standard . . . tended to establish a price-stability between countries." —D. T. Jack, *Economics of the Gold Standard*, London, 1925, p. 25.

sellers, and gold payments will have to be made to the country in question to redress the balance.[1]

It should be noted that this argument rests on the hypothesis that the price-level of any country is intimately connected with the quantity of gold in that country. So long as gold and convertible notes backed by a fixed legal ratio of gold constituted the sole medium of exchange, this hypothesis was likely to be justified. With the growing use of bank credit to augment the supply of monetary units, the theory was only modified by the assertion that the volume of bank deposits subject to transfer by cheque would be tied in a fairly steady ratio to the quantity of gold in the country by reason of orthodox banking policy.[2] We shall find that the belief that price-levels are still closely connected with gold holdings, so that gold flows tend

1 "The Territorial Distribution of money is effected through the agency of Prices. If the stock of money in any country becomes so large that, its rate of movement being what it is, goods offered in the market for money can be exchanged as often as required, and yet a higher level of prices be maintained than in other countries, that country becomes a good country to sell to, because prices there are high, and, for the same reason, becomes a bad country to buy from. The immediate consequence is that exports of domestic products from a country having such a scale of prices are diminished, while its imports of foreign merchandise are increased. If, then, the money of that country is such as has equal acceptance in foreign countries, a movement for its exportation to settle the disturbed balance of exchange at once begins."—F. A. Walker, *Money, Trade and Industry*, New York, 1879, p. 42.

2 "It will be obvious that no man engaged in business, and no bank, will keep more gold on hand than is held to be necessary for business purposes. . . . If a banker holds a larger amount of gold than he considers necessary, he extends his business until the excess is absorbed. . . . A fall in prices or a rise in prices is due to the fact that bankers adjust their business to the quantity of gold which they hold. They will neither allow gold to lie idle nor run the risk of carrying on their business with insufficient cash. I need hardly say that if the gold imported into a country is hoarded, it produces no effect on prices in that country."—Sir D. Barbour, *Influence of Gold Supply on Prices and Profits*, London, 1913, pp. 10–11. We shall find reason to believe that the "hoarding" of imported gold cannot be dismissed so lightly.

to correct themselves automatically by their effects upon the price-levels of the respective countries, is one of the most prominent fallacies in contemporary thought upon the problems of the gold standard.

This automatic self-regulation in the distribution of gold, then, was the first of the influences whereby the gold standard was, according to orthodox theory, aided in the discharge of its function of facilitating world commerce. So long as the system worked automatically, maldistribution would be impossible and every gold-standard country would be able to continue to quote the prices of its commodities in terms of the world currency—gold.

§ 4. With the growth of commerce during the nineteenth century and with the accompanying development of money markets, to and from which both domestic and foreign funds could be freely transferred, it became evident that the international flow of funds would not be confined solely to the settlement of commodity transactions. There now always exists in any financially developed country a certain amount of money which is not destined for the immediate purchase of goods but for investment at the most profitable rate of interest available. This money, when intended for short-term investment, because its owners wish to be able to recall it at short notice if necessary, usually finds its way into one of the money markets of the world. The growth of these and similar financial transactions led to the appearance of a new phenomenon, an international gold flow based not upon goods but upon the purchase and sale of securities. Here lay the first stumbling-block in the way of the automatic self-regulation of the world distribution. Evidently a country might continue to lose gold, even in the face of a falling international price-level, if the resultant favourable commodity trade balance were more than outweighed by the draining off of investment funds under the lure of a higher rate of interest in some foreign money market. In such conditions the gold reserve requisite to support the volume of internal circulation necessary for a healthy home trade might be imperilled.

The instrument relied upon to control this phenomenon has always been the rate of interest at which the Central Bank of any country will lend money, the so-called Bank rate. Because of the ultimate dependence of other lenders upon the Central Bank, it has been assumed that the latter through its rate can control, or at least profoundly influence, the rates which shall prevail in the money market of any country. According to orthodox theory, therefore, a country which found its gold reserves threatened could quickly rectify the situation by raising its Bank rate and so attracting back the expatriated funds of its own nationals together with foreign funds to the required extent.

Moreover, in so far as a rise in the Bank rate was reflected in a rise in other interest rates, it would have the effect of discouraging domestic entrepreneurs from borrowing funds. This in turn would have two reactions upon the financial situation of the country. In the first place, it would contract credit and therefore bank deposits, thus raising the ratio of reserves to deposits, and so strengthening the reserves against internal circulation.[1] In the second place, by thus reducing deposits it would decrease the supply of monetary units and therefore increase their value, i.e. increase the value of gold and lower prices, thus leading to an influx of gold to redress the commodity balance of international trade.[2]

[1] "An increase of bank rate brings with it an increase in rates both for short money and for bank loans. It works both on the international position by attracting funds to this country and preventing funds from moving outwards, and on the internal position by discouraging borrowing from commercial banks and so tending to a reduction of their deposits."—*Report of Macmillan Committee on Finance and Industry*, p. 32.

[2] "The Bank of England as Central Bank is in complete control of the creation of the cash base of the country . . . by which it can regulate the volume of bank deposits. . . . These in turn measure

For these reasons, orthodox theory has relied with great confidence upon the Bank rate as an instrument for furthering the smooth operation of the international gold standard by securing to each country such a share of the world's gold as is necessary to enable it to continue to measure the prices of its goods and services in terms of the international standard through the medium of a unit of account freely convertible into gold.

§ 5. In the previous section it was assumed that changes in the Bank rate are always reflected in changes in open-market interest rates. Indeed, were it not so they could exert no influence upon the international flow of funds. The Central Bank itself is never a borrower, while foreign borrowers, even when they are allowed to avail themselves of the facilities offered by the Central Bank, can normally find cheaper accommodation in the open money market, and so are unlikely to be affected directly by a change in the lending policy of the Central Bank.

Now so long as the money market or the private banks of a country are only slightly indebted to the Central Bank, a rise in the Bank rate may have but little effect upon open-market rates, for the money market may be adequately supplied with funds without recourse to the loan window of the Central Bank. Yet this independence of the Central Bank is the normal state of affairs for a money market. Except when pursuing a deliberate policy of easy money, the Central Bank is mainly concerned with the preservation of its gold reserves and will therefore keep its rate slightly above the market rate. Particularly is this likely to be the case when conditions are such as to lead the Central Bank to raise its rate. Such a step is likely

the amount which banks are prepared to employ particularly by lending to trade and industry. Money so lent is disbursed in wages, etc., and spent on commodities. Thus credit creation affects prices."—Op. cit., p. 44.

to be taken when an undesirable ease prevails in open-market rates, and threatens to occasion a heavy outflow of gold from the country or an undue expansion of domestic borrowing.

In order that the Central Bank may retain control of the financial situation at such times, it is commonly endowed with the power to buy or sell certain classes of securities in the open market. Supposing, for instance, that the Central Bank wished to make a rise in its rate effective upon open-market rates at a time when the market was but slightly indebted to it, it could sell securities to the market, payment would be made by cheque, and the cheque would ultimately be collected from one of the banks holding reserve balances at the Central Bank. If the process were steadily repeated, private banks would find their reserves at the Central Bank as steadily reduced, until the ratios of their reserves to their deposits had dwindled below the customary or legal level. In order to restore them to this level, they would then be forced to borrow from the Central Bank or to call in their most liquid loans. In either case, a hardening of open-market interest rates towards the level of the Bank rate would result, and the process could be continued until that rate had become effective over as large a section of the money market as required. Having thus "prepared the market," the Central Bank could raise its rate with the knowledge that this rate too would become effective to the same extent as the previous rate.

Open-market operations, then, have taken their place as a necessary item in the armoury of Central Banks for their control of the internal money market, and through it of the national and international gold situation.[1] Without them, we have seen that the Central Bank might on occasion be powerless to make its influence felt upon the money market through

[1] For the testimony of many expert American economists to the importance of open-market operations in the workings of the Federal Reserve System, see *Stabilizations Hearings*, H.R. 11806, Washington, 1929.

use of its interest rate. These operations, therefore, supply a necessary complement to manipulation of the Bank rate, and with the latter constitute the normal equipment of the Central Banks of the world for the bolstering up of the supposedly automatic tendencies of the world's gold supply so to distribute itself as to enable all gold-standard countries to continue to link their currencies to gold, the international currency, while at the same time pursuing a healthy internal development.

§ 6. It is in the reconciliation of these two aims of financial policy, the linking of the national currency to gold and a healthy supply of the internal medium of circulation, that the present-day dilemma lies. Orthodox theory has been wont to treat the former as the paramount aim and to neglect the latter because, as we have seen, gold was supposed to flow towards the country whose internal development warranted the flow, and gold holdings, upon which the supply of internal currency depended, would therefore automatically adjust themselves to the legitimate demands of each country. Thus a double benefit would accrue from a maintenance of the gold standard in any country; the prices of that country's goods quoted in terms of its own particular currency would be gold prices and therefore easily expressed in terms of the currencies of other gold-standard countries, a valuable asset to the development of a healthy foreign trade; at the same time the internal disorders which result from prolonged inflation or deflation would be precluded by the automatic inflow or outflow of gold, which would speedily bring the internal price-level back into line with world prices. The regulation of currencies with a view to internal requirements has, therefore, until very recent years been constantly subordinated to the task of retaining a sufficient gold reserve to link the currency firmly to gold.

A survey of world conditions at the present time, however, shows conclusively that, despite all efforts to retain the desired gold reserves, with all the hardships which these efforts inevitably impose upon home industry, maldistribution of the world medium has ensued. Table I on pp. 26–7 shows the progress of this maldistribution up to the end of 1932. The table shows how, particularly during the latter half of 1931, the gold reserves of certain countries were increasing at the expense of drastic reductions on the part of other countries. Despite a violent deflation which reduced the wholesale price-level by more than 40 per cent in seven years,[1] Great Britain, for instance, was forced to abandon the gold standard in September 1931 at a time when the United States held some $600,000,000 more reserves of gold than her laws required.[2] In the course of the world depression which set in in 1929, one after another countries have been compelled to restrict or suspend gold payments in an endeavour to protect their rapidly dwindling holdings of the metal, thus giving up the fight to maintain an international value for their respective currencies.[3]

Maldistribution of the world's gold supply has therefore led to the suspension of the international gold standard as the measuring rod for the determination of the value of a number of national currency units. But this is not all, for the fight to retain the gold standard entails, while it is in progress, steps which if prolonged are normally inimical to internal industry. As we have seen, the factors which are relied upon to redress a threateningly heavy outflow of gold are falling

[1] The British Board of Trade index of wholesale prices based on the average of 1924 as 100 stood at 59·7 for September 1931.

[2] The subsequent suspension of the gold standard in the United States in March 1933 is to be attributed to internal causes rather than to the international maldistribution of gold.

[3] From the viewpoint of international trade, measures which "peg" the value of a national currency in terms of gold or of the currency of some other gold-standard country by restricting by law the amount of foreign currency which may be bought or sold are almost as disastrous as complete suspension. Foreigners will be as chary of trading with a country whose foreign exchange market may be closed to them without warning as with a country where exchange rates are allowed to fluctuate freely.

prices and rising interest-rates, both of which act as dampers upon the activity of home entrepreneurs. Thus there may be long periods during which efforts to maintain the gold value of a currency will be in direct opposition to, rather than identical with, as orthodox theorists have supposed, the internal interests of a country. If these efforts succeed, they will at best merely link the development of internal industry to the international situation, and the internal price-level, whose stability is the key to healthy development, will be laid open to whatever fluctuations occur in world prices. If they fail, as they appear to have failed in many countries recently, the question of whether it is not more important to govern financial policy in the interests of internal price stability, while abandoning the international gold standard altogether if necessary, and allowing the rate of exchange with other currencies to fluctuate freely, will come more sharply than ever to the fore.

The fact remains that there are two ends toward which monetary policy must be directed in order that the financial mechanism may subserve the goal of increasing and facilitating production, distribution, and exchange, for which purpose it was created, and may not become an end in itself; the maintenance of a stable internal level of prices in order to combat the alternating waves of inflation and deflation which make up the business cycles which appear to have become chronic phenomena in modern industrial society; and a steady rate of exchange between the national currency and the currencies of other countries without which international trade must inevitably suffer some degree of dislocation. Orthodox theory has assumed that these two desiderata are automatically connected, so that a policy which is guided in the interests of the latter will *per se* react to the attainment of the former. Certain modern insurgents claim that the two aims are generally so thoroughly incompatible that the governors of monetary policy must confine themselves to pursuing the one at the expense of the other, and that, inasmuch as internal stability is of

TABLE I

GOLD HOLDINGS OF VARIOUS CENTRAL BANKS

Source: *Federal Reserve Bulletin*

		United States (Treasury and Federal Reserve Banks)	England	France	Germany	Argentina
1925*		3,985	695	711	288	451
1926*		4,083	725	711	436	451
1927*		3,977	737	954	444	529
1928*		3,746	748	1,254	650	607
1929*		3,900	710	1,633	544	434
1930*		4,225	718	2,100	528	412
1931	January† ..	4,285	679	2,176	535	397
	February†	4,309	685	2,192	544	390
	March† ..	4,343	699	2,200	553	378
	April† ..	4,373	712	2,180	564	370
	May† ..	4,445	735	2,181	569	362
	June† ..	4,593	703	2,212	339	350
	July† ..	4,587	643	2,290	325	322
	August† ..	4,632	649	2,296	325	309
	September†	4,364	656	2,326	310	281
	October† ..	3,905	660	2,534	273	270
	November†	4,031	587	2,659	239	265
	December†	4,051	588	2,699	234	253
1932	January† ..	4,009	588	2,808	226	252
	February†	3,947	588	2,942	221	249
	March† ..	3,986	588	3,012	209	249
	April† ..	3,956	588	3,052	205	249
	May† ..	3,717	608	3,115	206	249
	June† ..	3,466	663	3,218	198	249
	July† ..	3,522	670	3,221	183	249
	August† ..	3,639	676	3,224	183	249
	September†	3,748	678	3,241	190	249
	October† ..	3,819	678	3,250	195	249
	November†	3,885	678	3,267	197	249
	December†	4,045	583	3,254	192	249

* End of year. † End of month.

TABLE I—*continued*

CONVERTED INTO MILLIONS OF DOLLARS

Source: *Federal Reserve Bulletin*

Australia	Belgium	Brazil	Canada (Ministry of Finance and Chartered Banks)	Japan	Netherlands	Switzerland
162	53	54	157	576	178	90
110	86	56	158	562	166	91
106	100	101	152	542	161	100
109	126	141	114	541	175	103
90	163	150	78	542	180	115
75	191	11	110	412	171	138
76	191	0	92	415	175	126
76	197	0	94	417	179	124
77	200	0	96	415	179	124
74	201	0	99	419	181	124
74	201	0	102	422	181	124
75	199	0	87	425	200	162
66	214	0	87	412	236	225
52	221	0	89	406	260	229
52	346	0	83	408	282	328
53	357	0	86	342	336	422
51	356	0	82	271	362	425
52	354	0	78	234	357	453
51	352	—	80	215	351	472
52	351	—	78	215	353	482
52	349	—	77	214	354	471
52	351	—	77	214	364	471
52	353	—	78	214	384	493
52	357	—	78	214	394	503
42	365	—	79	214	408	509
42	364	—	80	214	415	510
42	359	—	81	214	416	509
42	363	—	85	214	416	509
42	362	—	86	213	415	493
42	361	—	84	212	415	477

greater importance than a well-regulated foreign trade, the former must be given priority.[1] It will be the double task of this book to show how far new world conditions have falsified the hypotheses of the orthodox theorists, whose notice they appear to have escaped, and at the same time to examine the possibility of yet devising a form of "managed international gold standard" which may reconcile the two aims of financial policy.

[1] "It is for the present quite impossible to stabilize both the exchange rate and internal prices. We cannot fix both the internal and the external value of our money."—G. D. H. Cole, *Gold, Credit, and Employment*, London, 1930, p. 29.

CHAPTER II

GOLD MOVEMENTS AND THE PRICE-LEVEL

§ **1.** It is now our unpleasant duty to descend from the blissful realm of orthodox theory, where the economic man is not only perfectly self-seeking but also perfectly intelligent, where markets are free and competition is unrestricted and universal, where "other things" are always "equal," and where the stars in their courses fight to create a paradise whose daily history can be prognosticated with peaceful assurance by the economist at his study desk. Instead we have to concern ourselves with a world populated by the animal called *homo sapiens*, most sapient perhaps in his realization that there are other whims which motivate his actions besides mere self-interest, a world where competition may be so restricted by ignorance and laziness that two stores in the same street may sell two identical commodities at differing prices, where the multiple interplay of an infinite number of economic forces renders the task of studying any one of them in isolation practically impossible, where "other things" are numerous and weighty and very seldom "equal." This is the world in which the question asked of any theory is not "Is it plausible?" but "Is it borne out by the facts?" The answer to this latter query is so frequently negative in the case of economics that the world is apt to despair of ever obtaining aid from this gloomy science. In the face of this challenge, it is the task of economics to set its house in order by testing every theory in the light of factual and statistical evidence before embracing it, and by ridding itself of all the deadwood of antiquated, traditional theory, which cannot bear this cold, clear, penetrating test.

One of the first of the theories of orthodox economics, which still enjoys considerable respect, but which deserves to be most searchingly studied, is the theory of the automatic tendency of gold to distribute itself in due proportion between the several gold-standard countries. It has already been pointed out that maldistribution of gold undeniably exists, and may in fact be blamed for playing an important part in the present world depression. It is obvious, therefore, that the so-called automatic tendency is either an illusion or has been completely nullified by other factors.

Now it must be noted that the simplest form of the orthodox theory of the self-regulation of the international gold flow could only work with anything approaching complete accuracy in countries where an inflow or outflow of gold was reflected in an equivalent or proportional increase or decrease in the volume of the internal medium of exchange in circulation. Only so could gold movements be expected to have that proportional effect upon prices which it is necessary to this theory that they should have. The ideal conditions for the operation of this theory would exist in a country where gold itself were the only, or at any rate the main, internal medium of exchange, for then an influx or efflux of the metal might be expected to reflect itself immediately in an equivalent, or nearly equivalent, increase or decrease in the volume of national currency units. In this case a decrease or increase in the value of the currency, i.e. a rise or fall in prices, might be expected to follow reasonably quickly. Unfortunately for the theory, however, such conditions no longer obtain in any of the large gold-standard countries.

Instead we have two very important modifications which have become incorporated in the monetary mechanism of the gold-standard world since its birth. In the first place, gold itself has now almost completely disappeared from hand-to-hand circulation and has been replaced by paper of greater or less convertibility. Since it is inconceivable that these notes should all be presented for payment in gold simultaneously, they are never backed by a hundred per cent gold reserve, but usually a minimum gold reserve is provided by law expressed sometimes as a percentage of the outstanding note issue, sometimes as a hundred per cent reserve against every note in circulation beyond a certain "fiduciary" issue.

Now the most immediate and obvious corollary to this state of affairs is that an influx or efflux of gold need have no direct connection with the volume of money in circulation in the form of currency notes. Since no Central Bank or other agent issuing notes will make it its policy to have always the legal maximum of notes outstanding, even supposing it had the power to force them all into circulation, there is no immediate reason why an influx or efflux of gold should lead it to make an equivalent, proportional, or any increase or decrease in its note issue. In actual practice the size of the gold reserve is customarily well above the legal minimum so that notes can be, and are, passed into circulation as demanded quite irrespective of whether or not gold is at the moment flowing into the country (cf. Chart I on p. 32).[1]

This alteration in the financial structure of nations makes necessary a profound modification in the philosophy behind orthodox gold-standard theory, for currency notes have now generally displaced gold in universal desirability. "Money is as money does," and money is universally desired because of its power to purchase goods and services. If pieces of paper possess this power just as fully as gold ever did, and if at the same time gold is deliberately withdrawn from circulation, men will cease to desire gold except for ornament or for fillings for their teeth and will make the possession of currency notes, or claims to currency (see § 2), their objective. The fact that

[1] The outstanding feature of both charts is the large outflow of currency at the end of each year in response to the demands of the public for the Christmas season and various year-end settlements. In the case of the United States, this outflow was greatly enhanced in 1931 by an unprecedented outbreak of hoarding, consequent upon a large crop of bank failures throughout the country. Both charts illustrate plainly the independence of movement in the two curves.

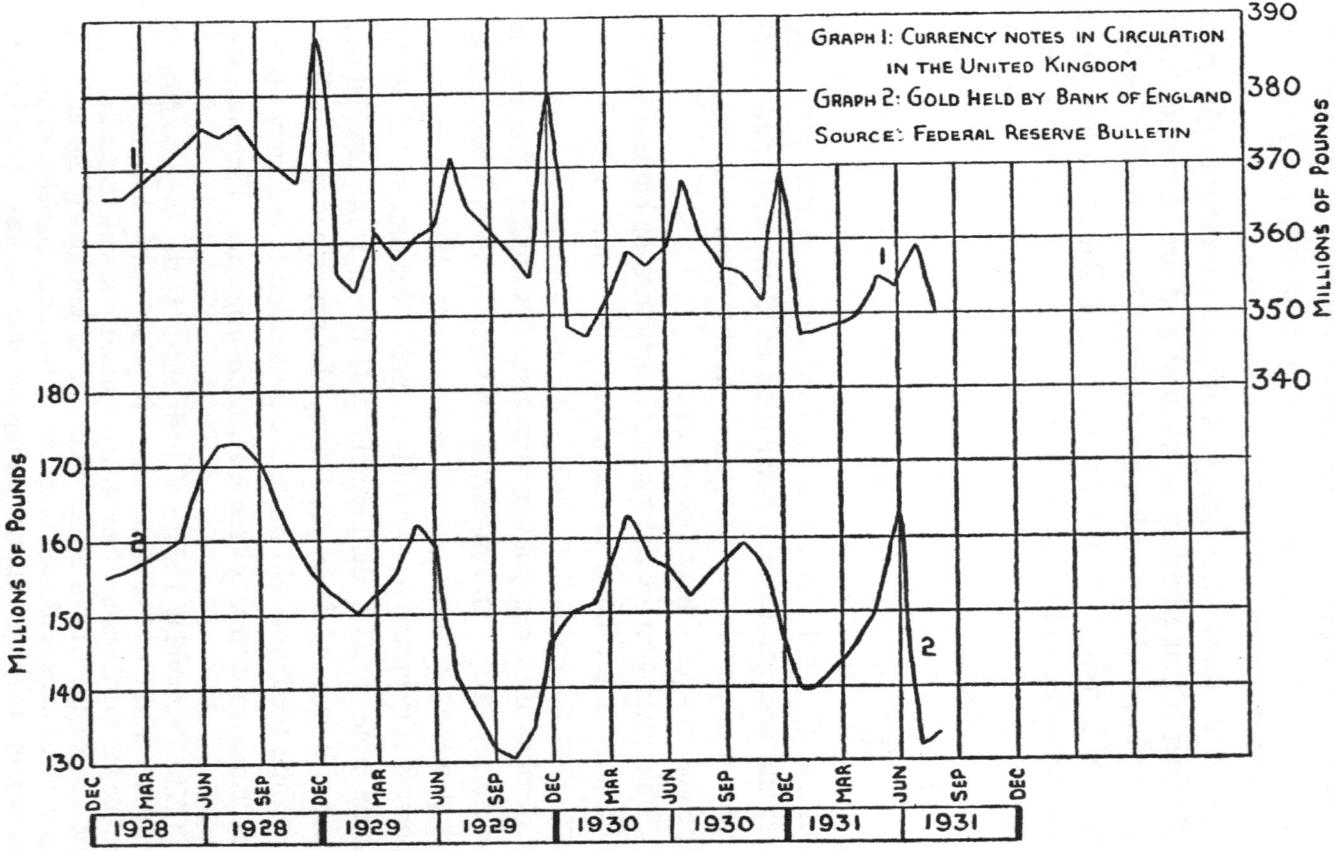
Graph 1: Currency notes in Circulation in the United Kingdom
Graph 2: Gold Held by Bank of England
Source: Federal Reserve Bulletin
Millions of Pounds
390
380
370
360
350
340
Millions of Pounds
180
170
160
150
140
130
1
2
DEC
MAR
JUN
SEP
1928
1929
1930
1931

CHART I

such notes are in certain quantities convertible into gold at some central institution will not interest them unless they desire gold for some commercial purpose, or unless they are foreigners anxious to repatriate their money, or nationals owing money to foreigners.[1] The notes are desirable for their own sake and not as representing claims to so many ounces of gold. Even for purposes of hoarding, notes have supplanted gold in all but the more primitive communities. When citizens of the United States hoard money they employ notes for the purpose; one has to go to countries like India to find perennial hoarding of gold.

It is therefore no longer accurate to say that "the market price of any commodity is certain to be the result of at least two sets of circumstances, namely, those which determine the demand and supply of the commodity, and those which determine the demand and supply of the gold."[2] The demand for gold for arts and trades being small in comparison to the demand for it for financial purposes, the most important "demanders" are the Central Banks of the gold-standard countries, whose demand is practically limitless at the price at which they are obliged by law to give out currency notes in exchange for gold. It is true that these Banks may accentuate or temper their demand by manipulation of their respective interest rates and that this may in turn affect prices (see ch. vi), but here the causal chain from the supply and demand of gold to prices is long enough to make the choice of gold as the first cause practically illegitimate.

[1] "The other banks look to the Central Bank as the sole source of legal tender money. . . . The banks and the public do not trouble themselves about the interchangeability of gold and credit. That is the affair of the Central Bank alone."—R. G. Hawtrey, *The Gold Standard in Theory and Practice*, London, 1931, p. 25.

[2] W. A. Scott, *Money and Banking*, New York, 1916, p. 46; cf. Harrison H. Brace, *Gold Production and Future Prices*, New York, 1910, p. 107: "The principal element in determining prices is the relative facility in producing commodities and of producing the standard."

§ 2. Before discussing the factors which determine the supply and demand, and therefore the value, of currency units which have displaced gold in the estimation of the public, it is necessary to introduce the second fundamental modification which has been made in the world's monetary structure since the birth of the gold standard, namely, the tremendous growth in the use of bank credit. The contribution which the device of creating purchasing power by a few strokes of a bank-clerk's pen has made to the progress of modern civilization can hardly be fully appreciated. If gold and convertible notes had continued to constitute the world's sole medium of trade and commerce, it is quite possible that industrial development and production would have been so restricted that the world's real wealth in 1932 would have been little greater than it was half a century ago. How vastly more important than money in hand-to-hand circulation that part of the community's purchasing power consisting of bank deposits has become in Great Britain and the United States is shown in the table on p. 35.

Yet here in the volume of deposit currency is an item whose supply, consisting as it does of so many figures in bankers' ledgers, is unlimited by niggardly Nature and therefore seems at first blush to have no visible connection with an inflow or outflow of gold, and yet which, by reason of its size, may profoundly affect the value of the country's currency, i.e. the price-level.

In actual practice, however, there are of course limits to the volume of bank credit that may be created. These limits are set in the first instance not by the quantity of gold which the earth can be made to disgorge but by the prudence of bankers. A banker may without difficulty increase the purchasing power of any client by lending him a certain sum of credit, i.e. by agreeing to honour cheques drawn by his client up to this amount. Difficulty arises, however, if and when the client or those in favour of whom the client draws his cheques choose to realize the claims which these cheques constitute against the lending banker by presenting them for payment in cash. A banker, in order to remain in business, must be prepared to meet all "demand claims" against him in cash without

RELATION OF DEPOSIT CURRENCY TO MONEY IN CIRCULATION

United States

(Figures in Millions of Dollars)

Date	Money in Circulation	Total Deposits of all Banks (excluding Interbank Deposits)
October 3, 1928	4,836	53,720
October 4, 1929	4,814	55,180
September 24, 1930	4,469	52,784
September 29, 1931	5,176	49,152

Source: *Federal Reserve Bulletin.*

British Isles

Notes in Circulation		Total Deposits*		
Date	Total	Date	Number of Banks	Total in Millions of Pounds
1928, Dec. 26	378,294,483	1928	43	2,600
1929, Dec. 25	379,573,841	1929	44	2,560
1930, Dec. 31	368,801,566	1930	44	2,698
1931, Dec. 30	364,150,042	1931	44	2,527
1932, Dec. 28	371,193,057	1932	45	2,800

Source: *Bank of England Weekly Return.*

Source: *The Statist*, May 20, 1933, *British Banking Supplement.*

* Total deposits of banks of Great Britain and Ireland (including the Bank of England).

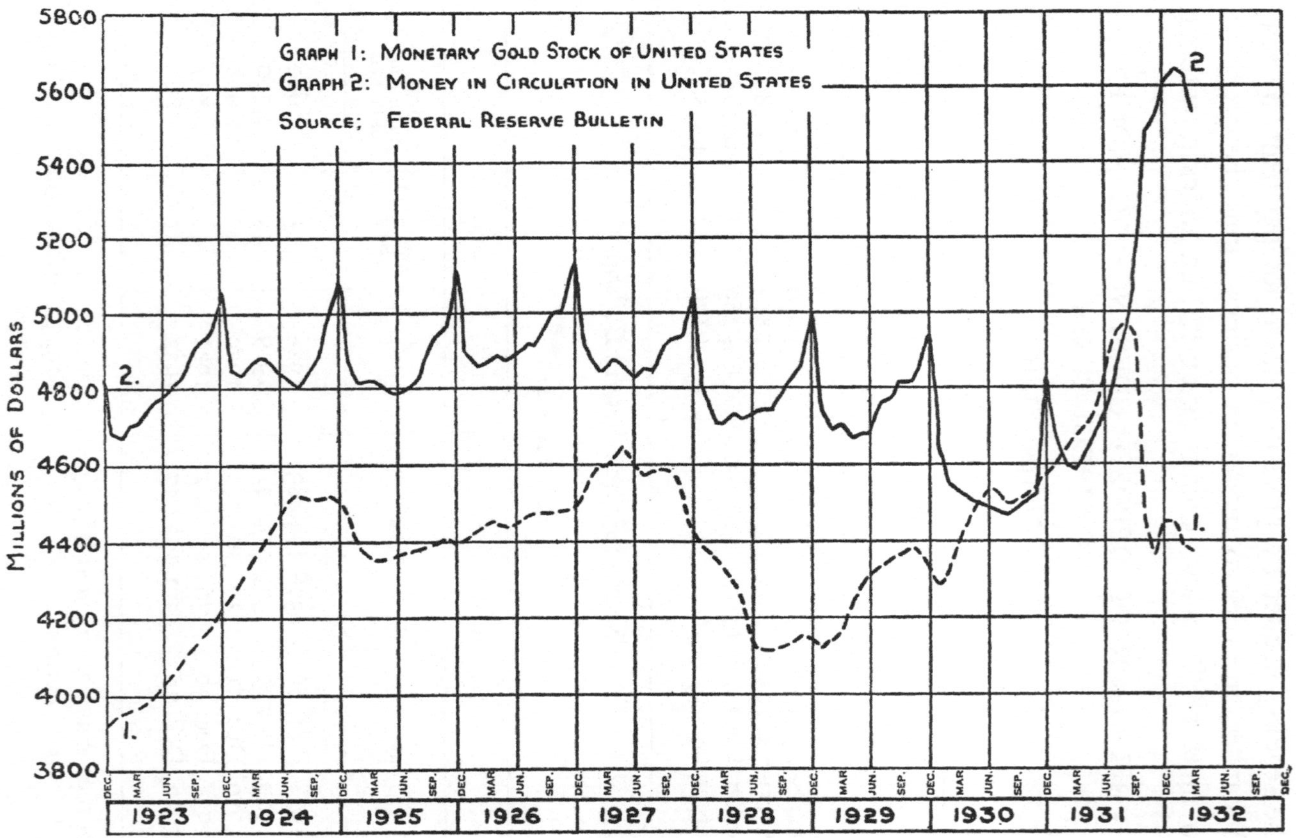
Graph 1: Monetary Gold Stock of United States
Graph 2: Money in Circulation in United States
Source; Federal Reserve Bulletin
Millions of Dollars
5800
5600
5400
5200
5000
4800
4600
4400
4200
4000
3800
1923
1924
1925
1926
1927
1928
1929
1930
1931
1932

CHART II

warning, and against this contingency he has, if he is prudent, to keep a certain percentage of these "demand claims" in cash or assets readily convertible into cash (e.g. deposits at a Central Bank).

As in the case of the gold reserves retained by Central Banks against their note issues, this percentage is not likely to remain rigid at the minimum compatible with the individual banker's estimate of safety. It will in practice fluctuate widely enough to allow considerable elasticity to the volume of bank credit outstanding without necessitating proportionate fluctuations in the volume of the reserves themselves. As an illustration of the variability of this "reserve ratio," figures are appended below showing the percentage of "Cash in hand and at the Bank of England" to "Current, Deposit and Other Accounts" for the "big five" banks in England during 1931.

PERCENTAGE OF "RESERVES" TO "DEPOSITS" IN THE "BIG FIVE" BANKS IN ENGLAND

(*Weekly Averages*)

1931	Barclays	Lloyds	Midland	National Provincial	Westminster
January	10·39	10·78	11·08	10·65	10·26
February	10·09	10·42	11·12	10·56	10·29
March	10·22	10·62	11·09	10·43	10·02
April	10·23	10·37	10·52	10·51	10·09
May	10·34	10·45	10·57	10·41	10·18
June	11·02	10·84	10·46	10·25	10·34
July	10·36	10·54	10·17	10·44	10·22
August	10·17	10·68	10·37	10·38	10·28
September ..	9·99	10·47	10·56	9·72	10·13
October	9·87	10·49	10·62	10·01	10·18
November ..	9·82	10·39	10·50	10·06	10·12
December.. ..	11·18	10·69	10·43	10·45	10·44

These figures show that among English banks it is considered expedient to maintain a reserve of between 10 and 11 per cent of total deposits, and at first sight it appears that this figure is adhered to with considerable rigidity. It should be remembered, however, that a fluctuation in reserves amounting to one per cent of deposits is equivalent to a fluctuation of approximately ten times that amount in the deposits themselves when reserves are standing at about one-tenth of deposits. Thus it would seem that the deposits of the Midland Bank, for instance, may have a variability range of 10 per cent in volume without any necessary change in the volume of its reserves. In other words, without any change in their reserves it would seem that the English banks might in certain circumstances be able, by increasing advances to, or purchasing securities from, their clients, to increase their deposits 10 per cent, i.e. to add anything up to 10 per cent to that part of the community's purchasing power which consists of bank accounts, without being guilty of a breach of the accepted standards of prudence with regard to their reserve ratios.[1] When it is remembered that the volume of deposit currency in England is as a rule some seven times as large as the volume of money in circulation, it may be seen that there is nothing in recognized banking practice to prevent the total purchasing power of the country from being raised by some 9 per cent by this means, without so much as a change in the volume of the bank reserves, let alone a change in the total gold holdings of the country.

A very similar illustration may be found in the case of the United States, though here allowance must be made for the fact that a minimum ratio is prescribed by law for the reserve ratios of member banks of the Federal Reserve System. The legal ratio is, however, a somewhat fictitious figure, for any

[1] For instance, supposing at any given time the banking system held total reserves of £220,000,000 against total deposits of £2,000,000,000, these deposits could be raised over a period to £2,200,000,000, without any increase in reserves, and yet without the reserve ratio falling by more than the recognized 1 per cent from 11 per cent to 10 per cent.

member bank that finds its reserves falling below the legal minimum can quickly relieve the situation by rediscounting the requisite volume of its eligible assets, i.e. selling them to its Reserve Bank, and so building up its reserves to the point required by law. On the other hand, any bank finding itself in possession of more than the legally required reserves may immediately increase its security holdings, loans, and advances to the maximum that its reserves can carry. Thus it is customary for all members of the Federal Reserve System to keep their reserve balances at the Reserve Banks at the legal minimum, and to redress any diminution which may occur in the reserve ratio, from a decrease in the absolute volume of the balances or from an increase in deposit liabilities, by rediscounting eligible paper at the Reserve Banks, and so reinforcing their credit there. Were it not for the tradition that it is bad policy to remain long "in debt" to a Reserve Bank by exercising the rediscount privilege at that Bank, it is possible that funds obtained by rediscounting would constitute a far higher percentage of total member bank reserve balances than they normally do. In actual practice, however, member banks endeavour to remain as little as possible in debt to the Reserve Banks. It is the elasticity of their willingness to remain in debt (if the phrase may be excused) and the elasticity of the Reserve Banks' willingness to countenance the indebtedness, that measure the elasticity of total deposits of member banks without any more alteration in their reserve balances than can be brought about by a further exercise of the rediscount privilege.

It is therefore to the ratio of member banks' "free reserves," i.e. total reserves less borrowings from Reserve Banks, to total deposits that one must look to find a true counterpart to the "reserve ratio" of the English banks, for we have seen that these free reserves can be built up to the legal minimum automatically by the member banks by the simple process of retailing some of their eligible assets to the Reserve Banks.

Any member bank wishing to increase its deposits by making an advance of $10,000 to a client can do so without more ado than by rediscounting some $1,000 worth of paper to build up its balances at the Reserve Bank to the required extent.[1] As the borrower makes use of the loan by drawing upon the lending bank cheques which are deposited in other banks, the lending bank's reserves will be depleted in favour of the banks receiving the cheques. The former will then have to build up its reserves yet further, but this also may be done by the same process of rediscounting paper at the Reserve Bank.

The knowledge that its reserves will be diminished as soon as the borrower draws cheques against his loan serves in fact normally to deter any individual member bank from issuing loans to the full amount of ten times any excess reserves which it may come by through the rediscounting of eligible paper or otherwise. As the borrower's cheques are redeposited by the recipients in other banks, however, these banks become possessors of additional claims against the lending bank. These the latter will pay by means of a cheque against its reserves at the Reserve Bank. The receiving banks will then find their reserves at the Central Bank enlarged, and will increase their loans accordingly. It is the total resultant deposit expansion of the whole banking system, rather than the initial expansion of the bank which first increased its loans, which will bear a ratio of ten to one to the new Reserve Bank credit created by the latter's sale of paper to the Reserve Bank.

It is not to variations from the legal minimum reserve ratio, therefore, that we must look for elasticity in the volume of deposits that may be built up on any given volume of member bank reserves, but to the ratio of deposits to the real, legitimate,

[1] The legal reserve requirements against member banks deposits are 3 per cent against time deposits, and 7 per cent, 10 per cent or 13 per cent against demand deposits according as the member bank in question is situated outside a reserve city, in a reserve city, or in a central reserve city respectively.

"free reserves" that member banks hold in their own right and not through an exercise of their rediscount privileges. In so far as they respect the tradition of remaining out of debt to the Reserve Bank, member banks will strive to keep these free reserves equal to the legal reserves. Their willingness to allow them to fall below this figure and to make good the difference by rediscounting will measure the extent to which they are willing to create purchasing power *ex nihilo*, i.e. without any real increase in their reserves, but only the makeshift increase obtained by retailing bills to the Reserve Banks.[1]

Chart III on next page shows the free reserves of all member banks expressed as a percentage of their total deposits during the period 1928–31. It is, of course, difficult to choose any period which can be claimed to have been perfectly normal, and it may very plausibly be said that this period, characterized as it was by heavy outflows and inflows of gold and by the stock exchange boom and collapse, was very far from normal. This must undoubtedly be conceded, but for that very reason statistics for this period will be unusually serviceable in revealing the degree of elasticity of deposit currency of which the Federal Reserve System is capable on occasions.

From this chart it will be seen that during the fifteen odd months from the spring of 1928 to the autumn of 1929 the percentage of free reserves to total deposits lay always between $3\frac{3}{4}$ per cent and $4\frac{3}{4}$ per cent. Though this period was one of

[1] The rediscount privilege was, of course, incorporated in the Federal Reserve Act for the express purpose of giving elasticity to the deposit currency of the country. "Prior to the establishment of the Federal Reserve System, our deposit currency, though not as inelastic as our bank-note currency, was none the less deficient in the quality of elasticity. . . . The Federal Reserve System increases the elasticity of our deposit currency in a number of ways . . . of which the most important is found in the machinery enabling member banks to borrow funds of their Federal Reserve Banks" mainly by rediscounting eligible paper. —E. W. Kemmerer, *A B C of the Federal Reserve System*, Princeton, 1919, pp. 58–61.

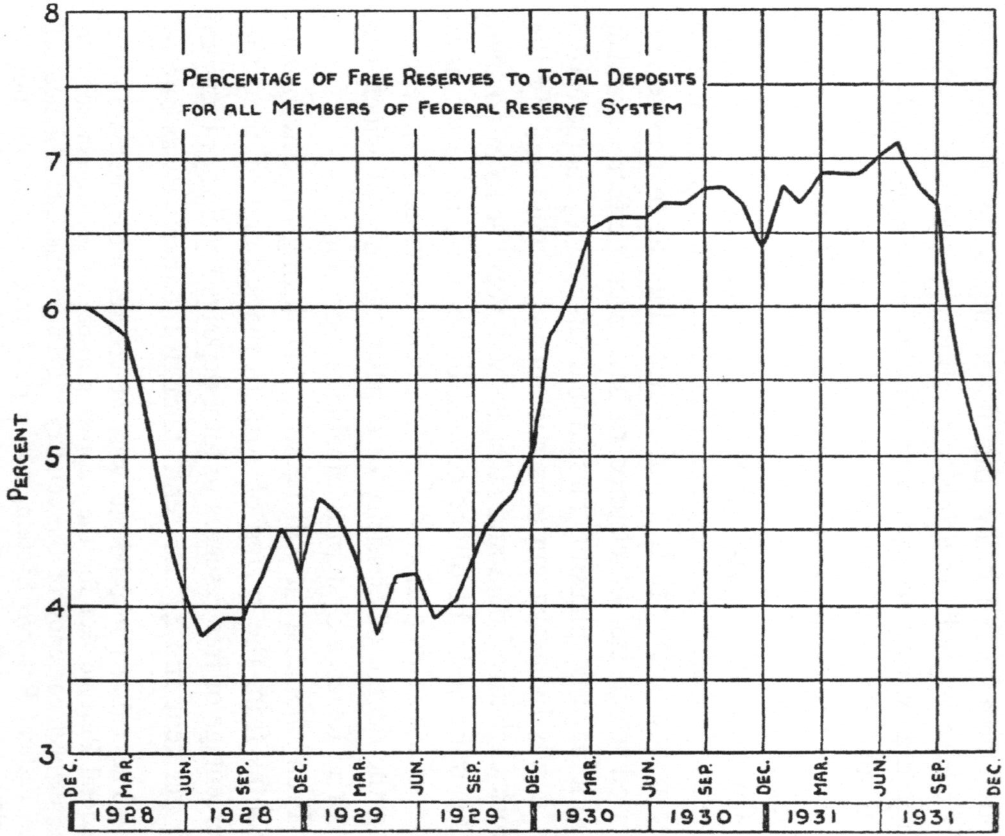

Percentage of Free Reserves to Total Deposits
for all Members of Federal Reserve System
Percent
8
7
6
5
4
3
Dec.
Mar.
Jun.
Sep.
Dec.
Mar.
Jun.
Sep.
Dec.
Mar.
Jun.
Sep.
Dec.
Mar.
Jun.
Sep.
Dec.
1928
1928
1929
1929
1930
1930
1931
1931

CHART III

unusual industrial and financial activity, the fact that so low a percentage was maintained for so protracted a time indicates that it is perfectly possible for a 4 per cent ratio to recur at any time.

On the other hand, at the outset of the period covered by the chart, and again from February 1930 until the autumn of 1931, when a heavy outflow of gold from the United States together with a drastic increase of money in circulation forced member banks to draw heavily upon their cash balances at the Reserve Banks in order to satisfy their clients' demands for money and so cut severely into their free reserves, the ratio moved between 6 per cent and 7 per cent. The years 1930 and 1931 were as abnormally stagnant as the years 1928 and 1929 were abnormally active, yet the facts that, first, during the later period with all its fluctuations in industrial and financial activity the ratio remained continuously between 6 per cent and 7·1 per cent for twenty consecutive months, and secondly, at the end of the comparatively "normal" year 1927 the ratio stood at 6 per cent, indicate that it is reasonable to expect that, as a result of the individual policies of the member banks rather than of a coherent policy of the whole system, free reserves will customarily amount to between 6 per cent and 7 per cent of the total deposits of all member banks. Indeed, if member banks are holding true to the tradition of attempting not to remain long in debt at the Reserve Banks, so that they are aiming at making their free reserves equal to their total required reserves, the ratio may confidently be expected not to fall much below 7 per cent since required reserves customarily amount to some 8 per cent of total deposits.[1]

Thus it appears that the member banks' "true reserve ratio," i.e. percentage of free reserves to total deposits, while standing normally in the neighbourhood of 6½ per cent, may

[1] Including time deposits. The legal reserves against demand deposits alone amount to approximately 10 per cent of such deposits for the system as a whole (see note, p. 40).

be reduced at will to 4½ per cent or less should demands from clients for accommodation suddenly become large enough to warrant the creation of a sufficient volume of new deposits. It would, of course, be unjustifiable to assume that, because the ratio may thus be reduced by one-third, the volume of deposit currency is ever likely to be suddenly increased in that proportion. What the statistical evidence does show, however, is that the "fictitious" portion of member banks' reserve balances obtained by rediscounting may frequently rise from say 1 per cent to 3 per cent of total deposits, or from one-eighth to three-eighths of total reserves. If this rise is brought about by an increase in the absolute volume of rediscounts rather than by an absolute shrinkage of free reserves, there is here an even wider margin for the creation of credit *ex nihilo* than exists under the English banking system.

It should be remembered that the period covered by the statistics cited was chosen because it represented the course of events during part of a credit cycle which, though severe, may easily recur in times which are not troubled by political complications. If statistics had also been adduced from the period of the Great War, even more extreme conclusions might have been drawn as to the expansibility of credit upon a stationary volume of member bank free reserves. At one time during that period, member bank borrowings actually exceeded the whole of their reserve balances, so that the proportion of their free reserves to total deposits was a negative quantity. The statistics here used, therefore, represent a normal course of events rather than an extreme possibility. For the purposes of the main argument, of course, this is a detail, since it is merely desired to show that a potential supply of deposit currency exists at all times rather than to attempt to determine the exact volume of this supply. It should be unnecessary to add the analogous conlusion that a large volume of outstanding purchasing power may also be destroyed at any time without any decrease in free reserves.

§ 3. From all this it will appear that under present-day conditions private banks are able at any ordinary moment to add at will a considerable mass of purchasing power to that already existing without any change in the volume of their own reserves, let alone a change in the total gold holdings of the country. It may easily be seen what a drastic blow such a situation deals at the orthodox theory of the automatic self-distribution of the world's gold. This theory, it will be remembered, was based on the argument that if one particular gold-standard country were to begin to enjoy a period of business prosperity and increased production and trade, more gold, or currency convertible into gold, would be required to act as the medium of exchange for the products of the boom. Demand for gold would then rise, and, its supply being temporarily fixed at the existing level of the country's gold holdings, its value in terms of commodities would rise, i.e. prices would fall, until an inflow of gold occurred from some country where its value was not so high.

It will now be seen that, in the first place, an increase in business activity will call for an increase in currency, either deposits or cash, and not necessarily in gold holdings; and, in the second place, that this call can now be satisfied to a large extent by an increase in deposit currency *ex nihilo* instead of necessitating a fall in the value of goods relative to currency, i.e. a fall in prices. Thus neither an outflow of gold nor an increase in trade and industry need involve a fall in the price-level provided that the banks are still willing and able to increase the outstanding volume of deposit currency; while similarly neither an inflow of gold nor a slackness of trade need involve a redundance of money if deposit currency is being simultaneously annihilated.

It is not suggested as likely that the banks of any country would suddenly and concertedly increase the amount of deposit currency in the country by 10 per cent merely for "devilment," e.g. by embarking on a policy of gigantic purchases of government securities. It is, however, not only likely but almost certain that the demands for bank advances, coming mainly from entrepreneurs and speculators, will rise and fall quite closely with the rise and fall in business activity.[1] It is now apparent that instead of producing a rise or fall in the value of gold, or even of currency, these rises and falls in demand may be met by a rise or fall in the supply of currency, unless and until the banking system has reached the points where a further increase or decrease in deposits upon existing reserves is deemed dangerously inexpedient. The value of the national currency as reflected in the general price-level may by this means remain relatively stable during either a boom or a depression without either an inflow or an outflow of gold taking place in order to adjust the internal value of the metal to its international value.

It is interesting to note in passing that it is in their ignoring of this potential source of supply of currency that the adherents of the old form of the quantity theory of money, which attributes to changes in the volume of currency the initiative in changes of the general price-level but never vice versa,[2] make their fundamental error. In actual fact, transactions will frequently take place in commodities at an agreed price some time before the money with which they are to be financed has come into being, and subsequently exactly the requisite amount of currency to finance each transaction at the agreed

[1] "Banks are able to supply the various forms of currency needed. . . . Any business man can get the money he needs, at the time and in the form that he needs it, provided his banker will discount his notes. The only limit to the increase in bank currency, therefore, is the capacity of the banks to discount mercantile securities, and within that limit its increase is in direct response to business needs."—W. A. Scott, *Money and Banking*, p. 113.

[2] Cf. Irving Fisher, *Purchasing Power of Money*, p. 169: "Except to a limited extent during transition periods, or during a passing season, there is no truth whatever in the idea that the price-level is an independent cause of changes in any of the other magnitudes in the 'equation of exchange.' "

price will be called forth when the buyer draws a cheque against his banker who is allowing him a line of credit or an overdraft. From the speculator in the Chicago wheat pit, who obtains advances from his banker to pay for wheat which he has already bought at a fixed price, to the English country squire, who pays his grocer's bills with a cheque on his bank where his account is already overdrawn, men are constantly "creating" the money required to finance transactions already concluded. This being so, it is futile to deny that changes can occur in the price-level without any causative or even simultaneous change in any of the other factors in the equation of exchange ($PT = MV + M'V'$) but with only a subsequent change in M', the volume of deposit currency. Changes in the price-level are not only not necessarily caused by the other factors but may themselves be initiators of changes in those other factors, e.g. in M'. It is impossible to deny that, so long as his credit stood high with his banker, the Chicago speculator could have agreed to pay 2 c. more per bushel for his million bushels of wheat, and then $20,000 more of deposit currency would have been called into existence when he made payment in the form of a cheque drawn against a banker's advance on the security of the wheat and/or other assets; or the English squire could have agreed to pay 6d. more per bottle for his whisky and a correspondingly greater amount of new deposit currency would then have been created when he paid by a cheque against his already overdrawn account.[1]

Orthodox theorists, therefore, err when their arguments

[1] Cf. J. M. Keynes, *Treatise on Money*, New York, 1930, vol. i, p. 247: "A speculative rise in the wholesale standard (index number of prices), unaccompanied by a rise in the consumption standard, is particularly unlikely to be held back by a shortage in the quantity of money. Moreover, there is a further time-lag between the price-rise and the demand for money, in that the current price quotations reflect the prices at which contracts for future completion are now being entered into; so that it is not until the date of completion that the higher prices will call for increased Business deposits."

imply that the value of a national currency is determined by the demand for it from all the various agents using it in their daily life or business acting upon a supply which is rigidly connected with the gold holdings of the country in question. The potential supply of deposit currency which may be called into being at any moment (or the volume of outstanding deposit currency which may be withdrawn) either in response to demand, when it will take the form of increased bank loans and advances, or by spontaneous action of the banking system, when it will show itself in larger purchases of securities by banks, is apt to be very large, and to bear no relation to contemporary gold movements.

§ 4. While, however, it is evident that banking systems customarily possess some degree of elasticity in the creation of deposit currency, it is equally apparent that sound banking principles impose a continual restraint upon the power to create deposits *ex nihilo*. Just as in mechanics "the tension varies as the extension," so in banking it is natural that the willingness of banks to increase their liabilities against a stationary reserve will vary with the height of their reserve ratio above the most conservative estimate of the desirable size of that ratio. Thus, if Lloyds Bank in London finds that its reserve ratio stands at 11·5 per cent, it will be much more ready to create currency by increasing its advances or by purchasing securities than if its reserve ratio were at 10·5 per cent, while when the ratio falls to 9·5 per cent it will probably flatly refuse to accommodate any new customers, and may perhaps charge its old clients a higher rate for renewing or continuing their borrowings. Conversely, when the National City Bank in New York has allowed its free reserves to fall to 4 per cent of its total deposits, it will be much readier to use any new funds that it may acquire for the reduction of its indebtedness at the Federal Reserve Bank of New York in preference to employing them as the basis for new loans or advances than when its free reserves amount to 6 per cent of total deposits.

Although the power to create *ex nihilo* a little more than the already outstanding volume of deposit currency will always theoretically exist, the resistance to such a tendency will therefore naturally increase as the reserve ratio falls below the generally accepted "prudence figure"; similarly, although the power to withdraw a portion of the outstanding volume always exists, this power is likely to be less and less exercised as the reserve ratio rises above the "prudence figure." It is for this reason true that the outstanding volume of deposit currency in any country is to a loose and uncertain degree connected with the size of the reserve balances of the private banks in that country.

Now the aggregate volume of the reserve balances of private banks is affected primarily by the changes which take place in three factors, (1) the monetary gold stock of the banking system, (2) the volume of money in circulation, and (3) cash transactions with the Central Bank.

(1) When gold flows into a country, the importer of the metal,[1] or the man who buys it in the open market immediately upon importation, either deposits it directly with his bank, or sells it to the Central Bank at the legal rate, obtaining in payment a cheque which he deposits at his bank. In either case, a private bank comes into possession of a claim against the Central Bank for the value of the gold. If it receives the gold directly from its client, it will promptly transfer it to the Central Bank, since it keeps practically no gold on hand itself, and so will increase its reserves at the Central Bank. If the client sells directly to the Central Bank and deposits the cheque with which he is paid at his bank, this bank by presenting the cheque for payment will become the possessor of exactly so much more reserve balances at the Central Bank. Thus in

[1] Except when the importer is the Central Bank itself, in which case the reserve position of the private banks will not be affected.

either case, some member of the banking system will find both its deposits and reserves increased by an exactly equivalent amount, the value of the gold imported, say $1,000,000. But if the normal reserve ratio of the system as a whole is 10 per cent, the banking system will tend to increase its collective deposits by $10,000,000 on the basis of this addition to its reserves, while in actual fact this transaction itself has only increased its liabilities by $1,000,000. Thus every import of gold strengthens the reserve position of the banking system of the importing country by causing an equivalent rather than a proportionate increase in both reserves and deposits of the system. Conversely, an export of gold will diminish the reserves of the banking system to exactly the same extent as its deposits, and consequently weaken its reserve position.

(2) Similarly, when money flows into the banks from circulation the effect will be reflected to an equivalent rather than a proportionate degree in the reserve balances of the banking system. No bank holds in its tills more cash than it deems expedient in normal times to meet the day-to-day demands of its clients. When it finds this amount increasing abnormally, it will transfer the excess over the "prudence figure" to the Central Bank where the money may count as reserve upon which remunerative loans, advances, or security holdings may be built up. Similarly, if an abnormal outflow of cash from the banks into circulation occurs, this will have to be met by the private banks drawing upon their reserves at the Central Bank in order to replenish their till-money, which, on account of its small size, will be quickly depleted below the "prudence figure" by any unwonted outflow of cash.

(3) The Central Bank stands in the same relation to the private banks as they in turn stand to their private customers. Just as a bank's customers will settle their debts with each other by drawing cheques against the balances which they hold at their respective banks, so the banks themselves will settle the accounts which arise between each other by a transfer

from the account of the debtor bank at the Central Bank to the account of the creditor bank. Thus, if on any day depositors in bank A pay more by means of cheques against their accounts at that bank to depositors at bank B than depositors at bank B are paying to depositors at bank A, at the end of the day bank A will find itself in debt to bank B to the extent of the excess. This debt it will settle by means of a cheque drawn in favour of bank B against its (bank A's) account at the Central Bank. Such transactions, while affecting the reserve ratios of individual banks, and therefore their several lending policies, tend to cancel out in the long run, so long as no bank is pursuing either a radical or an ultra-conservative policy. Since they do not in any case affect the aggregate reserves of the whole banking system, being but a transfer of possession of part of these reserves from one bank to another, they need not here be discussed.

A different case arises, however, when there is a debt to be settled between the Central Bank itself and one of the private banks. Such debts appear when the Central Bank buys securities from (or sells them to) some private individual or bank in the open market. Suppose for instance that the Federal Reserve Bank of New York buys $1,000,000 of government securities from a New York stockbroker. The broker will deposit the cheque with which he is paid at his bank, which then becomes possessor of a claim against its own Central Bank. In this case, as soon as it has deposited the cheque exactly the same situation arises as in the case of an import of gold; the deposits and the reserves of the bank in question are both increased to exactly the same extent, and its reserve position becomes correspondingly stronger. Should the Reserve Bank buy the securities direct from the member bank instead of from a private individual or non-member bank, i.e. a bank not using the Reserve Bank of New York or any other Reserve Bank as its Central Bank, the position is slightly modified by the fact that only the reserves of the member bank, and not its deposits, will be increased by the amount of the purchase. Its reserve position will then become even stronger than in the former case. In both cases the reserves of the banking system as a whole are built up without a proportional increase in total deposits. Similarly, when the Central Bank sells securities the reserves of the banking system are diminished without a proportionate decrease in total deposits.

It may readily be seen how powerful an instrument in the hands of a Central Bank is the authority to deal in open-market securities. By exercise of this authority, a Central Bank may negative the effects upon the reserves of the private banks of an inflow or outflow of gold or a flow of money into or out of circulation, while on the positive side it may apply the screw to the banking system of the country by embarking upon a persistent sale of its holdings of securities, thereby diminishing the free reserves of the banks as a whole. This whole subject of the open-market operations of Central Banks will be discussed in the following chapter. For the moment it is sufficient to remember that, so long as this authority is actively utilized, and so long as the volume of currency in circulation does not remain perfectly stable, an inflow or outflow of gold will not be exactly reflected by an equivalent increase or decrease in private bank reserves, but may in fact be completely nullified by the behaviour of these other two factors.

§ 5. It may now be profitable to sum up the conclusions reached in this chapter. In order that the orthodox theory of automatic self-distribution of the world's gold supply should hold good, it would be necessary that an inflow or outflow of gold should act directly upon the value of the currency of a country in terms of goods, an inflow above the amount required by commercial and industrial conditions causing a depreciation of the national currency, i.e. a rise in prices and hence a compensating outflow of gold to countries where it is more highly valued, and vice versa. In present-day conditions, however, gold has been displaced from use as the medium of exchange in all important gold-standard countries and replaced by (1) currency notes, the volume of which in circulation is unconnected with the gold holdings of the country, except in so far as the latter impose a maximum limit, which is seldom called into operation in practice, to their issue, and (2) deposit currency, whose volume, amounting in England to some seven times, and in the United States to some eleven times, the volume of money in circulation, is at best only loosely connected with the size of the reserve balances of the private banks of the country, and therefore only very indirectly with the flow of gold in so far as the effect of the latter upon these reserves balances is not nullified by other factors.

It may be seen, therefore, that the supply of any gold-standard currency, and so, according to the orthodox theory, its value at a given level of industrial and commercial activity, no longer depends to any close degree upon the gold holdings of the country. In fact, an inflow of gold may be accompanied by a decrease in the supply of currency and hence possibly by a fall in the price-level, and vice versa. In view of these facts, the Commission of the British Government on Finance and Industry has well said: "The sense in which the gold standard can be said to be automatic is very limited; it is automatic only as an indicator of the need for action and of the end to be achieved."[1] To a consideration of such "ends" and "actions" we must now pass.

[1] *Macmillan Report*, p. 19.

CHAPTER III

CENTRAL BANK POLICIES AND THE QUANTITY OF MONEY

§ 1. We have seen that the plausibility of the assumption in orthodox gold standard theory that gold will distribute itself automatically among gold-standard nations on the basis of their respective needs for the metal involves the hypothesis that an inflow or outflow of gold will reflect itself in an increase or decrease in the outstanding volume of currency in the country in question. This, it is assumed, will raise or lower the supply of currency relative to the demand of the country's inhabitants. Unless the inflow or outflow is in proportion to the expansion or contraction of the demand, it is maintained, the value of the currency, and therefore of the gold into which the currency is convertible, will depart from its international value and a counteracting gold movement will take place. But we have also seen that the important currencies of the world no longer consist of gold, but of two items, namely, currency notes and bank deposits. Over both these items Central Banks can exercise a considerable degree of control, over the former as being the chief issuers of notes, and over the latter through their power to affect the volume of the reserve balances of the private banks upon which the latter create the "pyramid" of bank credit.[1] It is now necessary to consider how far Central Banks have used, or are likely to use, their powers in such a way that excessive international gold movements will continue to carry with them the seeds of their own destruction.

[1] "The value of the monetary unit in commodities depends upon the action of the banks in creating credit. That action the Central Bank is in a position to control. For the one limitation upon the creation of credit is the supply of cash, and the supply of cash is in the hands of the Central Bank."—R. G. Hawtrey, *The Gold Standard in Theory and Practice*, pp. 25–6.

With regard to that part of a country's currency which is composed of notes, the work of the Central Bank is inevitably little more than a routine. In countries where the gold standard is functioning freely, the Central Bank is obliged by law to give its notes in exchange for any amount of gold offered it at its statutory buying price, and to sell gold at the statutory price when any of its notes are presented to it for payment. In actual practice, however, the purchase or sale of gold by the Central Bank is unlikely to have any effect upon the volume of notes in circulation, since the transaction will nearly always be financed by cheque. In case notes are used on any such occasion, the effect will probably show itself fairly quickly by a corresponding increase or decrease in the till-money of the private banks. The latter will then adjust the situation by returning to the Central Bank the notes which the seller took out (or by withdrawing the notes with which the buyer paid for his gold), and the ultimate result will be a change in bank reserves but not in the volume of money in circulation.

Like any other bank, the Central Bank is in addition obliged to be prepared to meet the claims of its depositors for cash. These latter claims, depending as they do upon the cash requirements of the whole community, vary in accordance with a number of factors: the habits of private citizens, the frequency with which corporations pay wages, the general price-level, the activity of retail trade, and so on. Some of these factors are necessarily outside the control of the Central Bank. Others, such as the general price-level, may be influenced to some extent by the credit policy of the Central Bank, which will be discussed later in the chapter. But at least it is evident that whenever changes in this complex of factors initiate a drain upon the till-money of the private banks, and these banks "cash their cheques" at the Central Bank in much the same way as a private individual cashes a cheque at his bank, there is no alternative for the Central Bank but to pay out notes as demanded. A maximum limit to the issue of notes by any

Central Bank is customarily fixed by law in some relation to the Bank's gold holdings, but so long as the gold standard is functioning normally this limit is in fact always above any issue of notes that may be demanded.[1] Similarly, when for any reason an excessive amount of currency returns from circulation to the tills of the private banks, the latter will deposit the excess at the Central Bank in order to build up their reserves there. The Central Bank cannot then refuse to accept the notes for this purpose.

Thus legal tender money flows into or out of circulation in accordance with the demands of the public, and changes in the flow are not dependent on changes in the gold holdings of the country except in so far as the latter are reflected in the credit policy of the Central Bank and so transmitted to the general price-level and the activity of trade and industry in the country.[2] "The tendency of to-day is to watch and to control the creation of credit and to let the creation of currency follow suit, rather than, as formerly, to watch and control the creation of currency and to let the creation of credit follow suit."[3]

§ 2. The idea that a Central Bank should regulate its credit policy in accordance with the needs of internal stability is a

[1] For an admirable summary of the statutory provisions governing the reserves of the Central Banks of twenty-one different countries see "The International Gold Problem," *Collected Papers of the Royal Institute of International Affairs*, Oxford University Press, 1931, pp. 131–40.

[2] "In present-day conditions, when the active circulation of notes is mainly required for the purpose of meeting wage payments and small transactions usually settled in cash, an expansion in the active note issue is likely to be a result of active trade ensuing with an appreciable interval after an expansion in the Central Bank's deposits. Thus it is the latter which is now the factor of dominating importance . . . while the note issue which was a hundred years ago the initiating cause of inflation is to-day the factor which is the latest to be affected by the forces of expansion or contraction."—*Macmillan Report*, pp. 138–9).

[3] J. M. Keynes, *Monetary Reform*, New York, 1924, p. 200.

comparatively recent one. Central Banks are the historical descendants of powerful private banks, and as such they have inherited the natural desire to operate at the maximum profit. It was therefore logical that they should keep their earning assets at a maximum compatible with their reserves. As their ultimate reserves consisted of the gold which they held in their vaults, this tendency was the equivalent of the regulation of their credit policy in accordance with the direction of the flow of gold between the country in question and the outside world. When the foreign exchanges were moving adversely and a gold efflux was impending or actually in progress, a wise Central Bank would be ready to raise its rate of interest on its discounts and advances. Such means would serve to protect its reserve ratio by discouraging borrowers and attracting foreign lenders to help it to accommodate its compatriot clients. When the exchanges were tending in a favourable direction, on the other hand, it would be ready to lower its rate and increase its purchase of securities and other earning assets.

Within the last two decades, however, a new philosophy of Central Bank policy has grown up mainly as a result of three factors; a growing trend towards Socialism with its emphasis upon the rights of the State as against those of individual citizens and corporations; the tremendous price dislocations caused by wartime finance and crying aloud for all possible regulation in the future; and the disappearance of gold from circulation rendering unnecessary the holding of the traditional proportion of gold reserves to liabilities from fear of a national run on gold. The new philosophy is the outcome of the impatience of economists, bankers, and politicians with a system whereby national credit structures were dominated through the medium of foreign exchange rates by world forces over which they themselves had no control. The realization has gradually grown that it is highly important for the health of the national body economic that the supply of credit should be regulated as far as possible in obedience to the internal needs of the country (however these may best be discovered) rather than to autocratic fluctuations in foreign exchange rates.

How far the new philosophy had progressed in the United States by 1926 is well brought out by the following list, quoted by the late Governor Strong of the Federal Reserve Bank of New York in his testimony before the House Committee on Banking and Currency (H.R. 7895, April 9, 1926), of the charts which hung on the walls of the directors' room at that bank to aid the directors in their decisions as to the credit policy which they should follow at any time. "These charts are, first, the indices of money rates, employment, production, and prices, quite a variety of them. Then statistical information with regard to retail stores, which includes department stores, chain stores, and the 5-and-10-cent stores. We get reports from about 125 separate establishments in our district every month. Then sales and stocks of wholesale dealers, savings bank deposits, changes in rent, changes in wages, movements of funds about the country, foreign exchange rates, business profits, volume of buildings, failure statistics, the reports of car loadings, the consumption of electrical energy, all the crop statistics, all the foreign trade reports, such information as we can get on stocks of goods on hand—inventories, speculation, bank clearings, what the bank deposits show as to the changes in the deposit and loan account. I have not by any means listed them all." Such is the information on the basis of which the leaders of the Federal Reserve System attempt to formulate their credit policies; the mention of "foreign exchange rates," the erstwhile single fingerpost in the days of the unregulated gold standard, humbly sandwiched in among a mass of purely national statistics, is almost ironical.

The rise of this new philosophy implies, of course, a faith in the possibility of the realization of its end by means of a judicious use of the instruments at the disposal of Central Banks. These instruments are two in number, the power to raise or lower the Bank rate, or rediscount rate, and the power to buy and sell securities in the open market.

The task of attempting to secure internal price stability with so minute an armoury seems at first sight rather a staggering one. The theory upon which confidence in the adequacy of these two instruments is commonly based may be briefly summarized as follows:

The Central Bank is the creator of the cash upon which the credit structure of the country is built. It is used by the private banks as their own Bank at which they keep those reserves, realizable at any time in cash, which laws or prudence oblige them to hold against their liabilities. In normal times the cash reserves of the private banks, the sum of their till-money and their reserves at the Central Bank, are approximately equal to the minimum amount necessary to support the outstanding volume of deposit currency, though in the United States this involves the justifiable assumption that private banks remain true to the ideal of attempting to keep their free reserves equal to their legal reserves by remaining out of debt to the Reserve Banks. Now suppose that some private bank or banks have been overexpanding their earning assets, loans, advances, or security holdings. This expansion will immediately be reflected in an increase in the total deposits of the banking system, for even if the credit thus extended is immediately realized by the borrowers' drawing cheques against it, these cheques will be deposited by their recipients in other banks of the system, where they will swell total deposits. Against this increase in total deposits an increase in reserves will be required. Unless there has been a simultaneous rise in the gold holdings of the country and/or a simultaneous return flow of currency from circulation, this increase in reserves can only be obtained by increased borrowings from the Central Bank.[1] By raising the "Bank rate," the rate of interest at which it will satisfy this increased demand for borrowings, the Central Bank can make

[1] See above, p. 48.

such new borrowings unprofitable unless the private banks in turn increase their interest rates to their clients, and so discourage them from further borrowing and encourage the repayment of any unnecessary advances that are already outstanding. Thus by raising its Bank rate the Central Bank is able to dampen an expansion of deposit currency, or, if the financial community is already indebted to it, even to encourage liquidation of already existing advances. Conversely it is able at other times to discourage liquidation by lowering its rate and thereby prompting private banks and other lenders to proffer easier accommodation to their would-be clients.[1]

Should the Central Bank itself wish to initiate either a tighter or easier credit situation, it may do so through its power to deal in open-market securities. For instance, if cash is so plentiful in the open market that the reserve ratio of the banking system is considerably above the "prudence figure," private banks will be in a position to expand their deposits without recourse to the Central Bank, whose interest rate will therefore be powerless to prevent such expansion. If in these circumstances the Central Bank deems a further expansion of deposit currency unhealthy, it may soak up the redundant funds by selling a portion of its security holdings. Buyers of these securities will pay by means of cheques drawn on the banks where they keep their accounts, and these banks will find their reserves at the Central Bank reduced and their reserve ratio tending back towards the "prudence figure." They will then be discouraged from following too easy a loan

[1] Under the English system the effect of a rise in the Bank rate is not transmitted through the banks to the open market, since the banks are never themselves borrowers at the Bank of England. When it becomes necessary, either through an expansion in the deposits of the private banks or through a contraction in their reserve balances, to build up these reserves, the banks recall a portion of their most liquid assets, i.e. advances to bill brokers and other finance houses "in the City." These in turn are forced to have recourse to the Bank of England, whose rate of interest they then transmit to the open market.

policy towards their clients, and the impending expansion will be checked. By pursuing such a policy in the equilibrium position when the reserve ratio of the banking system already stands close to the "prudence figure," the Central Bank may actually induce liquidation if it deems that the volume of deposit currency already outstanding is excessive. Similarly, by pursuing a consistent policy of security purchases the Central Bank can so increase the reserve balances of the private banks as virtually to compel them to increase their loans and investments in order to avoid the wastefulness of carrying idle excess reserves.

It seems likely that this instrument of open-market operations is of greater value to a Central Bank than the power of altering the Bank rate itself, though it is of course difficult to compare the relative values of two instruments which are customarily used in such close conjunction. The fact that is of the most vital concern to the private banks is the actual size of their reserves, since these must be carefully conserved against the possible demands of the banks' various creditors. The increase in the cost to the financial community of maintaining such reserves resulting from a rise of two, three, or even four, per cent in the Bank rate may be a matter of small concern if open-market rates are high and so long as borrowings at the Central Bank are not heavy—particularly when it is remembered that for every dollar or pound borrowed the banking system as a whole may expand its earning assets up to some ten times that amount.[1] But any marked reduction in

[1] "Under the assumption that one dollar of reserve, maintained by the member bank by continuous borrowing, would enable it to keep outstanding interest-bearing loans variously estimated at from two to ten dollars . . . a rediscount rate to operate as a true penalty rate would have to be set at a point far above the rates found in Federal Reserve or other central banking practice."—A. C. Whitaker, Speech at Annual Meeting of American Economic Association, December 1929. Of course, to the extent that the borrower of the loan immediately withdrew part of the proceeds from the lending

the size of reserve balances as a result of the open-market policy of the Central Bank will call into operation a factor different in kind from the dislike of the financial community for paying high rates for its accommodation, namely, its dislike of being appreciably indebted to the central institution at any price.

§ 3. Such are the instruments with which Central Banks are generally endowed for the execution of their policy of credit control. How adequate they are to the task of attaining internal price stability is a question which will be considered in a later chapter (ch. vi). It is significant that M. Jacques Rueff in summing up his conclusions in an article submitted to the Gold Delegation of the Financial Committee of the League of Nations[1] can only say, "A systematic investigation of the possibilities of influencing the general price-level is likely to lead to the conclusion that one cannot hope to arrive at complete stability of the purchasing power of the monetary unit and that one can only try to reduce the breadth of the variations." For the moment suffice it to admit that it is at least possible for any Central Bank, equipped with the two instruments of the Bank rate and open-market operations, to aim at such stability; that there is a growing sentiment in favour of Central Banks adopting this aim; and that the United States, one of the two most important financial nations of the

bank and paid them to individuals who failed to redeposit them in the same bank, the bank's reserves would be reduced and its borrowings increased correspondingly; it would itself therefore have to increase its borrowings by more than one-tenth of the increase in its earning assets. Only if the whole loan were withdrawn, however, and none of it redeposited at the same bank, would the borrowings of the lending bank be increased by as much as its earning assets. Even then, if the rate of return which it obtained on the loan were higher than the rate which it had to pay to the Reserve Bank, the transaction would be profitable.

[1] *Selected Documents submitted to the Gold Delegation of the Financial Committee of the League of Nations*, Geneva, 1930, p. 51.

world, has been openly committed to this policy for the last decade.

Now the first and most obvious step that any Central Bank which set out to attain internal price stability would take towards that end would be the negativing of the effects of an inward or outward movement of gold. Nothing could be more at variance with the ideal of stability than that the banking system of any country should be laid open to the full effects upon its reserves which result under an "unmanaged" gold standard from a change in the gold holdings of the country. These effects can be promptly negatived by the Central Bank's carrying out the necessary operations in the open market, soaking up an inflow of gold by selling an equivalent volume of securities, or compensating the banks for an outflow of gold by the requisite security purchases.[1] Such operations would tend to become almost a matter of routine to any Central Bank which had resolutely set its face towards the pursuit of internal stability.

Unfortunately the policy of sterilizing gold movements not only negatives the theoretically automatic self-distributive tendency of gold but actually substitutes a gold flow which carries with it the seeds of its own perpetuation, since the corrective changes in the price-level of the gold-losing or gold-receiving country will not take place, and the cause of the disequilibrium will continue. The countries which will be best able to sustain this policy for any length of time are those whose balance of international payments is consistently favourable, since their gold reserves will tend to be superabundant, thus giving them a free hand for the execution of their policies. In the case of these countries, the necessary operations will

[1] Actually these transactions should involve securities to the value of about 90 per cent of the value of the gold movements rather than an equivalent volume if the gold is imported or exported by someone other than a bank, since the banking system's deposits will then be altered by an equivalent amount, necessitating a change of about 10 per cent of that amount in their reserve balances (cf. p. 49).

consist of the sterilization of the steady gold imports occasioned by their favourable balance, in order to preserve price stability by obviating the inflation which might otherwise result. On the other hand, if their favourable balance is due to deep-seated causes, such as large annual interest payments on capital held overseas, or a high level of industrial efficiency, the inflow of gold is not likely to be checked unless some rise of internal prices occurs to correct the country's "advantage" in world markets.[1]

Meanwhile, the Central Banks of those countries which are losing gold owing to a persistently unfavourable balance of payments will but tend to perpetuate their gold losses if they attempt to negative their deflationary effects. So long as the causes of their unfavourable balance continue, their chief hope of escape must lie in an attempt to correct their "disadvantage" in world markets by a fall in their internal prices. Sooner or later, in any case, if this situation continues, a Central Bank in a gold-losing country will find its supplies of gold so diminished and its liabilities so increased by its operations in the open market that the necessity of preserving its reserve ratio will compel it to desist from further counteracting operations. It will then be faced with the task of initiating a policy of credit deflation. This deflation will tend to be all the more severe, first, because it has been postponed until gold reserves have sunk to a precariously low level, and secondly, because it will not be aided by the gold-receiving country in adjusting its position of relative international disadvantage, as it would have been under an unmanaged international gold standard, since the latter will continue to avoid a price inflation by sterilizing its gold imports.

An excellent illustration of the prolongation of disequilibrium in the commodity balances of payments which may occur when

[1] The possibility of a correction of an unbalanced international payments account by means of international transfers of capital will be considered in the next chapter.

a gold-receiving creditor country does not force her imports of gold to have their orthodox effects of increasing the volume of the country's total currency in circulation is found in American economic history in the period 1921–24. "In these four years, but little less than $1,500 millions net gold was imported. Normally according to traditional theories, such an import of gold would have led to a very considerable general rise in prices. But no such rise occurred. The inflowing gold went instead to the Federal Reserve Banks in payment of member bank borrowings. In this way, these huge supplies of the money metal were absorbed. American commodity prices, meanwhile, after 1920, continued a decided though gradual downward trend, while those in gold-losing countries, under rigid price-maintenance policies, declined but slightly more rapidly. Thus the usual price stimulus to a reduction in (American) exports and to an increase in imports simply did not appear. Hence the normal correctives expected by many for balance of trade adjustments completely failed."[1]

Thus it seems an inevitable corollary of the new philosophy of Central Bank management of credit that gold movements should only be allowed their "automatic" and self-destructive effects in countries which are consistently losing gold, in which countries the effects will of course be drastically deflationary. In all other countries where the new philosophy holds sway (and it already does so in high economic circles in the majority of important gold-standard countries)[2] Central Banks will tend as a matter of routine to negative the effects by their operations. In doing so, they will deal the death-blow to the hopes of orthodox theory in the automatic functioning of the inter-

[1] J. H. Rogers, *America Weighs her Gold*, Yale University Press, 1931, pp. 96–7.

[2] Cf. Speech of Rt. Hon. R. McKenna, Chairman, at the general meeting of shareholders of the Midland Bank, London, January 29, 1932. "Deliberate, skilled, and resolute monetary management, with or without gold, is a *sine qua non* of steady economic progress."—Quoted from *Bankers' Magazine* (London), March 1932, p. 479.

national gold standard. Perhaps, however, orthodox theory will not be missed. "The conception of the gold standard prevailing before the War must doubtless be made largely responsible for the false ideas that inspired monetary policy during the War and the years immediately following. The whole lesson of the world's sad experiences of monetary mismanagement can only be drawn if we realize that the gold standard is nothing else than a paper standard, the value of which is entirely dependent upon the way in which the supply of means of payment is regulated."[1]

The logical conclusion of the new philosophy of monetary management would seem to lie in the attempt of the financially important Central Banks of the world through international co-operation to secure so firm a control over the values of their respective currencies that the value of gold itself, into which these currencies would be convertible, should be completely subject to international control. Such an end, if achieved, would mean the exact reversal of the conditions under which orthodox gold-standard theory evolved. Instead of the value of gold determining the value of currency, the managed values of the various currencies would now determine the value of gold. We shall return to a consideration of the possibilities of such a situation in a later chapter (ch. viii).

§ 4. One further factor making for the falsification of the orthodox assumption of the automatic self-regulation of the gold supply must here be noted, though its discussion in detail will be postponed to a later chapter (ch. vi). The reasoning upon which this assumption is based involves the postulation of a high adjustability of the internal prices of any country. It is assumed by many orthodox theorists that not only do prices respond readily to a change in the volume of total currency, but that they respond in the same direction, if not

[1] Gustav Cassel, *Post-War Monetary Stabilisation*, New York, 1928, pp. 4–5.

to the same degree, in all classes of commodities and, be it added, services.

Unless this hypothesis is accepted, it is conceivable that the whole of a rise in the general price-level might be accounted for by a rise in the prices of domestic goods and services which do not enter into the country's foreign trade. These "sheltered" commodities form a large part of the annual production of every country. They include almost all forms of service, from professional services down to manual labour, perishable commodities, commodities whose bulk makes the cost of their transportation high, the services of retailers, which customarily become more costly in times of a fall in wholesale prices, the benefit of which is not wholly handed on to the consumer, rents, transportation, communication, taxes, etc. These commodities may vary widely in price from one country to another. "Anyone who has travelled abroad must have come to the conclusion, even on superficial observation, that, in exchange for the same value in money, much more can be obtained in one country than in another."[1]

The greater the proportion of the total production of any country which these sheltered commodities compose, the greater the proportion of any alteration in the total volume of currency which they will tend to absorb. In the extreme case, where they absorb the whole of any new emission of credit due, say, to an inflow of gold, the price-level of the products of the country's "unsheltered industries," i.e. those industries whose products enter into international commerce, would be unchanged, the country's relative advantage in international commodity trade would be maintained, and the inflow of gold would continue, unchecked by the rise in internal prices. Similarly, if a country is losing gold through standing at a relative disadvantage in foreign trade, the fall in prices, which must, according to orthodox theory, ensue upon the

[1] L. J. A. Trip, *International Price-Level Adjustments*, League of Nations, *Selected Documents*, p. 82.

outflow of gold, will not bring any relief to the situation unless the price-level of the country's foreign trade products shows at least some degree of adjustability.

Now, in actual practice, the assumption that the price-level of unsheltered commodities will be as responsive to an inflation of the currency as the price-level of sheltered commodities is likely to prove far from justified. It is, of course, impossible to expect that all prices will rise proportionately in response to an increase in the volume of currency in circulation. The price-rise is caused by the increased spending of those members of the community who come into possession of the new currency, and will, therefore, in the first instance at least, be confined to those commodities which they choose to buy in excess of their previous purchases. But, even allowing for this inevitable unevenness of movement in different commodity-prices, there is a strong reason for believing that unsheltered industries will not experience as great an increase in the demand for their products in proportion to their existing output as will sheltered industries. The new currency will pass into the hands of citizens of the country, and be spent by them, but even if they were to increase their purchases of all types of goods, international and domestic, in an equal proportion, the effect upon the prices of all goods would not be the same. For, supposing the increase in the volume of the currency were such as to warrant an increase of 10 per cent in the spendings of the community for all types of goods, this would mean an increase of 10 per cent in the demand for the products of the sheltered industries, whose sales are, by hypothesis, purely local, but only an increase of, say, 5 per cent in the total demand for the goods of an unsheltered industry whose sales were 50 per cent foreign and 50 per cent domestic.

Indeed, the prices of international goods, the produce of unsheltered industries, which are, after all, the prices which must be affected by an expansion or contraction of the currency if the necessary relief is to be obtained according to the orthodox theory, are likely to be determined by international considerations fully as much as, if not more than, by purely national influences. The improvements in the methods of transportation and communication, the forces of money, credit, and investment, and the intensive development of the mechanism of foreign trade, all make for a closer internationalization of the prices of any goods for which there is an international demand. It is, therefore, for this reason also unlikely that an alteration in the outstanding volume of the currency of a country will have an equal effect on the price-level of both international and domestic goods.

Again, the adjustability of all prices has been much reduced with the progress of trade unionism and with the consequent resistance to wage reductions. Such resistance is apt to place industries in which labour is strongly unionized at a great disadvantage relative to other industries at times when deflation is necessary, since a disproportionate share of the burden of falling prices has then to be borne in the former group by the factors of production other than labour. If the unsheltered industries of any country happen to be strongly unionized, the resistance of labour to a reduction of its money share of the proceeds of production at a time when world prices are falling may place that country for a considerable time at a relative disadvantage in international commodity trade, and may thereby initiate and prolong an outflow of gold. "Speedy adjustment of the international balances of payment has been much impeded in post-War years by the growing rigidity of the social and economic structure. . . . From the standpoint of the working of the international gold standard, such a rigidity of social structure and of the scale of money incomes implies that the adjustment, which might under more elastic conditions have been made by movements in the domestic price and income structure, is at best delayed, with the inevitable effect that gold movements, or . . . changes in the holdings of foreign exchange assets at the command of the Central

Bank, take place on a larger scale than would otherwise have been necessary. At worst, adjustments are not made at all."[1] It is evident that an export industry whose labourers are strongly unionized, and whose market is largely abroad, will be both less able and less willing to reduce its prices in response to a decrease in the volume of currency in the country resulting from an outflow of gold than the champions of orthodox theory have commonly supposed.

§ 5. Reviewing the conclusions of this chapter, we find that the Central Bank's control of the note circulation is merely a routine affair of issuing or withdrawing notes in accordance with the demands of the public. The Central Bank has, however, a considerable degree of control over the volume of deposit currency through the employment of the instruments of the Bank rate and open-market operations, by means of which it can do much to influence the size of the reserve balances of the private banks, upon which the pyramid of the country's credit rests. With the rise of the new philosophy of attempting to regulate the volume of the currency in accordance with the demands of internal stability, rather than, as of old, in accordance with movements in the foreign exchange rates, Central Banks now tend to use these instruments to make the value of their currencies independent of variations in the value of gold as shown in the movements of world prices, particularly by "sterilizing" inflowing or outflowing gold streams. Such a policy divorces the volume of total currency outstanding from any direct connection with the volume of the country's gold holdings, and thus aims the crowning blow at the orthodox theory of the automatic self-regulation of the distribution of the world's gold according to the requirements of the various gold-standard countries. Even when gold movements are still allowed to have something of their tradi-

[1] T. E. Gregory, *The Gold Standard and its Future*, pp. 33, 36.

tional effect upon the total volume of the currency, and even if the corresponding rise or fall in the domestic price-level ensues according to the orthodox theory, there is no guarantee that the rise or fall will occur in the price-level of the foreign trade commodities of the country to anything like the same extent as in the price-level of purely domestic commodities. If it does not, the country's relative advantage or disadvantage in international commodity trade, which set the gold flow in motion, will continue unabated. In any case, few prices possess the high degree of adjustability presupposed by the orthodox theory.

Thus it is no longer true that international gold movements carry with them the seeds of their own destruction.

CHAPTER IV

CENTRAL BANK POLICIES AND INTERNATIONAL CAPITAL MOVEMENTS

§ 1. We have now seen that there is little hope of an amelioration of the maldistribution of the world's gold from the supposed automatic tendency of commodity prices so to respond to international gold movements as to destroy the forces which caused the flow of gold. Owing to Central Bank management of the internal credit situation of each country, gold movements, particularly when inward, are not allowed to work their normal effects upon domestic prices, so that when their causes are more deep-seated than a mere seasonal or other purely temporary disequilibrium, there is little prospect of their being removed by an adjustment of commodity-trade balances.

The excess of the value of a country's imports over its exports or vice versa is, however, by no means the only factor that leads to that disequilibrium in balance-sheets of international payments which it is the purpose of a gold movement to correct. Mr. Keynes has divided the flow of foreign exchange transactions into three classes, (1) balance of payments on income account, (2) balance of payments on capital account, and (3) balance of payments on speculative account.[1] It is only into class (1) that the balance of payments on commodity account enters. What then are the prospects of checking the tendencies towards a maldistribution of gold through an adjustment of the balance of payments of the last two types? For the purposes of this question, the two types may be considered together as being payments on capital account, since the speculative movement of funds constitutes

[1] J. M. Keynes, "The Prospects of the Sterling Exchange," *Yale Review*, Spring 1932, p. 434.

in fact a species of short-term loan from the speculators' countries to those countries in which the funds are put to use.

Now capital is to the saver who accumulates it as the finished product is to the entrepreneur, a source of income to be traded to the highest bidder. Being, moreover, in the form of money, its universal acceptability and easy "transportation" render it extremely fluid,very much more so than commodities. The price of a tooth-brush may be considerably higher in France than in Czechoslovakia before tooth-brushes will be exported from the latter to the former. The exporter must first make contact with the importer who deals in his particular wares, must then convince him that Czechoslovakian tooth-brushes are at least as good as the brand which he is used to handling, and finally must obtain a contract at a price sufficient to allow him a safe margin to cover transportation costs, customs duties, and so on. The price of money, on the other hand, will normally not vary considerably between different gold-standard countries without initiating a flow of funds from the market of one nation to the market of another. Money is money, i.e. the power to purchase goods and services, the world over in a sense in which Czechoslovakian tooth-brushes are not French tooth-brushes. So long as the gold standard is functioning freely, crowns may be changed into francs at will; there is generally only one money market in each country, and the rates current in that market are widely published, so that the necessary preliminary of making contact with the appropriate foreign importer is immensely simplified; and finally the cost of transportation, including customs duties, is almost negligible between gold-standard countries. Thus it would seem natural that of the two impulses which lead to an international transfer of funds, the impulse arising from the attractiveness of prices of commodities in one country relative to those in another, and the impulse arising from the attractiveness of interest rates in one country relative to those in another, the latter should be the more flexible and the more powerful in the short run.[1]

Here then is an item of high liquidity in balance-sheets of international payments which in normal times might be expected to respond immediately to a disequilibrium between the interest rates of different money markets, and which should therefore fall directly under the influence of Central Banks who are able to retain some degree of control over the rates obtaining in their respective money markets. Indeed, in so far as international payments on income account are extremely unlikely even to approximate to a position of balance now that the automatic corrective effects of gold movements upon commodity prices have been destroyed, the ability of Central Banks operating on the gold standard to influence the balance of payments on capital account through manipulation of interest rates is a matter of greater importance to them than ever before if they hope to obviate heavy international gold movements.[2]

[1] Cf. G. D. H. Cole, *Gold, Credit and Employment*, p. 31. "The chief cause that normally makes gold move from London to New York, or from New York to London, is the possibility of getting more for it in the one place than in the other. This may mean that it will buy more goods, of the sorts that pass current in world trade; or it may mean that it will earn more interest or profit in one place than in the other. . . . The fact that most influences international gold movements under normal conditions is the movement of interest rates."

Monthly Letter of the National City Bank of New York, November 1928, p. 178. "Trade balances and income from investments have become subordinate factors in the international balance of payments, opportunities for the advantageous employment of capital being the decisive influence."

J. A. Todd, *The Fall of Prices*, London, 1931, p. 53. "The old idea that the normal method of adjusting the balance of trade between nations is to pay the difference in gold dies very hard, though it is of course no longer true. . . . The real equilibrium of indebtedness between nations is maintained not by the passing of gold but by the creation or extinction of debts either temporary or permanent."

[2] "The entire gold standard is based on the functioning of capital movements, on their elasticity in view of relative changes of interest

§ 2. The nations of the world fall fairly readily into two groups, capital-exporting nations and capital-importing nations. Before the War, Great Britain, itself for a prolonged period the most important nation in the former category, possessed in London the great free gold market of the world. This market was *par excellence* the meeting place of the member nations of the two categories. The Bank rate of the Bank of England, which, on account of the high degree of centralization which characterized the country's banking structure, could be made "effective" in the open market almost at will, enjoyed therefore a world-wide influence. This influence was consistently used towards a proper regulation of the net export of capital in accordance with the contemporary course and volume of the balance of payments on income account. And that not from altruistic motives but in obedience to the natural functioning of the laws of supply and demand in the money market; for movements of funds in settlement of a balance of payments on capital account tend to counteract the forces which set them in motion in exactly the same way as, according to orthodox theory, do movements of funds on commodity account. "Under normally healthy financial conditions, should a gold outflow temporarily tighten money rates, a resulting increase of foreign short credits is almost sure to arrest the flow. Similarly, a gold inflow, by reducing money rates, is almost equally sure to correct itself by a resulting outflow of foreign and domestic short-term funds seeking more profitable markets."[1]

It was under just these "normally healthy financial con-

rates; if a country is not able to attract foreign capital by raising the interest rates, then it may lose gold until the gold standard breaks down. The amount of gold moved and the directions in which it moves are largely based, in their changes at least, on the changes in the capital movements all over the world."—Dr. M. Palyi, *Some Problems of International Banking Policy*, Collected Papers on *The International Gold Problem*, pp. 118–19.

[1] J. H. Rogers, *America Weighs her Gold*, p. 60.

ditions" that the London money market had the good fortune to be able to operate prior to 1914. "A very considerable surplus was due to Great Britain on current international account, and this, if no steps had been taken to avert the natural consequence, would have been settled largely by imports of gold. Simple but adequate measures were, however, adopted by the Bank of England. If gold was coming to London in excess of our currency requirements, the rate of interest was lowered and foreigners were encouraged to borrow from us. If, on the other hand, through excessive lending abroad, too much gold was being taken, the rate for money was raised; foreign borrowing was thereby discouraged, and the favourable balance of payments rapidly replenished our gold stock. Thus the surplus on current international account was used according to the needs of the time to reinforce our gold reserves or to provide accommodation for debtor countries to develop their economic resources."[1]

The influence of this Bank rate policy upon the course of the foreign exchanges in London, and hence upon the movements of gold to and from Great Britain, is strikingly brought out by the remarkably stable level at which the gold holdings of the Bank of England remained over the long period of development in overseas trade prior to the Great War. It is at first sight puzzling that during this period, when very considerable fluctuations were occurring annually in the balance of payments on income account, gold movements into and out of the world's financial centre should have been so consistently small. Figures for the net import of gold bullion and specie into the United Kingdom for the ten whole years prior to the Great War are as follows:—

[1] Rt. Hon. R. McKenna, Speech at the General Meeting of the shareholders of the Midland Bank, January 29, 1932, *Bankers' Magazine* (London), March 1932, p. 479.

NET IMPORTS OF GOLD BULLION AND SPECIE INTO THE UNITED KINGDOM[1]

	£
1904	837,450
1905	7,738,053
1906	3,425,323
1907	6,222,538
1908	3,823,783[2]
1909	7,343,293
1910	6,423,321
1911	8,593,213
1912	6,150,412
1913	13,446,190

Over the same period, the total value of exports, including re-exports of goods previously imported from abroad, ranged between £380,000,000 and £635,000,000, while the total value of imports varied from £550,000,000 to £770,000,000.[3] It will, therefore, clearly be seen what a small percentage of the total of Great Britain's international payments was composed of the "corrective" flow of gold. Actually such gold as was imported seems to have been devoted to artistic and industrial uses rather than to monetary purposes, for during the whole of this period the figure for the quarterly average of the gold holdings of the Bank of England remained continually between £30,000,000 and £40,000,000 with the exception of the autumn quarter of each of the last three years. Indeed, the figures for the net imports seem to represent a very fair proportion of the world's annual gold production for Great Britain to have retained for her growing monetary and industrial needs. Certainly they fade into insignificance when compared with post-War international gold movements. Chart II above (p. 36) shows the gigantic fluctuations which occurred during the period 1923–32 in the size of the monetary gold stock of the

[1] Figures from Board of Trade Annual Statistical Abstract for the United Kingdom.

[2] Net export.

[3] Board of Trade Annual Statistical Abstract.

United States, apart from gold imports for industrial purposes. During the first three years of this period, this stock grew at an average rate of $280,000,000 per year; in the twelve months from June 1927 to June 1928 it fell by $500,000,000; between January 1929 and August 1931 it again rose at an average annual rate of some $300,000,000; while during the three autumn months of 1931 it decreased by over $600,000,000. Between April and June 1932 a further fall of $400,000,000 occurred, only to be followed by an increase of $600,000,000 during the last half of the year. Finally the loss of $200,000,000 of gold in three weeks during February 1933 hastened the suspension of the gold standard in the United States. Beside such vast fluctuations, Great Britain's small annual net imports of the pre-War decade take on the aspect of normal increments under a sanely ordered international system. A large portion of this February outflow of gold was paid out to hoarders in the country, and was not actually exported from the United States.

§ 3. Unfortunately the very fluidity which endows the international movement of capital with the power to become the balancing factor, by means of which gold shipments may be obviated, also makes it a strong potential force for evil. Some transitory, and often non-economic, phenomenon may react upon the minds of international lenders or borrowers without previous warning, and may precipitate immediately a concerted flow of funds to or from some particular market or markets. Such a flow may far outweigh in suddenness and size any international disequilibrium of payments which could ever arise on account of relative maladjustments in commodity price-levels and may therefore entail heavy international shipments of gold. The most common of such phenomena which have appeared from time to time in recent years is an outbreak of speculation in some money market, which may compel the Central Bank to raise interest rates there in an effort to check the speculative tendency and thereby add the attraction of high open-market rates to the already strong encouragement to holders of foreign balances to seek profitable employment for their liquid funds in the speculative market; a breakdown of the confidence of lenders in the solvency or good faith of borrowing countries; a breakdown of the confidence of lenders in the soundness of conditions in their own country; and considerations of policy which may divert lending or borrowing governments or Central Banks from the pursuit of their purely economic interests to the pursuit of some special end.

The first of the above types of forces making for disequilibrium in international lending was well exemplified by the flow of funds to the United States during the Stock Market speculation of 1928–29, when rising interest rates and the glamour of speculative fortunes sucked Europe's liquid resources into the New York market as into an insatiable sponge. This type of force differs from the other three types mentioned above in that it is an ordinary economic phenomenon, funds flowing from one market to another in response to a differential, actual or anticipated, in interest rates. As such, it should fall within the range of Central Bank control and will not be discussed here (see ch. vi).

The other three types, however, are not ordinary economic phenomena in the sense that the determining motive of the lending agents is not simply their greatest economic advantage, in the form of the highest available interest rates, but some non-economic purpose, such as security or a political end. All three types of forces appear to have been actively militating against the adjustment through lending of the disequilibrium in international payments during the years which have ensued since the autumn of 1929.[1] It is unfortunately

[1] Cf. J. M. Keynes, "The Prospects of the Sterling Exchange," *Yale Review*, spring 1932, p. 439. "Huge capital transactions both ways [in London] have been swamping the income balance and have been temporarily depriving it of the decisive importance which it must possess in the long run."

impossible to obtain anything like an accurate figure for the net import or export of short-term capital in the case of any country. At least, however, the palpable maldistribution of the world's gold at the present time makes it safe to say that the "surpluses of lender countries on current international account" are no longer being "used according to the needs of the time to reinforce their gold reserves or to provide accommodation for debtor countries to develop their economic resources." These three types will therefore now be examined in turn.

§ **4.** For the successful functioning of international lending as a means of obviating gold movements between countries with a favourable and countries with an unfavourable balance of international payments on income account, two closely related psychological factors are necessary to creditor nations, the disposition not to "hoard" money, and a liberal attitude towards foreign investments. These two factors are, of course, merely different degrees of the same psychological phenomenon, confidence. They are, however, worth distinguishing, since the situation, confidence in which may be lacking, is in the first case the internal situation and in the second case the situation abroad. Mistrust of conditions in foreign countries is continually present to some degree in every creditor country, and is the explanation of the differential which normally exists between the rate of return on domestic and foreign bonds. The question of "hoarding," dependent as it is upon confidence in domestic conditions, belongs to the second type of factors making for a breakdown in foreign lending and will be discussed below (§ 5). For the moment attention will be confined to the question of mistrust of conditions outside the creditor countries.

From the middle of the nineteenth century till the outbreak of the Great War, conditions were wellnigh ideal for a steady transference of capital from creditor to debtor countries. The political horizon was comparatively clear with no such sore spots as a chaotic China or a recalcitrant Australia obtruding themselves as nightmares into the dreamless sleep of international financiers. Even Latin America confined its turbulence to local politics, and for the sake of its international standing treated its economic obligations as sacrosanct. At the same time, the borrowing countries consisted for the most part of those areas of the world which were crying for economic development, and seemed to promise ample returns on any capital invested in them; bankruptcy must have seemed unthinkable for countries with the untapped resources of Argentina or Brazil.

Conditions have changed sadly with the post-War period, and particularly with the great depression of 1929–? (it would be dangerous to attempt to substitute a date for this question mark as yet). While the appearance of a huge volume of international obligations contracted during the War added greatly to the difficulties of debtor nations in their attempts to secure the amount of foreign exchange necessary for their annual repayments of interest and principal on commercial debts, the drastic scaling-down of War debts which necessarily followed during the post-War reconstruction period popularized a somewhat unethical attitude towards international obligations in general. No fire or even brimstone was seen to descend upon debtor governments who flatly declared themselves unable to meet the debts which they had contracted for war purposes. It was, therefore, natural that governments who had had no part in the War, States, Provinces, even perhaps municipalities and railroads, should begin to wonder whether they had been wrong all along in exerting themselves so strenuously to keep their word with foreign capitalists. While debtor countries were pondering this problem, they were overtaken by the great depression. With the sweeping decline of international trade after 1929, their difficulties were enormously enhanced by an unprecedented "transfer problem," the problem, that is, of how to secure currency of the creditor countries, when the latter's imports, and therefore purchases of foreign exchange, were being cut to the bone. Largely as a result of these circumstances, there ensued the era of international defaults, which has banished for an indefinite period the disposition to lend abroad without a high "risk differential" in interest rates.

An immediate effect of the disappearance of international confidence is that funds no longer flow from one market to another in obedience to differences in the interest rates obtaining in the various money markets of the world. It was for this reason that many English authorities have maintained, in answer to overseas criticism, that it would have been worse than useless to raise the Bank rate in London in the autumn of 1931 in an effort to save the gold standard in England. Such action, they argue, would merely have accentuated the suspicion of foreigners, who were already withdrawing their liquid balances at an alarming rate, and would have led to an even more rapid outflow of funds. This contention is at least well supported by the following extract from a London report published in the *New York Times* of February 29, 1932. "The recent reduction of the bank rate seems to have greatly strengthened foreign confidence in Britain's financial future. This is now finding expression in substantial Continental buying of sterling bills, sterling securities, and sterling itself. . . . The same change in foreign sentiment is held largely responsible for the week's rise in sterling exchange. . . . French bankers visiting London this week predict that much of the gold lost by London to France will eventually find its way back." No clearer example could be found of the way in which lack of confidence not only negatives, but may actually reverse, the normal tendency of funds to flow to those markets where they may command the highest rate of interest.

The most unfortunate result of this phenomenon lies in the consequent inability of Central Banks to influence the international flow of capital by a manipulation of their interest rates, a power which we have seen cause to believe to have been of paramount importance in the proper regulation of the pre-War gold standard. But the breakdown of confidence brings with it more deep-seated difficulties than simply the contemporary disequilibrium of the balance of payments on capital account. So far no distinction has been made between short-term and long-term capital, but the distinction is an important one where foreign confidence is concerned, since a lack of confidence will be reflected in a disinclination on the part of lenders to embark on further long-term foreign loans some time before a similar disinclination makes itself felt in the short-term money markets. So long as a country remains upon the gold standard, short-term funds advanced to it may be withdrawn at will on the suspicion of impending trouble; or if the borrowing country is one which has no money market of its own, but which obtains short-term funds for the financing of its current trade requirements through the acceptance market of a creditor country, the credits so advanced fall due at short intervals, and renewal can then be denied if the creditor feels any doubt as to the future solvency of the borrower.

The situation is, however, very different in the case of long-term loans. In this case, the capital cannot be extracted at will from the borrowing country, should the latter show any sign of impending insolvency or unwillingness to meet its obligations. The holders of the bonds in question will therefore attempt to realize their assets on the markets which deal in them, lest they become worthless on their hands through a default of the borrowers. The rush to sell depresses prices in the foreign bond market, where the supply of bonds will greatly exceed the demand. This in turn will make the market in question unreceptive to any new foreign bond issues. Until a rise in the demand for this type of bonds relative to the supply is reflected by a rise in their price, local promoters will be unwilling to undertake the flotation of any new long-term issues for their foreign clients, and the outflow of long-term capital to the debtor nations will be peremptorily cut off. Indeed, in so far as the latter are meeting their sinking fund requirements on previous issues on time, they will be repaying capital to their former lenders, and the flow of long-term capital will be definitely reversed.

This is the situation which appears to have arisen in the money markets of the chief creditor countries since the autumn of 1929. "Difficulties have resulted from the international lending power of the creditor countries being redistributed, favourably to two countries, France and the United States, which have used this power only spasmodically, and adversely to the country, Great Britain, which was formerly the leader in this field and has the most highly developed organization for the purpose. . . . This redistribution of lending power need not, however, in itself have interfered with the working of the gold standard. The difficulties have arisen through the partial failure of the two recipients, during the last two or three years, to employ the receipts in the way in which Great Britain had always employed hers, namely either in the purchase of additional imports or in making additional foreign loans on long-term. On the contrary, they have required the payment of a large part of their annual surplus either in actual gold or in short-term liquid claims. This is a contingency which the normal working of the international gold standard does not contemplate and for which it does not provide."[1]

This increased preference for liquid assets over long-term claims is the crux of the whole situation induced by a loss of confidence in overseas borrowers. While the continuance of international lending on short-term account may help to ease the transfer problem for debtor nations for the time being, it is fraught with danger if not accompanied by a continuance of foreign lending on long-term account. In the first place, countries, in whose money markets is held an ever-increasing volume of foreign short-term funds, are living upon a potential

[1] *Macmillan Report*, p. 107.

quicksand, inasmuch as these funds are liable to be withdrawn with such suddenness as to dislocate the entire financial structure of the country. It is possession of just such vast short-term balances in many foreign money markets that has recently given France her great politico-economic influence in the councils of the world, an influence which has dwindled considerably now that abandonment of the gold standard has become a fashion, not a crime.

But the increased preference for lending money abroad on short, rather than on long, term has a second unhealthy reaction upon the financial structure of the debtor countries. To many countries, particularly those which are relatively backward, or which include territories which are still in process of being developed, a steady inflow of long-term capital has become a virtual necessity. In so far as this normal supply is suddenly cut off, or "short-circuited" into the short-loan market and perhaps a counter-flow set up for the purposes of amortization of the already outstanding foreign debt, an erstwhile source of purchasing power will be withdrawn from the market for investment goods and investment services, which were formerly produced for the development of the country, and a fall in prices is likely to ensue.[1] This fall in prices is likely to be reinforced by the increased competition for foreign exchange which will result from the necessity of the debtor country's now having to attempt to meet its foreign obligations without the accustomed assistance of an inflow of foreign funds on capital account. With the drying up of this source of supply of foreign exchange, competition for the remaining supply will be heightened, and the price-level of the country's export commodities will tend to be forced down still further.

Moreover, no country in the world can maintain a high level

[1] According to the writers of the *Macmillan Report*, "The effect on prices internationally of the increased preference for employing resources in the purchase of liquid claims, including gold, is the same as that of hoarding in a primitive community."—*Macmillan Report*, p. 68.

of industrial efficiency or enjoy full economic expansion if consistently starved of capital for the maintenance and development of her productive capacity. It is for this purpose that the debtor countries who are not yet in a position to satisfy their own capital requirements are so essentially dependent on imports of foreign long-term capital. "There is a serious consequence of this situation," international lack of confidence, "with regard to the prospect of overcoming the depression. Whereas, in countries which have an average or greater than average accumulation of capital, that capital collects in the banks during a period of depression and thereby makes it possible for rates of interest to be reduced, thus lessening production costs, the resuscitation of production in countries which are poor in capital depends on capital being offered from abroad on sufficiently favourable terms, and this again frequently depends on events which it is quite impossible to foresee."[1]

If the need for long-term capital is very great, the would-be borrowers may be tempted to avail themselves of the comparative ease prevailing in the various short-term money markets to raise there the funds which they will subsequently use as though they had been borrowed on long term. This practice appears to have been widely resorted to by European countries, Germany in particular, during 1930 and the first half of 1931, when the long-term money markets of the world were virtually closed to them, while short money was available at a highly attractive rate.

In New York the practice was reflected in the astounding growth in the volume of acceptances "based on goods stored in or shipped between foreign countries." This item, which,

[1] Karl Pribram, *World-unemployment and its Problems,* Norman Wait Harrison Memorial Foundation lecture, University of Chicago, June 1931. Cf. Lansing Warren in *New York Times* of December 19, 1931, "The very flight of capital, which is uncontrollable, becomes a factor to prevent Germany benefiting fully from her favourable trade balance, since a large part of the returns are believed to be never repatriated."

prior to 1925, had been practically peculiar to the London acceptance market, made its debut on the New York market in February of that year, at a time, significantly enough, when the New York acceptance rate had been less than the London rate for nine consecutive months. After making but slow progress during the first three years of its career, this item registered rapid gains during the years 1928–30. By February 1930 it had become the largest of the various classes of acceptances outstanding on the New York market, and in December of that year reached a high record of $561,000,000. In reply to a questionnaire on the subject of the increase of this item circulated by the Senate Committee on Banking and Currency in January 1931, one of the Reserve Banks stated, "With regard to the large increase in the volume of acceptances drawn for foreign storage and shipment between foreign countries, it appears that a substantial amount of this business originates in Germany and other central European countries, and that it results, at least to some extent, from a continued shortage of capital, and is not likely to be reduced until long-term loans can be floated in this country or in London or in Paris. If long-term capital were readily available, it is the belief that the amount of bills of this class would be reduced to a considerable extent."[1]

The instability which this practice of substituting money raised on short-term for funds which should in the nature of things be obtained on a long-term loan, lends to the structure of international finance was disastrously illustrated during the summer of 1931, when the precipitation of internal credit crises in Germany and Austria led to a mad rush by foreign lenders to withdraw their short-term credits from those markets.[2] The flood of liquidation is again well exemplified

[1] *Hearings before Senate Sub-Committee of Committee on Banking and Currency, S.R.* 71, p. 450, February 18, 1931.

[2] The situation was further complicated by the fact that Germany, while "borrowing short" abroad, had been "lending long" to Russia in order to facilitate her sales of machinery to that country.

in the volume of American acceptances based on goods abroad; this item fell from $494,000,000 at the end of June to $338,000,000 at the end of September, owing to "the practical cessation of dollar acceptance financing in Europe since July 1931."[1] American investors were of course not alone in the scramble to realize their liquid claims; lenders of all nations were anxious to save what they could from the avalanche which threatened to freeze for an indefinite period all assets that were not withdrawn from its path.

Called upon thus to repay at short notice an immense volume of funds, much of which was being employed in non-liquid form, the European debtors were unable to meet their obligations in full. "The situation of the banks and industries perhaps would not have had such far-reaching results on the German banking system were it not for the fact that an enormous amount of short-term foreign debts was thereby set in motion, which Germany, suffering from a shortage of capital, could not withstand. By a concert of action of the banks of the creditor countries, which is unprecedented in the history of international commercial relations, the withdrawal of the short-term indebtedness was postponed for six months by the Standstill Agreement of last autumn and it has been renewed under different terms for one year by the agreement initiated by Mr. Wiggin in Berlin last Saturday."[2]

Similarly in the case of Austria; "some time last summer [1931] the banks with short-term credits in Austria made a gentlemen's agreement that they would continue their credits pending the arrangement of a formal standstill agreement."[3] In other words, the pseudo-short-term advances extended by foreign lenders to these two countries were commuted through the policy of the borrowers and the exigencies of the crisis

[1] *American Acceptance Bulletin*, March 1932, p. 16.

[2] William C. Cannon, Address before the American Acceptance Council, January 25, 1932. *American Acceptance Council Bulletin*, January 1932, p. 11.

[3] Ibid., p. 15.

into loans of a comparatively long term. The effect of the standstill agreements with European debtors was reflected in the fact that American acceptances based on goods abroad remained practically stationary in volume between November 30, 1931, and April 30, 1932. Some $60,000,000 of these acceptances were liquidated during the summer of 1932, but from the end of September to the end of March 1933 their volume again remained constant at between $230,000,000 and $240,000,000. At the same time, the failure of this figure to rise at any time between the autumn of 1931 and the spring of 1933 illustrates the inability of the Central Banks of the former European borrowers to attract back even short-term foreign capital, despite the maintenance of a wide differential between their own discount rates and those of the Central Banks of the principal debtor countries.[1]

The far-reaching effects which the practice of borrowers applying short-term loans to long-term uses may have upon the financial structure of the creditor countries themselves is illustrated by the fate which overtook England in the late summer of 1931 as a result of the crises on the Continent. London, as one of the world's two great money markets, is liable at all times to be subjected to a heavy foreign demand for funds both from overseas holders of balances in the market and from would-be borrowers. With the shock which the confidence of foreign creditors had received over the Austro-German crisis, suspicion spread to London and a gigantic exodus of funds from that centre set in. In the normal course of events this drain might have been met by a sharp rise in

[1] During the greater part of 1932, the Reichsbank's discount rate stood between 2 per cent and 3 per cent higher than the rates of the Federal Reserve Bank of New York and the Bank of France, though this differential was reduced to 1½ per cent with the reduction of the Reichsbank's rate to 4 per cent towards the end of September. The rate differential was even higher in the case of the Austrian Central Bank, whose rate only declined from 8 per cent to 6 per cent during the year.

the Bank rate which would have recalled short funds lent abroad and offered a restraining inducement to foreigners to leave their balances in London undisturbed. In this case, however, the normal source of response to such a rise, short-term loans to foreigners, was largely frozen; money which had been placed in the London market on short term, and had been reloaned abroad also on short term, had been commuted to a long-term basis by factors outside the influence of the British creditors. It was therefore felt that a rise in the Bank rate would have a much reduced effect in recalling balances from abroad, while it might be the signal for panicky withdrawals of balances owed by London to foreigners. The expedient of raising direct credits abroad for the support of the exchange was therefore resorted to, and, when that in turn failed to stem the onslaught on the pound, there was no alternative to a suspension of gold payments.

The similar onslaught on New York, the other great money market of the world, which ensued during the autumn of 1931, might have ended in a like result but for the strong reserve position of the United States at that time, which enabled the Federal Reserve System to view without undue emotion the withdrawal of a huge volume of foreign balances and to offer the domestic market compensating accommodation at a remarkably steady price. As it was, these withdrawals, coupled with the more prolonged outflow of short-term foreign funds from New York during the first six months of 1932, seriously weakened American reserves, and thereby directly contributed to the forces which caused the suspension of the gold standard when the domestic crisis supervened in February 1933.[1]

[1] It is interesting to note that, whereas the United States withstood a net export of $338,000,000 of gold in one month in October 1931 and a net export of $620,000,000 during the first six months of 1932 without suspending gold payments, she eventually went off the gold standard at the beginning of March 1933 after seven consecutive months of net imports of gold.

It is, therefore, in the first instance in the curtailment of the flow of long-term capital from creditor to debtor nations that a weakening of foreign confidence works its vicious results upon the balancing of payments between the two classes of nations, and only in the last resort in a breakdown of short-term lending.

§ 5. The same preference for liquid over long-term claims on the part of creditors may also arise from conditions which are still further removed from the control of the Central Banks of the debtor countries, namely, the soundness of conditions in the creditor countries themselves. That even the financially strongest communities may experience difficulties in the heavy liquidation which accompanies a period of prolonged business depression was well illustrated by United States history from the summer of 1931 to the time of the suspension of the gold standard in March 1933.

Bank failures are the stuff of which old-time financial crises were made. Now as formerly, if a number of failures occurs simultaneously, a run on neighbouring banks is likely to ensue in sympathy, even though the latter are absolutely sound. Since gold has been withrawn from general circulation, these runs can now be met to a large extent by the paying out of currency against which a full hundred per cent gold backing may not be required. The reaction upon the reserve position of the whole banking system will not therefore be as severe as in pre-War days. At the same time, a heavy outflow of money into "circulation" in response to the demands of hoarders will weaken the reserve position of individual banks to a considerable extent. This in turn may lead to the repatriation of balances held abroad, particularly if the individual banks who are feeling the pressure of the demand for currency happen themselves to own such balances.

The United States is rendered particularly susceptible to an infection of hoarding by two factors; an enormous number of small, unitary, unsupported banks, who inevitably find it difficult to obtain outside aid when their own front line of liquid assets grows thin, and whose dead bodies, if they fall, provide excellent breeding ground for further infection; and a large class of thrifty immigrants from parts of Europe where banking is undeveloped, who are prone to suspicion and panic at the first rumour.[1]

A violent infection broke out during the summer of 1931 as the result of an unprecedented and ever-growing crop of bank failures during the year. As a result, the volume of money in circulation, which, even during the business activity of 1928–29, had remained generally below $4,800,000,000, and which had stood consistently under $4,500,000,000 throughout the summer of 1930, after registering an ominous unseasonal rise throughout the spring of 1931, mounted rapidly during the autumn and reached a high point of $5,650,000,000 in January 1932.

It is of course impossible to argue that this display of preference for the most liquid available asset, currency, over other forms of money was the cause of a repatriation of balances held abroad. In actual fact it coincided with a heavy outflow of gold in response to withdrawals of balances from New York by panic-stricken foreigners. The hoarding of currency did, however, tighten money rates somewhat abruptly in the New York market by weakening the reserve position of the banking system, and even became so menacing to the position of the Reserve Banks themselves as to compel them to abandon the easy money policy which they had been pursuing earlier

[1] The story is told of a foreign-born cook who was found by her American employer to have sewn up $1,000 in her mattress during the panic of the autumn of 1931. The employer after much talk persuaded the cook to redeposit the money in the local bank, but two days later the bank failed. The embarrassed employer went to the kitchen to offer his condolences, but was met with a broad smile. "I no trust dem banks," said the cook, "so I took my money out again next day."

in the year.[1] It therefore militated strongly (had any further militancy been necessary for the purpose) against the ability of any foreign borrowers to raise new loans in the New York market. At the same time, it is likely to have offered some added inducement to the repatriation of balances held abroad.

During 1932 a lull ensued. Bank failures, which had occurred at an average of 268 per month during the last six months of 1931, declined considerably soon after the beginning of the year, and from March to November only averaged 93 per month. The volume of money in circulation remained comparatively steady near the high figure reached in January. A sudden heavy outflow of gold during June was counteracted at the time by large purchases of securities by the Reserve Banks and balanced subsequently by a steady return flow during the latter half of the year. As a result, the Reserve authorities were able, by means of unprecedentedly vigorous open-market operations during the first half of the year, to reduce open-market interest rates to the low level of the previous summer, and to that extent to restore conditions favourable to an outflow of short-term capital.[2]

Once again these conditions were upset by an internal panic when a fresh crop of bank failures during December 1932 and January 1933 shook the confidence of the American public in their banks and led to a severe outbreak of hoarding during February. Between January 28th and March 4th, money in circulation rose by $1,185,000,000 to the hitherto unknown figure of $6,805,000,000. This outflow of funds from the banks was rendered the more serious by the fact that a considerable part

[1] Rates on prime bankers' acceptances, 90 days, in New York City rose from $\frac{7}{8}$ per cent early in September 1931 to 3–$3\frac{1}{4}$ per cent towards the end of October.

[2] During April, New York rates on 90-day prime bankers' acceptances fell from $2\frac{1}{8}$ per cent to $\frac{5}{8}$ per cent, and continued to decline throughout the year till they reached a low point of $\frac{1}{4}$ per cent in January 1933.

of it took the form of gold coin and gold certificates, $300,000,000 of which were paid out betweeen February 15th and March 4th.

This new assertion of the community's preference for gold and notes over even the most liquid of other assets again resulted in abruptly weakening the reserves of the banking system and in making the banks both less willing and less able to lend. The excess reserves of member banks, which had become very considerable during the easy-money period of 1932, suddenly vanished, and in their place reappeared a larger volume of rediscounting by the Reserve Banks than had been known since the panic of 1931. Bills discounted at the Banks rose from $256,000,000 on February 11th to $847,000,000 on March 4th, and further to $1,421,000,000 on March 11th. In consequence of the fall in the reserves of private banks, interest rates rose sharply, the New York acceptance rate, for instance, leaping from ½ per cent to over 3 per cent within three weeks.

The effect of this rise in interest rates alone would probably have been sufficient to upset any outflow of short-term capital that might have been in progress or pending at this time. This was not all, however, for by the first week in March the hoarding fever had forced so many banks all over the country to suspend business that on the evening of March 5th a national bank holiday was proclaimed, and the entire financial mechanism of the country came to a virtual standstill. Subsequent events are still too recent at the time of writing for a clear picture to be drawn, but it would seem safe to assume that the temporary embargo on the export of gold on March 10th, subsequently confirmed as a more permanent measure on April 20th, the resultant fluctuations in the dollar exchange rates, and the general uncertainty regarding American financial policy in the immediate future, must all have served to interrupt the flow of investment funds from the United States to debtor countries. In so far as these events were caused by a domestic panic in the United States, completely outside the control of the Central Banks of other, and particularly of debtor, countries, they afford another illustration of the frequent inability of Central Banks to influence appreciably the international flow of capital by a mere manipulation of their own interest rates.

Similar outbreaks of hoarding occurred about the same time in France. The French public has always been notoriously fearful of investments of all sorts and the French peasant's preference for the sock over the bank as a repository for his savings has become proverbial. With the widespread breakdown of confidence in the autumn of 1931, the note circulation underwent a rapid increase. Having varied between 77 and 80 billion[1] francs during the first nine months of the year, the figure rose 5½ billion in October to 83½ billion. At the same time, as in the United States during February 1933, hoarding was not confined to notes; part of the French public when duly frightened loses confidence in the security of even a currency note and demands gold coin. A considerable quantity of gold coin is said to have been shipped from New York for this purpose, and figures show clearly that a large part of the gold imports which took place at this time were not finding their way into the vaults of the Bank of France. During the first six months of 1931, the gold holdings of the Bank of France increased by 2,850 millions of francs as against net imports of some 2,400 millions in gold. During the last three months of the year, the Bank's gold holdings only increased by 9½ billions of francs as against net imports of 10½ billions. No doubt a large part of the one billion francs of gold unaccounted for was retained in the tills and vaults of the private banks against the demands of would-be hoarders. It seems reasonable, however, to suppose that some part of it was

[1] The word "billion" is used throughout this book in the American sense of one thousand million, rather than in the English sense of one million million.

actually withdrawn by just those clients against whose demands the banks wished to be prepared.[1]

This increased preference for liquid assets on account of domestic fears again resulted in a large repatriation of balances held overseas. The New York money market was the logical one from which withdrawals should take place, the gold standard having been suspended in England. The tremendous outflow of gold, mounting to $612,000,000, which occurred from the United States during the three autumn months offers a clear example of an interruption of foreign lending (in this case, lending of European balances to the New York money market) through lack of confidence in the domestic situation of the creditor, rather than of the debtor, country. It is true that persistent rumours were circulating at this time in many European monetary centres that the United States would soon follow England off the gold standard, but such rumours could hardly have found ready credence in informed circles at that time. The hoarding of international short-term capital, which resulted in this heavy drain of gold from the United States, was the second factor which contributed to the already mentioned hardening of short-term rates in the New York money market.

The Bank of England having suspended gold payments, a dead loss would be suffered on any funds repatriated from England owing to the depreciation of sterling. At the same time, open-market interest rates in London had risen to a point which offered a considerable differential in favour of the market over Paris.[2] In spite of these two deterrents, however, Conti-

[1] According to Mr. Todd (*Fall of Prices*, p. 55) private individuals in France were already hoarding gold late in 1930. "Many French balances were withdrawn from London in the autumn of 1930, and a good deal of them was taken in gold; and this movement was again accentuated by the bank failures in France which led many monied people in France to strengthen their position by laying in more gold."

[2] The London rate for 3-month bills remained between 5½ per cent and 6 per cent from the time of the suspension of gold payments till

nental balances appear to have been withdrawn from London also. Mr. Neville Chamberlain, British Chancellor of the Exchequer, speaking in the House of Commons on December 10, 1931, said, "There have no doubt been withdrawals from this country of balances held by foreign holders. *These holders include neither the French Government nor the Bank of France,*[1] but there have been others who have removed their balances, partly because of want of confidence, not in the state of things over here but in their own countries, and they thought it desirable to have liquid resources available." When the balances began to return to London, it was paradoxically enough in response to falling, rather than to rising, interest rates. So much for the ability of Central Banks to control the flow of investment into and out of their countries by manipulation of their interest rates!

As a result of the disturbances in the United States, hoarding broke out afresh in France in March 1933 in which month the note circulation rose by over two billion francs. During April about half this amount returned from circulation, but meanwhile gold was much in demand for private storage. The large imports of gold during March and April seem to have been completely absorbed in meeting this demand, for while, according to provisional figures available at the time of writing, about 1,600,000,000 francs of gold was imported during these two months, the gold holdings of the Bank of France were actually 150,000,000 francs lower on April 28th than on February 24th. These figures would suggest that over one and a half billion francs was withdrawn from investment outside France during these two months, converted into gold, and transferred straight to the cash boxes of individual Frenchmen, who did not even dare entrust it to the safe keeping of their own banks.

the end of the year, while, according to the *Federal Reserve Bulletin*, the Paris private discount rate during the same period averaged less than 2 per cent each month.

[1] The words in italics are the writer's own.

In so far as these individuals were determined to withdraw their money from interest-bearing investment in any market into the safe keeping of their own homes, no amount of interest-rate manipulation by the Central Banks of the countries where these balances had previously been employed would have served to stem this return flow of capital to France.

§ 6. The last of the three main types of international transactions on capital account which are undertaken from some other than the purely economic motive of obtaining the highest available rate of return on the capital is the type of transaction carried out by Central Banks or governments for reasons of general policy. These non-commercial transactions, which were relatively uncommon before the War, have played a very large part in the international gold movements of the post-War period.[1]

The commonest examples of these transactions were those undertaken during the post-War reconstruction period, when a number of countries were making efforts to restore their currencies to a gold basis. Obviously it would be impossible for any country not on the gold standard to obtain gold by means of commercial transactions unless its exchange had risen to parity, since it is always cheaper to make remittances to countries with depreciated currencies in their own bills of exchange rather than in gold. It was therefore necessary for Central Banks aiming at stabilization to take special steps

[1] Mr. Einzig, writing in 1929, asserts, "Though no figures comparing amounts of commercial and non-commercial transactions before and after the War are available, there is no doubt that the ratio between them has changed considerably in favour of the latter. . . . Those who expected that special transactions would be reduced to comparative insignificance have been disappointed. Notwithstanding the return to the gold standard of a great number of countries, special transactions continue to occupy a prominent place."—P. Einzig, *International Gold Movements*, London, 1929, pp. 22–3. We shall find cause to believe that this statement still held good after the re-abandonment of the gold standard by certain countries.

to obtain the required gold. This end was achieved in a large number of countries during 1927 and 1928, mainly with the aid of the Federal Reserve System and the Bank of England. Commenting on the heavy outflow of gold from the United States during the latter part of 1927, the *Monthly Letter of the National City Bank of New York* (January 1928) says, "It is evident that the greater part of the shipments have not been due to ordinary exchange conditions, but to transactions for special purposes. . . . The Government of Argentina, in contemplation of the restoration of the gold standard, placed a loan of $40,000,000 in New York in August, withdrawing the proceeds in gold. . . . The movement to Brazil was the result of a loan flotation in this market, the proceeds to be used in placing the monetary system of that country on a gold basis. The $5,000,000 sent to Poland was part of the proceeds of a loan of $72,000,000 in October for the purpose of restoring the monetary system of that country to a gold basis. Very likely more gold will go out on this account. The $10,000,000 taken for Paris on December 27th was on account of the funds which the Bank of France and the French Government were accumulating here in 1927, partly by shipments from London and the Continent and partly in exchange for private funds transferred to France. The latter transactions were in pursuance of the policy of stabilizing the French exchanges."

Inasmuch as stabilization is wont to require the active co-operation of the more powerful monetary centres, however, these movements were usually sanctioned by mutual agreement of the gold-losing and gold-receiving parties. A type of special transaction, more dangerous to international stability because requiring no such mutual agreement, has recently become more common, namely, the movement of gold from one market to another by Central Banks or governments of countries whose currencies are already on a gold basis, and who therefore own the gold in the sense that they can buy it at a trifling loss compared with the expense incurred in making the same transaction by the Central Bank of a country with a depreciated exchange. Transactions of this type may therefore be undertaken at will by any gold-standard bank holding balances in other gold centres. At the same time, it may often be prompted by no more economic motive than a desire for prestige or impatience at the slowness of the gold flow under the influence of purely commercial transactions.[1]

After the suspension of gold payments by Great Britain in September 1931, a new impetus was given to the repatriation, even at a loss, of balances held abroad by Central Banks. After the War, the custom of Central Banks holding large foreign balances found great favour under the system of the "gold exchange standard," whereby certain Central Banks were allowed to substitute liquid claims which they held in other gold centres for at least a part of their gold reserves. By this means, part of the Banks' reserves were at the same time earning assets, while they could be used to buy the country's own exchange in any foreign centre where it threatened to depreciate, or could be increased by a sale of their own currency in centres where it showed a tendency to rise above par. From an international viewpoint, moreover, this practice was encouraged as tending towards a desirable economizing of gold reserves in place of the competition for gold which would be likely to ensue from a world-wide attempt to return to the pure gold standard.

In September 1931, a large volume of such balances were held in the larger monetary centres of the world, not only by the Central Banks of countries still operating the gold exchange standard, but also by many Banks of gold-standard countries, the Bank of France in particular. These Banks received a rude shock with the suspension of gold payments in Great Britain, since their balances in London immediately

[1] For an interesting discussion of the causes which may give rise to gold movements on non-commercial account, see P. Einzig, *International Gold Movements*, London, 1929, chapter iii.

depreciated in the same extent as sterling exchange. This may well have sounded the death-knell of the gold exchange standard for all who could afford to dispense with it.

Certainly it is hardly to be wondered at that many Central Banks, whose fingers had been burnt by London's suspension, should conclude that after all "there's no place like home" for holding one's most liquid resources, and should have repatriated much of their balance held in other gold centres. This in fact took place on a large scale between September 1931 and June 1932, France, Belgium, and Holland in particular drawing a considerable quantity of gold from New York. Thus a Paris despatch to the *New York Times* of January 11, 1932, says, "In connection with the deflation of sterling credits held by the Bank of France, it is understood here that the Bank's future policy will tend towards reducing its foreign balances. This policy will be adopted in response to pressure from the Government, which took over the main part of the risk of exchange fluctuations incurred by the Bank on such foreign holdings, and which, therefore, is naturally desirous of avoiding further losses than have already been created through the fall in sterling."

In many cases, the assets were realized and the golden proceeds set aside in the foreign market under earmark for their owners without or before being actually shipped home. Unless, however, earmarking is a mere temporary measure adopted to strengthen the gold reserves of a Central Bank until the gold earmarked may be released again in the same market to seek profitable employment once more, it possesses no advantage over the retention of the gold in the securer keeping of the domestic vaults of the Bank which owns it. The prolongation of the depression throughout the winter and spring of 1932 seems to have led most of the European holders of earmarked gold in New York to the conclusion that it would be some time before their funds, if released from earmark and invested in the New York market, would again earn a rate high enough to justify their being left abroad, and as a result much of the earmarked gold was shipped home before the summer of 1932. Quoting again from the *New York Times* of April 21, 1932, "Last September, following the suspension of the gold standard in England, several European central banks converted their holdings of dollar balances in this market into gold, which they placed under earmark in the Federal Reserve Bank in order to strengthen their positions. This gold has since been carried by these institutions in their public reports in the same class with gold actually held in their own vaults. Since the first of the year there has been a tendency for European Central Banks to call home their earmarked gold, since no purpose is served by leaving it abroad. Between January 15th and March 15th, the Bank of France took $170,000,000 of its holdings of earmarked gold, and the National Bank of Belgium repatriated a smaller amount. The decision of the Bank of the Netherlands (to withdraw all the gold that it holds abroad) is in line with this policy. . . The conversion of the foreign balances of the Bank of the Netherlands into earmarked gold last fall was revealed in the rise of its gold holdings and in the simultaneous fall in its holdings of devisen. Between the end of August and the end of November the bank's gold holdings rose $79,600,000, or from $280,800,000 to $360,400,000, while in the same period its holdings of foreign bills dropped $65,600,000." This repatriation of balances held abroad by European creditor countries continued up till the end of June 1932. By that time the process appears to have been completed, for similar movements of funds were not in evidence during the latter half of the year.

In consequence of their timely action, the Central Banks of these creditor countries escaped the heavy losses which they would otherwise have incurred when the dollar went off gold in March 1933. This event, therefore, did not occasion the heavy return flow of funds which followed the suspension of the gold standard in England. It did, however, render the possibility of a revival of the gold exchange standard more remote than ever.

Such is the principal type of non-commercial transaction involving heavy gold movements which has, for the present at least, supplanted the movements of 1927–28 which took place mainly in aid of national efforts to rehabilitate currencies. While they last, such transactions not only may be carried out in a direction contrary to the disideratum of distributing international capital where it is most needed, as indicated by the relative heights of different interest rates, but also, by the uncertainty of their date, duration, and volume, may cast an added blight of doubt and pessimism over the already harassed market from which they are drawn.

§ 7. As a general conclusion from the evidence which has been considered in this chapter, it must inevitably seem that the proudest weapon in the armoury of orthodox gold-standard theory, the power of Central Banks to manipulate their own discount rates, has become obsolete at least for the purpose, so important in pre-War conditions, of influencing the international balance of payments on capital account. Fear, which will not without great difficulty be allayed after the era of international defaults and bankruptcies heralded in during 1931, seems for the moment to have entirely eclipsed in the minds of lenders the purely economic motive of seeking highest interest rates. The risk differential demanded on foreign loans has risen out of all proportion to the pure economic rate of interest which would formerly have sufficed to induce creditor nations to keep up a steady export of capital. Until fear has sufficiently subsided for this risk differential to return to normal proportions, the changes of a few per cent which Central Banks are able to make in their discount rates will be powerless to bring about those adjustments in international balances of payments on capital account which are essential to the smooth workings of an international gold standard.

CHAPTER V

WAR DEBTS, REPARATIONS, AND TARIFFS

§ 1. It has become so fashionable to blame the majority of the difficulties in which the world finds itself upon the evil genii whose names form the title of this chapter that there is a temptation for any writer, who wishes to avoid the trite, to assume in his readers an understanding of the effects of these factors upon the adjustment of international balances of payments. Inasmuch, however, as these three factors are of paramount importance among the new phenomena which have falsified the hypotheses upon which orthodox gold-standard theory has been based, it is necessary for the purposes of this book to dedicate a special chapter to their consideration.

We saw in the last chapter that international indebtedness is in itself no new or disturbing phenomenon; in fact, the burthen of the argument there was that the breakdown of confidence, and consequently the drastic reduction of the secular flow of international capital, was deeply to be deplored. For generations prior to the War Great Britain was continuously amassing a vast quantity of foreign investments. There can be little doubt, moreover, that this outflow of capital to different parts of the world worked great benefits not only to herself, but also to those countries who received the loans, and to the rest of the world, which was able to partake of the enjoyment of the addition to total wealth which resulted from the employment of these funds. The repayment of principal and interest seldom caused even local difficulties. Certainly it was never seriously accused of causing or even abetting a world-wide depression. What, then, are the features characterizing the growth of international indebtedness since 1915, which make of it such an economic "sore spot" in the eyes of the world?

The outstanding difference between the present large volume

of international indebtedness and that to which the world was becoming accustomed before the War is that the latter was mostly contracted by the borrowers for productive purposes, such as the building of railroads or the establishment of new plant, for which the borrowers were unable to obtain the necessary capital in their own country owing to its relative poverty. A large part of the new indebtedness, on the other hand, grew up as a result of the unproductive expenses of the War, when the future productivity of the belligerents was in a manner of speaking mortgaged by their governments as security against loans raised for and spent on the unproductive occupation of blowing each others' heads off. The old pre-War loans were of a type calculated to render the borrower better able to pay than before, by increasing the productivity of the country in which they were invested. The building of railroads in South America, for example, might logically be expected so to increase the exports of that continent that the Republics, of which it is composed, would annually find at their disposal a larger volume than before of foreign exchange of the various countries, to which they had exported their raw materials in increased quantities. Meanwhile, the actual corporations or individuals who raised these loans would partake of this prosperity in the form of high profits, with which they could easily secure a necessary share of the plentiful supply of foreign exchange with which to meet their overseas obligations.

Much of the present outstanding amount of international indebtedness, however, represents no such productive enterprise. This fact is well illustrated by an examination of the long-term foreign investments of the United States. At the end of 1930, for instance, just before the era of defaults set in, the total value of America's claims on account of War debts and German obligations, capitalized at $4\frac{1}{4}$ per cent, constituted a little more than one-half of the remainder of her foreign long-term investments.[1] In other words, approximately one-

[1] J. H. Rogers, *America Weighs her Gold*, p. 47.

third of the total interest payments which had to be made to the United States on long-term account each year were incurred by the borrowers on loans raised for unproductive purposes. The United States as the chief Allied lender is, of course, an exceptionally large claimant on this account, but payments similar in kind, though different in degree, have to be made, according to existing agreements, between several other nations every year, the most important being Germany, who, at the other end of the ladder from the United States, constitutes the largest debtor on unproductive account with a debt of annuities, which, when capitalized at $5\frac{1}{2}$ per cent, represent a sum of some $8 billion.

Here then, in payment of interest and amortization on these unproductive intergovernmental debts, lies an item which must be settled in international balances of payments every year, but for the settlement of which no excess exports are likely to flow in the nature of things from debtor country to creditor. Indeed, in so far as the burden of the extra taxation necessary in the latter countries for the raising of the annual debt service charge raises costs of production, or otherwise exercises a depressing effect upon internal industries, exports might be expected to fall rather than rise as a result of these foreign claims.

In this connection, one in particular of the aspects of the changes in the long-term debtor-creditor positions of various countries is worthy of note. "At the outbreak of the War, the net debt of the United States on international balance was approximately three billion dollars made up largely of American securities and properties owned by Europeans."[1] In other words, the United States, as befitted a country whose resources were still not being fully exploited, and whose productivity, under the influence of continual additions of new foreign, as well as domestic, capital was still increasing by leaps and bounds, still ranked among the debtor nations of the world.

[1] J. H. Rogers, *America Weighs her Gold*, p. 46.

With the advent of European borrowing for the financing of wartime needs, particularly after the United States' entry into the War in 1917, the position changed almost overnight, until by the end of 1930 the United States was a net creditor on long-term account to the extent of some eighteen billion dollars.[1]

Now it is obvious that this sudden change of the flow of capital from a net import into the United States to a violent net export was not consummated to the detriment of domestic productivity. Even during the post-War decade of reconstruction, while the net export was continuing on a scale undreamed of before the War, the United States continued to enjoy a sizable net commodity export balance varying from $254 million in 1923 to $905 million in 1928. This condition places the United States in a very different category from the biggest international creditor of the pre-War days, Great Britain, who, during the greater part of her career as a capital exporter, and therefore as a receiver of annual interest payments from overseas, has had a consistent adverse balance on commodity account. Although it would be palpably short-sighted to maintain baldly that this fact alone made it impossible for the United States to receive the interest payments due her, at least it is evident that the ready recipience by Great Britain of the raw produce of the ever-developing resources of her immature debtors, and her need of many other commodities from overseas, which she herself as a mature and developed country was unable to produce, made the problem of her debtors in meeting their annual obligations very much simpler than that of the debtors of the United States, a far more self-sufficient country with not only considerably less need of overseas products but with a positive abhorrence of the import of goods which could be produced domestically.

We shall find how this abhorrence has demonstrated itself to the dismay of the remainder of the world, when we treat of

[1] J. H. Rogers, *America Weighs her Gold*, p. 47.

the question of tariffs. For the moment, suffice it to note that the debtor countries, struggling to meet their overseas obligations by creating and increasing a net export balance on commodity account, have not only had difficulty in obtaining a market for their goods in the territories of the chief creditor herself, but have actually had to face the severest competition from the goods exported by that creditor in other international markets. Meanwhile the chief debtor, Germany, is a country which, by reason of her advanced industrialization, would probably by now have come in the normal course of events to be a net commodity importer and a net capital exporter, but which now is confronted with the necessity of cutting her imports to the bone in order to obtain the net commodity export by means of which to acquire the foreign exchange demanded of her by her creditors. In such freak results does war upset the natural and healthy development of the flow of international capital.

§ 2. A second characteristic in which a large block of the newly-incurred international debts differs from the pre-War type is to be found in the fact that the new debtors are in many cases governments rather than the private individuals and corporations who commonly constitute peace-time borrowers. This difference is one of considerable importance. If a corporation suffers reverses, it passes its dividends and its shareholders endure the consequences with a certain degree of equanimity. The possibility of passed dividends is a risk which every investor in a corporation expects to take, no matter whether the corporation operates on foreign soil or at home. The creditors of governments, on the other hand, rightly or wrongly are apt to consider themselves the victims of an injustice if their dividends are not received regularly. After all, governments wield the power of taxation, and the foreign creditor naturally feels that he has a grievance against any government which does not appear to be using this power for the satisfactory meeting of its obligations. Particularly is this true when the creditor happens to be itself a government, as was the case with the majority of international debts incurred during the War. The national budget is the affair of every taxable citizen, and it is apt to be sadly deranged by the default of a foreign debtor government.

Meanwhile, a debtor government is liable to think more seriously than a corporation before defaulting on its bonds, and to use every means in its power before resorting to such a drastic expedient. A default on bond interest is a virtual declaration of bankruptcy. Whereas a corporation reduced to such a pass is not likely again to lift its head to the extent of ever trying to raise new capital, so that its future credit standing is no longer likely to be a matter of any great importance to it, a defaulting government is seriously prejudicing its chances of raising in the international market funds which it may expect to need in the future. "The credit of governments is not easily built up. It may be easily shattered."[1] Consequently the normal purgative method of passing dividends, whereby an overstrained debtor-creditor relationship is relieved in the case of corporations or private individuals, is not readily available where the debtor, and perhaps the creditor also, is a government. In this case, an enforced default is liable to have painful and far-reaching consequences.

Debts arising directly out of the War do not, however, constitute the only portion of the recently-incurred international indebtedness in which the debtor is a government. One of the most remarkable phenomena in the history of post-War international finance was the insatiable appetite of the American public for foreign bonds of all sorts, but particularly for foreign government bonds, which showed itself during the years 1924–28. In 1923 flotations of foreign government bonds in the United States amounted to $186 million; during the next

[1] Dwight W. Morrow, "Who Buys Foreign Bonds?" *Foreign Affairs*, January 1927.

five years these flotations averaged $561 million a year.[1] This immense increase was but the response of investment bankers to the clamorous demands of their clients, for whom the loans could hardly be floated fast enough. "During the World War, the American public in large numbers learned, entirely by accident, how to invest. . . . With the passage of the War and the rapid absorption of the Victory loans, the investment-thirsty American public began to hammer at the doors of the investment bankers. So great was the rush of business and so large their profits that many youthful upstarts matured overnight, and uninvited and unwelcome competitors sprang up on every side . . . until many of the big investment houses, forgetting their former dignity, began literally to comb the world for securities in sufficient quantity to meet the apparently insatiable demands of the American investing public."[2]

This tendency was attested by an investment banker himself in evidence before the Senate Committee on Finance on January 8, 1932, when Mr. Breck of J. & W. Seligman & Co. in reply to Senator Johnson's question, "What was it that led to the extraordinarily keen competition among international bankers for South American loans?" said, "I think it was an appetite on the part of the American public to buy foreign loans."[3] A few minutes later in the same Committee, Senator Johnson asked Mr. Strauss, a member of the same firm, "You found in the last few years a perfect madness for the acquisition of bonds and the selling of them to the public, did you not, among all those engaged in the same line of business as yourselves?" "I might qualify with an adjective," replied Mr. Strauss, "but in the main, yes; you are correct." "And there came a keenness of competition among international

[1] Figures from *The Commercial and Financial Chronicle*.

[2] J. H. Rogers, *America Weighs her Gold*, pp. 52–4.

[3] *Hearings before Senate Committee on Finance on S.R.* 19, January 8, 1932, p. 1323.

bankers to obtain loans in Latin America in order to sell them to the American public?" "Yes, sir."[1]

As might be expected in such a state of affairs, the vigilance of the investment bankers concerning the justification of the new foreign loans which they marketed to the public relaxed somewhat, and certain foreign governments took advantage of the appetite of the bond-buyers to borrow money on an unjustifiably lavish scale. Illuminating instances of this reckless financing by certain South American republics were brought out by Mr. Lawrence Dennis in evidence before the Senate Finance Committee on January 11, 1932. Speaking of a loan of some $22 million "made by Bolivia and floated in this country by Dillon, Read & Co. in 1928," Mr. Dennis said, "There was $5,061,000 paid on account of the Vickers contract for arms purchases. I thought that was a rather unusual thing, because the arms were supposed to be paid for in five years, and the debt was funded in 34-year 7 per cent bonds. A phase of that loan which was interesting to me was that they took $3,904,000 to pay off deficits, which included quite a large item for delayed salaries of Government officials. . . . Only $2,259,000 of the loan went for new public works. Of that amount I was told in the ministry of finance that $1,500,000 had been retained by the minister of war for use in connection with military activities in El Chaco. Of course he said, as I understood, that he was using the money for building roads down there."[2]

Again, speaking of a loan made to Peru in the same year, Mr. Dennis said, "The way things were going the loans had to be in default within five years. . . . With unbalanced budgets, and in view of the way in which the money was being spent, bankruptcy seemed inevitable. . . . With the budget unbalanced, and making foreign loans, a government could not go on indefinitely without going into default. I knew the

[1] *Hearings before Senate Committee on Finance on S.R.* 19, January 8, 1932, p. 1325.

[2] Ibid., pp. 1585–6.

resources of Peru and I knew from those resources that she was struggling under a heavy load. . . . The point is that the Peruvian borrowing increased much faster than the income of the country."[1]

Thus during this period a number of governments who had no direct connection with the War were busy incurring unproductive debts of a type similar to those contracted by the recent belligerents for their military needs. Their conduct bore its natural fruit when the world-wide fall of the prices of raw materials seriously reduced the value of their exports. Even if the new loans had been applied to productive purposes and had resulted in an increase in the volume of exports, the fall in prices would have cut severely into their favourable balances on commodity trade, and would thereby have greatly increased the difficulty of acquiring sufficient foreign exchange to meet their foreign loan obligations. As it was, the nominal burden of their interest payments rose at a time when the real burden was also growing rapidly with the fall in the price-level, while there was no factual basis for an expectation of an increase in the physical volume of exports. Default was the natural consequence.

§ **3.** The third outstanding difference between the new international obligations and those incurred prior to the War is that the former are owed largely to countries whose economic policy differs from that of the chief pre-War creditor, Great Britain. The United States and, to a much lesser degree, France have now assumed important rôles as creditor nations, yet both are strongly committed to a policy of protection, while Great Britain herself, the other great international creditor, has abandoned her time-honoured free-trade policy.

Allusion has already been made to the difficulties which arise when an important international creditor nation is not a

[1] *Hearings before Senate Committee on Finance on S.R.* 19, January 8, 1932, p. 1587.

"mature lender" in the sense that she herself is still largely self-sufficient, supplying the bulk of her own needs for raw materials, and therefore not receptive to the exports of her debtors. For a nation customarily builds up a creditor position by means of a high degree of industrialization, in the course of which she tends to become more than self-sufficient with regard to her needs of manufactured goods, exporting a considerable surplus to her debtors who supply her with raw materials. If at the same time she produces her own supplies of these raw materials, her debtors will have considerable difficulty in finding any goods which they can sell to her in order to obtain the amount of her currency necessary to meet their annual interest and sinking fund obligations to her.

Now the United States was becoming a lender of growing maturity in the few years prior to the Great War. This tendency is attested by the rapid increase in her exports of wholly or partly manufactured goods during this period as against her exports of foodstuffs, which suffered a heavy proportional decline from the beginning of this century onwards. By 1913 the proportion of her total exports which consisted of foodstuffs of all sorts, raw or partly or wholly manufactured, had declined from 42 per cent in 1900 to a trifle over 20 per cent, while during the same period, finished and partly manufactured goods had risen from 35 per cent to 50 per cent. The remaining item of crude materials rose slowly from 23 per cent to 30 per cent.

Commenting on this situation at the time, the Department of Commerce said, "The share which the United States supplies of the requirements of foreign countries in the three great groups of articles—foodstuffs, manufacturers' materials, and manufactures—is rapidly diminishing as to the first group, foodstuffs; is apparently not materially changing in the second group, manufacturers' materials; and is increasing in the third group, finished manufactures."[1] By 1929 the percentage of

[1] *Annual Review of Foreign Commerce of the U.S.*, 1913, Department of Commerce, Miscellaneous Series, No. 14, p. 26.

exports composed of foodstuffs had fallen further to 13·7 per cent.

On the other hand, although these figures indicate a proportional transference of productive energy from food-producing occupations to manufactures, a transference which implies increasing "maturity," the United States has as yet shown little sign of increasing dependence on overseas sources for her supplies of food or raw materials. Apart from the four chief imports of coffee, sugar, rubber, and raw silk, which constituted together 28 per cent, 27 per cent, and 24 per cent of the value of total imports in 1928, 1929, and 1930 respectively, with the possible addition of raw hides and skins, crude copper, and printing paper, which together made up a further 10 per cent of the imports of this period, the United States still satisfies the vast majority of her own needs.

The table opposite shows her balance of trade on account of the five grand classes of the International (Brussels, 1913) Classification for the years 1923–29.

From this table it will be seen that in only one of these grand classes has the United States had a consistently large net import balance, namely, in articles of food and drink. This import balance is more than accounted for by the two huge items of coffee and sugar, imports of which together amounted to more than half a billion dollars, or considerably more than half the total imports of foodstuffs, in each of the years covered by the table. The next largest import item in the foodstuff class is that of "nuts and fruit," which has never yet reached an annual value of $100 million. If the two items of coffee and sugar are omitted, therefore, the United States has a large export balance on account of all other foodstuffs. It would not be inaccurate to say that with the exception of these two items the United States is still independent of overseas sources for her food supply.

In the case of Class III in the table, the figure varied during the period from a net export of $322 million in 1924 to a net

TABLE II

NET EXPORT BALANCE OF UNITED STATES IN FIVE GRAND CLASSES OF COMMODITIES

(Millions of Dollars)

Source: *League of Nations Memoranda on International Trade and Balances of Payments, published periodically in Geneva*

	1923	1924	1925	1926	1927	1928	1929
I. Live Animals	− 1·2	− 3·2	− 3·3	− 8·4	− 18·5	−19·4	− 18·7
II. Articles of Food and Drink ..	−102·4	− 33·9	−104·1	−179·3	−125·0	−246·8	− 281·1
III. Materials, raw or partly manufactured	− 77·4	+321·8	− 76·0	−277·1	−114·0	+140·9	− 152·2
IV. Manufactured Articles ..	+480·0	+603·1	+775·6	+745·6	+831·6	+1064·0	+1209·7
V. Gold and Silver, specie and unmanufactured	−328·9	−222·1	+151·2	− 94·4	− 1·1	+382·7	− 176·3

(− indicates net import)

import of $277 million in 1926. Here again two items alone are more than sufficient to account for such net imports as did occur, namely, rubber and raw silk. Indeed, it is interesting to note how the figure in the table varies directly with the figure for the imports of these two items together, the highest net import figures of 1926 coinciding with the largest import of these two commodities, which in that year reached a value of $908 million, while the net export figure of 1924 synchronized with the lowest import of these two commodities for the period at a value of $509 million. In this class also, therefore, the United States shows a very high degree of self-sufficiency with the exception of two commodities.

It is again not inaccurate to conclude, therefore, that with the exception of the producers of the four above-mentioned commodities, coffee, sugar, rubber, and silk, the debtors of the United States, in endeavouring to sell her goods with which to acquire the exchange necessary for the meeting of their loan obligations, will run into competition with goods being produced in the United States. This situation stands in marked contrast to the case of Great Britain, the other chief creditor nation of the world. Opposite is appended the table of the latter's net export balance for the same five grand classes of commodities as were shown in the case of the United States. The figures in this table exhibit far less variability than those in the table for the United States, a characteristic which one would expect to find in a country of the maturity of Great Britain. The rigidity is particularly marked in the figures for Class II, which, if the depression year of 1930 is omitted, show a maximum variability of some 7 per cent during the period. Even the figures for Class III fall within £20 million of each other in four out of the seven years covered. These figures indicate that, as might be expected of a small island country, Great Britain has been consistently dependent upon overseas sources for her food supply and her raw materials. Nor is the value of her imports concentrated in a small group of commodities as in the case of

TABLE III

NET EXPORT BALANCE OF THE UNITED KINGDOM IN FIVE GRAND CLASSES

(Millions of Pounds)

Source: *League of Nations Memoranda on International Trade and Balances of Payments*

	1924	1925	1926	1927	1928	1929	1930
I. Live Animals	− 22·1	− 17·5	−17·3	− 16·2	− 16·8	− 17·4	− 19·8
II. Articles of Food and Drink ..	−447·8	−452·1	−426·1	−432·5	−423·4	−427·4	−378·9
III. Materials, raw or partly manufactured	−274·2	−209·7	−341·9	−268·3	−256·6	−265·1	−210·8
IV. Manufactured Articles ..	+407·6	+386·2	+322·5	+330·6	+345·1	+328·2	+223·1
V. Gold and Silver, specie and unmanufactured	+ 22·1	+ 9·8	−11·7	− 3·4	+ 11·7	+ 15·9	− 5·0

(− indicates net import)

the United States; her chief imports are butter, beef, mutton, bacon and hams, wheat, wool, timber, cotton, petroleum, and tea. This list is not only of greater length than that of the four main imports of the United States, but also only the last three items are the peculiar products of particular geographical areas, while the remaining items, with the possible exception of timber, are the natural exports of any agricultural country. Thus Great Britain is by nature and of necessity a much more ready recipient of the goods of other countries than is the United States. Without them she would be threatened with starvation and many of her great factories would lie idle. For only four commodities is the United States similarly dependent upon overseas commerce.

Although France is not a creditor nation to anything like the same extent as either the United States or Great Britain, it may, on account of the part which she is playing in the workings of the international gold standard, be of interest to include here a table of her export balances for the same classes of commodities as before (see table opposite). This table bears a greater similarity to the British than to the American table in that it shows a steady and not greatly varying import balance on account of Classes II and III throughout the period. Moreover, the list of her main imports, consisting of grain (flour and malt included), wine, "other foodstuffs," oleaginous fruits and seeds, mineral oils, coal and coke, wool, silk, cotton, and machinery and apparatus, is longer than that of the United States, though perhaps not so general as that of Great Britain. France would therefore seem *prima facie* to be a fairly easy payee of obligations, though it should be noted that she had not prior to the present depression developed any decided unfavourable balance on her total commodity trade, a fact which would lessen her receptivity.

§ 4. Now it is an axiom of elementary economics that a nation's exports pay for its imports. By this it is not meant

TABLE IV

NET EXPORT BALANCE OF FRANCE IN FIVE GRAND CLASSES

(*Millions of Francs*)

Source: *League of Nations Memoranda on International Trade and Balances of Payments*

	1924	1925	1926	1927	1928	1929
I. Live Animals	− 132	− 252	− 271	− 131	+ 97	+ 103
II. Articles of Food and Drink ..	− 4,562	− 5,097	− 6,152	− 8,243	− 6,346	− 7,162
III. Materials, raw or partly manufactured	−16,892	−19,550	−26,441	−18,087	−20,839	−24,067
IV. Manufactured Articles	+23,806	+26,862	+32,498	+28,663	+25,548	+23,044
V. Gold and Silver, specie and unmanufactured	+ 111	− 30	− 27	+ 585	− 6,125	− 8,506

(− indicates net import)

that the value of a country's commodity exports and imports must balance every year, for they palpably do not, but that over any given period of time a country's payments to foreigners on all accounts must balance its receipts from overseas. That is simply a matter of book-keeping. If during any period a country's receipts exceed her outward payments, due allowance having been made for such items as gifts from abroad, repayment of debt or interest, etc., the excess must be due to her having postponed some payments which will come due in the subsequent period, and therefore constitutes an increase in her short-term debt to foreigners. As such, it will be accounted for in her foreign payments balance sheet under the heading of "short-term credits."

This item acts as a compensating factor through which the two sides of any country's foreign payments balance sheet are made to tally. For instance, during almost any period the countries of the world will be importing some commodities for which payment will not be made till a subsequent period; in the interim between receipt of the goods and settlement of the account, the short-term foreign borrowings of the importing country will be increased by the value of the goods, while the short-term foreign loans of the exporting country will be increased by a similar amount. In actuality, however, the fact that "short-term credits" act as the compensating factor in balance sheets of international payments does not make the item an artificial concept. In practice, the greater part of this item is built up, in the case of the important commercial and financial nations of the world, on account of purely financial transactions entered into by the various holders of short-term funds in the money markets of the world. Its importance on that account has already been commented upon (ch. iv).

There are a variety of items which go to make up a country's balance sheet of international payments. Rogers classifies the various items which comprise the United States' balance sheet of international payments under the following headings: net short-term credits, tourist expenditures, immigrant remittances, charities, net export of long-term capital, commodity trade balance, return on war debts, net return on foreign credits, cinema royalties, and gold.[1] Of these the items of greatest importance for the commercial countries of the world in general are the net commodity trade balance, net return on foreign credits (including in certain cases war debt payments), and net new foreign credits of both short and long term. Gold is in all cases the ultimate balancing factor, and is only shipped between countries when the other items, including the highly adjustable "short-term credits," fail to strike a balance.

Thus for debtor nations, whose net return on foreign credits is always negative, because they owe more abroad each year on account of this item than they receive from it, and whose net capital export is increased by their obligations to amortize annually a part of their outstanding indebtedness, there are only three practical ways in which these net liabilities can be met; (*a*) by further borrowings abroad, which will tend to turn their net capital export into a net capital import; (*b*) by an increasing commodity export balance; or (*c*) by an export of gold.[2]

(*a*) During the years 1924–28, the problems of the debtor nations in meeting their overseas obligations were greatly facilitated by the appetite of Americans for foreign bonds. Dr. Ray O. Hall estimates[3] that the net long-term capital export

[1] J. H. Rogers, op. cit., p. 18.

[2] The potentialities of increased expenditures in a country by foreign tourists as a means of aiding debtor countries to meet their overseas liabilities is illustrated by the fact that this item constituted a debit in the United States balance sheet of from $440 million to $685 million in the years 1924–30. This item, however, is unfortunately outside the influence of the debtor countries themselves.

[3] *Balance of International Payments of the United States*, published annually by the Department of Commerce.

of the United States during this period averaged some $650 million a year. At the same time, loans on both long and short term were readily obtainable in the money markets of other creditor nations. As was noted in chapter iv, however, the era of defaults has now ushered in a drastic curtailment of foreign lending of all sorts, and the device of balancing their international payments by resorting to further borrowings is now virtually closed to the debtor nations.

(*b*) Debtor nations have therefore sought relief in the natural expedient of an enlarged favourable commodity trade balance, and have endeavoured to widen the gap between the value of their exports and the value of their imports. This is not only a natural, but also a healthy, tendency, for, although a temporary balance may be achieved in the international payments between debtors and creditors by the raising of further credits, if these credits are ever going to be successfully paid off, and if the interest charges upon already outstanding debts are going to be regularly met, such payments must in the long run be settled in terms of goods, a transfer of which cancels debts once and for all. Anything, therefore, which makes creditor countries less receptive of goods from overseas places one more difficulty in the way of the already harassed debtor countries who are striving to honour their foreign obligations.

It is here that the self-sufficiency of the United States noted above becomes a difficulty of primary importance, for by reason of it she is naturally less receptive of overseas goods than Great Britain, the historical creditor. This very self-sufficiency, moreover, has endowed her with a heritage from the days when she herself was a debtor nation with rapidly developing resources, the heritage of protection. Nor is she alone in this, for France is now busy tightening up her restrictions on incoming goods by placing quotas on a number of her imports in addition to already existing duties. Even Great Britain, after nearly a century of free trade, has now forsaken this unfashionable goddess for the orthodox worship of the god of tariffs. Thus we have the spectacle of these three large creditors, the United States, blessed with such a wealth of resources that without a tariff she would be an unreceptive customer, and Great Britain and France, both dependent upon foreign sources for the supply of a large portion of their requirements, all three united in demanding that their overseas claims be honoured, and yet also united in combating the efforts of their debtors to meet their obligations in the most effective way by paying their tribute in goods.

(*c*) For a time it is possible for debtor nations, precluded from the possibility of either raising new loans or selling more goods abroad, yet to continue to meet their obligations by shipping out gold. It is, of course, misleading to speak as though this course is taken nationally through the medium of the governments of the debtor countries, or even as though the individual nationals in the debtor countries realized that their meeting their obligations by purchasing foreign exchange with their own currencies is likely to cause an outflow of gold from their own countries. In actual practice, this process will work itself out through the medium of the foreign exchange market. As the demands of the various debtors for foreign currencies in which their obligations are payable increase in excess of the amount of such currencies available as a result of the sale of goods abroad, or of the raising of foreign credits, or of one of the other items which cause an inflow of funds from abroad, the dealers in foreign exchange will begin to charge more for the foreign currencies demanded in terms of the national currency, or in other words the national currency will depreciate. If the debtor nation in question is on the gold standard, a limit to this depreciation will be set by the gold export point, i.e. that point at which it becomes cheaper for the banks or other finance houses, through whom the payments are made, to ship gold to the creditor country rather than to buy its exchange. For gold may always be bought for the same price in terms of the currency of any gold-standard country, and may also be sold for the same price in terms of the currency of the creditor country, if she too is on the gold standard. Gold will, therefore, always buy all other currencies at par, due allowance being made for the cost of shipping it to the centre in which the particular currency in question is sold. Thus when the demand for foreign currencies so exceeds the available supply of them as to drive the national currency down to the export gold point, gold will flow out of the country. In this way gold acts, as it were, as an additional commodity export, thereby enlarging the commodity export balance, and helping to redress the deficiency in the international balance of payments.

The export of gold is in fact the expedient to which debtor countries have been increasingly forced to resort by the policies of the creditor nations. "The nations which have become large creditors since the War, France and America, both have policies of protection; though they want to be paid, they object to being paid in goods which means that they get paid in gold, because gold is one of the few things that they do not try to keep out by tariff."[1]

Obviously, however, there is a limit to this process set by the currency needs of the debtor countries. Their gold supply is far from limitless, and if they are to continue on the gold standard they must retain a certain minimum for their own needs. Yet we have seen that in modern conditions a gold flow no longer sets in motion those corrective forces which according to orthodox theory it should. "As a natural consequence, three-quarters[2] of the world's stock of gold has piled up in France and America, and the use of gold as the basis of world currency has become, for the time being, impracticable. Gold in international trade is like oil in an engine; it works only if

[1] *New York Times*, January 11, 1932, p. 2.

[2] Two-thirds of the monetary gold stock of the world would have been a more accurate estimate at this time.

it is well distributed and moves about; if it all sticks in one place, the machinery jams."[1]

The bearing of tariff policies upon the question of the maldistribution of the world's gold is now evident. Even though the new philosophy of Central Banking had never grown up, so that gold movements had continued to have their traditional effect on prices, the tariff policies of creditor nations would have largely, if not totally, nullified this effect by raising the prices of incoming goods, and so destroying the relative commodity trade advantage which should normally accrue to the debtor nations under the deflation of their prices caused by a steady drain of their gold. Even though international lending had continued at a normal rate, the current obligations of the debtor countries could not have been permanently met by further borrowings, so that, if tariff policies continually precluded them from paying in goods, defaults were inevitable as soon as their gold stocks had been sufficiently depleted.

The negativing of the traditional effects of gold flows upon prices and the breakdown of foreign lending are, therefore, merely defects in certain details of the workings of the international gold standard. The defect of paramount importance is the breakdown of international commodity trade under the widespread influence of tariffs. "International payments are made primarily by goods, with gold used only to settle small balances, and with credit used primarily to bridge over seasonal periods between the time of maximum imports and the time of maximum exports."[2] If it were only the "primary" means of payment, international commodity trade, that had broken

[1] *New York Times*, January 11, 1932, p. 2. Cf. Lord Bradbury, *Memorandum of Dissent*, *Macmillan Report*, p. 271, "Under the gold standard, gold in quantities which can be digested is a food, in excess it becomes a poison. The system ought to be worked in such a way as to leave to other nations what they require for food, not to take it and then have to lock it up so as not to be poisoned by it."

[2] Albert H. Wiggin, Chase National Bank of New York, in the *New York Times*, January 11, 1932, p. 4.

down, the strain on the two subsidiary means would have been far greater than they were ever intended to bear, but with the additional breakdown of one of these secondary means, international credit, a totally disproportionate burden has been placed upon the remaining means of payment, gold, which should normally only be used "to settle small balances."

§ 5. The normal effect of a prolonged drain of gold must be to force the gold-losing country off the gold standard, whether, as in the case of Brazil, the drain is allowed to continue until the whole gold holdings of the central institution are exhausted, or whether, as in the case of Great Britain, gold payments are suspended when gold holdings have sunk to a point where their further reduction might make a subsequent return to the gold standard a virtual impossibility. The suspension of the gold standard is, in a figure, Nature's way of rectifying a prolonged adverse balance of international payments. For, in the subsequent depreciation of the national currency, the price of imports is raised to a level which discourages importers, while the world price of the country's exports is lowered and the volume of the exports correspondingly increased. By this means a stimulus is given to the favourable export commodity balance.

Inflation is, however, almost inevitably involved in the process, and of inflation debtor nations, in Europe particularly, have had their fill. In the present crisis, therefore, debtor nations have been loth to abandon the gold standard altogether, particularly as in many cases they had only recently been at considerable pains to restore their national currencies to a gold basis. Instead, a new phenomenon has appeared in international finance, the maintenance of a nominal gold standard with varying degrees of control over transactions in foreign exchange.

There are two ways in which a favourable commodity trade balance may be achieved or increased; by means of an increase in exports, or by means of a decrease in imports. If the former method is debarred by the tariff policies of creditor nations, the latter is always open to any government which is willing to undertake some form of national control of foreign trade. Particularly does this expedient appeal to governments who are themselves debtors, and who are at the same time anxious to honour their obligations; for if the transfer problem grows so acute that there is a danger of their being unable to obtain sufficient foreign exchange for this purpose, their simplest course is to control the amount of the available exchange which may be sold to would-be importers of foreign commodities.

The members of the Economic Committee of the League of Nations were so perturbed at the growth of this practice by the end of 1931 that they devoted the whole of the first chapter of their *Report to the Council on the Work of the Thirty-seventh Session* to a discussion of it. "We have seen, under the pressure of circumstances, the appearance or reappearance in the economic sphere of a whole arsenal of restrictive measures—measures which have assumed the most varied forms: increased Customs duties, quotas, prohibitions, currency control, denunciation of commercial treaties, etc. . . . The situation has grown daily worse; one after another, nearly all the European countries have taken drastic measures to restrict their imports as far as possible and increase their exports. Since all the countries are acting in the same way, the second of these measures, needless to say, is generally without effect. The first, on the contrary, proves only too successful, resulting in a wholesale falling off of commercial exchanges. . . . All the measures taken by the different States in the matter of foreign exchange and the regulation of the exchanges are directed in the last resort towards two main objectives: they are designed either to protect the national currency and the country's credit against any weakening which would mean a reduction in its gold and stock of foreign currency, or, on the other hand, to protect national production against the dumping of cheap goods, that dumping in its turn being determined very largely by the monetary situation of other countries. Financial disorders were bound to affect in the first place debtor countries, whose foreign payments are becoming heavier and increasingly difficult, to the extent of jeopardizing their monetary stability. The majority of those countries are accordingly hastening to take measures which, simply from the standpoint of their financial administration, are perfectly comprehensible and justifiable: they are introducing control of foreign exchange and restricting their imports and are, for the same reason, endeavouring to increase their exports. The double consequence of this state of affairs in the creditor countries is that exports are diminishing, whereas imports would tend to increase if, to cope with this new situation, they, in their turn, did not take defensive measures. These countries find that their credits and exports are alike endangered. . . . The countries which are soundest financially and which are in the position of creditors should, it would seem, be in favour of an increase in the exports of the debtor countries, that the latter may become possessed of the means necessary for them to meet their obligations. But since, on the other hand, countries whose currencies and finances are sound are anxious at seeing their exports reduced as a result of the measures taken by the debtor countries, and feel some apprehension also as regards their own balance of payments, they too are setting up barriers against foreign imports. . . . In theory a country cannot pay its debts otherwise than by exporting gold or obtaining fresh credits or exporting goods. The first means is precluded by the smallness of the reserves held by most of the debtor countries. Complete loss of confidence is paralyzing the international operation of credit, so that until confidence is restored the export of goods is the only means whereby debtor countries can meet their obligations. These countries must therefore have a favourable trade balance, and the greater the volume of their debts the greater that favourable balance must be. Such a position would not be incompatible with the interests of the creditor countries;

on the contrary, it would give them a guarantee for the payment of the debts due to them. But under pressure of circumstances the extra-European and European creditor countries are following the general tendency to set up ever higher tariff barriers to imports from abroad."

From the point of view of international traders, the effect of this new phenomenon of governmental control of the foreign exchanges is virtually the equivalent of a complete suspension of the gold standard. Indeed, an added encumbrance is involved in that, whereas under a suspended gold standard and a freely fluctuating exchange rate the exporter of goods to the country in question has at least an approximate idea of what the currency he receives in payment for his goods is likely to be worth in terms of his own currency, under the system of official control he may be unable to buy any of his own currency whatsoever with the proceeds of his sales overseas. The essence of an international gold standard is the free interchangeability of all currencies based upon it with gold and therefore with each other. This criterion is evidently no longer satisfied when the government of any country places an embargo upon the export of gold and at the same time regulates autocratically the amount of foreign exchange which it will sell for its own currency, even though, when it does agree to sell foreign exchange, it does so at the gold parity rate.

A compilation prepared by Mr. Grosvenor Jones, chief of the Finance and Investment Department of the United States Department of Commerce, and issued on March 29, 1932,[1] revealed that, by that date, few countries were functioning on an unrestricted gold standard. In Europe, France, the Netherlands, Belgium, Switzerland, Poland, and Roumania, and in the Americas, the United States, Guatemala, Peru, and a block of minor Latin-American republics whose currencies were linked to the United States dollar, and in the rest of the world the Union of South Africa, remained alone the champions of

[1] *Department of Commerce, Special Circular*, No. 340.

the pure standard. In Europe, Austria, Bulgaria, Czechslovakia, Denmark, Esthonia, Germany, Greece, Hungary, Latvia, Lithuania, Norway, Portugal, Spain, Sweden, and Yugo-Slavia were all employing varying restrictions in their foreign exchange markets "with a view to safeguarding the value of their currencies abroad." In America, Mexico, Brazil, Chile, Argentina, Bolivia, Colombia, Costa Rica, Nicaragua, and Uruguay had all resorted to a managed currency system with rigorous control of exchange transactions.

By June 1933, the only country outside Europe functioning on a free gold standard, according to the *League of Nations Monthly Bulletin of Statistics*, was the Dutch East Indies. Peru had fallen from grace in May 1932, South Africa on December 28th of the same year, while Guatemala and the other Latin-American countries had followed the United States off gold in March 1933. In Europe the position remained the same as in March 1932, except that Roumania had succumbed to exchange control in May 1932, while her place among the unrestricted gold-standard nations had been taken by Lithuania, and that Norway and Sweden were no longer listed as controlling their foreign exchange rates, though the currency of each stood considerably below par. During the early part of 1932, government intervention spread from a mere control of the sale of foreign exchange to a prescription of the types of imports for payment for which the controlling authority would not issue any foreign currency. Under the heading of "Bulgaria Bars Baby Buggies in Move to Protect Currency," the *New York Times* of January 7, 1932, declared, "What amounts to an embargo on luxuries has been declared by Bulgaria in the form of more drastic restrictions on payments abroad to protect her currency. Payment abroad is forbidden for such imports as baby buggies, passenger automobiles, musical instruments, silks, toilet soaps, flowers and bulbs, biscuits, furniture, jewellery, wicker-work, woollen or fur clothing, motor-cycles, bicycles, phonograph records, and toys." The following extracts from other editions of the same newspaper are but further examples of the restrictions which were being announced almost daily during a large part of this period:

April 22nd. "The Central Bank of Bolivia suspended the sale of foreign drafts to-day in order to protect its gold reserve. . . . The Government has sent to Congress a special message asking enactment of a law to compel exporters to sell a minimum of 65 per cent of the total value of drafts for exports to the Central Bank, which would cover with these amounts the demand for foreign drafts by quotas among the different cities. It would provide that requests for drafts be filed with the Central Bank and studied by a special committee to consist of a delegate of each of the governments, commerce, industry, mines, and banks. It would consider only requests for drafts for articles not manufactured in Bolivia."

April 25th. "The Greek Government decided to-day to postpone for one year repayment due on May 5th of an advance of $7,500,000 on a loan for productive works made by Speyer and Seligman Companies of New York. It was announced difficulty had been encountered in finding sufficient foreign exchange, but that interest on the loan would be paid."

April 28th. "The Austrian Cabinet Council decided to-day to present to Parliament to-morrow a list of proposed import embargoes. Austrian farmers have demanded exclusion of United States fats, lard, and canned goods. Sugar, Southern fruits, cotton cloth, shoes and automobile tires and other rubber goods are almost certain to be on the prohibited list, while a further reduction of the quota for automobiles is being considered."

April 29th. "Two new decrees affecting the finance structure of Peru were put into effect to-day in a supreme effort on behalf of the Government to maintain the sol at its present par value of 28 cents United States gold. One of the decrees provided: (1) Deposits made by judicial or administrative order will not be made in foreign currency except when such deposits are destined for payment of obligations in foreign money. (2) Interest earned by deposits of foreign money in Peruvian banks will be taxed 25 per cent. (3) All contracts in foreign currency will pay an additional tax of 25 per cent besides taxes already imposed on such contracts. (4) All kinds of property or estates of foreign money or stocks willed to persons abroad will also pay a 25 per cent tax in addition to the usual levies. . . . Under another decree Peruvians living abroad and receiving government pensions must return to Peru within sixty days to prevent their pay being remitted in foreign currencies by proxies representing them here."

May 2nd. "The Turkish Government is about to assume more control of the export and import trade than now exists under the import quota system. The Minister of National Economy has announced that a monopoly of the importation of sugar and coffee will be created and the Government will use its monopoly rights to compel countries exporting these commodities to Turkey to buy Turkish tobacco. From to-morrow the purchase of foreign exchange will be permitted only through the State Banks, which will control purchases so that the value of goods exported to Turkey by any country shall be equalized by its imports from Turkey."

May 11th. "A bill empowering the Japanese Government to control the foreign exchange rate will be introduced at the forthcoming special session of the Diet."

The inevitable result of all these and other like measures, the majority of which have been applied from the purely financial motive of protecting national currencies, as against the traditional motive of protecting domestic industries, has been to reduce international commerce to an unprecedented degree, thereby enhancing the difficulties and perplexities of the severest world depression of modern times. It is estimated that during 1931 the total value of world trade fell to 57 per cent of its 1929 value, and declined further during 1932 to 39 per cent of the 1929 figure. During the early months of 1933, there was no sign of an improvement: "provisional figures for both February and April showed that during these two months the value of world trade had fallen to a new low figure of 33 per cent of the 1929 monthly average."[1]

It is interesting to note the comparative success which the debtor countries have achieved in their attempt to increase their favourable commodity trade balance. The National Industrial Conference Board of the United States in a survey published in April 1932 found that of twenty-two leading commercial nations, accounting for 75 per cent of the total trade of the world, the seven creditor nations had suffered a decline of 31·0 per cent in the value of their exports in 1931 as compared with 1930, as against a decline of only 21·8 per cent in their imports, while the exports of the fifteen debtor nations in the list had declined only 22·8 per cent as against a loss of 35·2 per cent in their imports. The moral of these figures appears to be that during 1931 the debtor nations were attempting to meet their obligations by reducing their standard of living, but that this reduction hit back at their creditors by the drastic curtailment which it involved in the foreign sales of the latters' goods. It is noteworthy that, according to the figures given in this survey, the United States, at once one of the largest creditors and one of the most thoroughly protectionist nations, showed the largest loss in exports of any nation on the list.

The moral of the 1932 figures is not so clear. Among the creditor countries, Switzerland, Belgium, and Holland again suffered a heavier percentage decline in the value of their exports than in the value of their imports as compared with 1931; in the case of the United States and Sweden, both imports and exports declined by practically the same percentage of the 1931 figures; while, for the United Kingdom and France, exports fell by a smaller percentage of the 1931 figures than did imports. For the group as a whole, imports and exports

[1] Figures from the *League of Nations Monthly Bulletin of Statistics*.

both declined by exactly the same percentage, 34 per cent, of the 1931 figures. Similarly, the exports and imports of the fifteen most important debtor countries fell in almost exactly equal proportion, exports declining 30·5 per cent and imports 31·7 per cent of the 1931 figures. These statistics would suggest that, while the process observable during 1931 was not continued during 1932, the *status quo* established by the end of the former year was maintained during the latter, the imports of debtor countries being again cut to the bone, while as a consequence the commodity trade balance of the creditor countries registered no improvement.

§ 6. The conclusions of this chapter may be conveniently summarized as follows. A large part of the heavy increase in international indebtedness which has occurred since 1914 is due to loans which differ from pre-War international loans in that (1) they were raised for unproductive purposes, (2) they were often raised by governments instead of by corporations or individuals, and (3) they are mainly owed to countries whose governments are not receptive of goods from abroad. All these facts complicate the problem of the debtor countries in their attempt to meet their obligations.

There are only three effective ways in which debtor countries can meet their annual payments of interest and principal to their creditors, (1) by raising new loans, (2) by increasing the value of their exports relative to the value of their imports, or (3) by exporting gold. The first expedient has been closed to them owing to the breakdown of foreign confidence in the era of defaults, the second is largely impossible owing to the tariff policy of the creditor countries, so the strain was for a time transferred to the third expedient of shipping gold. The rapid exhaustion of the gold reserves of the debtor countries has led to the wholesale suspension or restriction of the international gold standard, and in the process the new phenomenon has appeared of varying degrees of national control of foreign exchange transactions and/or foreign trade in countries who are unwilling to resort to an unregulated paper standard. By means of this control, debtor countries have so successfully achieved their end of reducing their imports relative to their exports that the exports of creditor countries have been severely curtailed, and international commerce threatens to approach a complete standstill.

CHAPTER VI

THE DILEMMA

§ **1.** We have now traced the various world phenomena which have combined to falsify the hope and belief of orthodox economists that the international gold standard, once established, would take care of itself, and would give to the world that universal measuring rod the existence of which would prove such a boon to international commerce. We have seen how, in actual practice, the effort to preserve and abide by this standard has reduced the commerce of nations to a low ebb, and how one nation after another has been forced to abandon the attempt to maintain the standard pure and undefiled.

The instruments which were formerly relied upon to guarantee the smooth operation of the system have been blunted and rendered ineffective by a set of new phenomena for which the orthodox gold standard made no allowance. The hoped-for automatic self-regulation of the distribution of the world's gold supply has inevitably weakened under the growth of the new philosophy of Central Banking. The total supply of the currency of any nation is now divorced from the volume of the country's gold holdings, while currencies tend to be managed with an eye to the internal needs of the various countries rather than to the movement of their foreign exchange rates. Those Central Banks, among which seem to rank those of the two most important financial nations of the world, who have embraced this new philosophy now employ the instruments of the Bank rate and open-market operations, which were formerly trusted to subserve the purpose of facilitating the work of the gold standard for the alternative, and often incompatible, aim of internal stability of prices. Meanwhile, in the hands of the nations who most need these instruments for the protection of their gold basis, the latter are often rendered nugatory by the spread of a feeling of distrust generated by the era of defaults.

The growing popularity of tariffs, particularly among those nations who have recently attained to a creditor position, has placed innumerable barriers in the way of international commodity trade, enhancing the tendency towards a maldistribution of available gold, and endangering the very basis of the international gold standard. The increased preference shown by two creditors in particular, at least up to the end of 1932, for gold over other kinds of wealth has resulted in a gigantic net inflow of the metal into their coffers and a corresponding outflow from the already weaker Central Banks of other countries. This in turn has caused widespread suspension or control of gold payments.

In such circumstances as these it is hardly surprising that there are widespread murmurings of a revolt against King Gold, murmurings which threaten to dethrone him permanently and renounce allegiance to him, even though such conduct might for the moment place those nations who are guilty of it outside the pale of the empire of nations who still remain faithful to him. Gold, the ringleaders of the revolt claim, instead of accepting the role of constitutional monarch which was wished for him by the pre-War champions of orthodoxy, has proved himself a despot whose rule is not conducive to the welfare of his subjects. Every constitutional means to curb him has been tried and proved vain; now nothing remains but revolution.

Revolution would not mean anarchy but simply a transfer of allegiance to the more democratic form of financial government known as the managed paper standard. The argument of the revolutionaries is briefly as follows. Under the gold standard the supply of currency for internal purposes is largely determined, particularly in the case of weaker countries who are threatened with a loss of gold, by world conditions which influence the course of the country's foreign exchanges. Any attempt to manage the supply of currency with a view to internal stability is apt to put the internal purchasing power of the currency out of alignment with its external value unless fortuitous conditions in the outside world are influencing the latter in the same direction as that in which the policy of the Central Bank is influencing the former. An inflation, for instance, induced by an extra emission of credit by a Central Bank for the express purpose of checking a fall in the internal price-level, would tend to place the country in question at a relative disadvantage in international commodity trade, unless the contemporary fall of world prices were simultaneously checked. The country in question would then tend to lose gold. "We cannot stabilize both exchange rates and internal prices—both the external and the internal value of our currency. We can do either, perhaps, but not both."[1] If the choice has to be made, argue the revolutionaries, better by far to retain control of the internal value of the currency, and to let exchange rates follow their natural course, than vice versa.

In the light of recent experience it seems undeniable that any attempt to adhere to the international gold standard involves the subordination of the credit policies of Central Banks to contemporary world factors over which the individual Banks may have no control. The drastic deflation which was forced upon all the important countries of the world from the end of 1929 until the time when one after another sought relief in the restriction of gold payments offers a convincing illustration of the truth of this contention. During the greater part of this period, with the increasing maldistribution of gold under the influence of the various factors discussed in the previous chapters of this book, not only was new gold merely being dug up from one set of holes in the ground in the various mining areas of the world to be quickly buried in another set in the vaults of the Bank of France and the Federal Reserve Banks of the United States, but these latter bottomless pits were at the same time swallowing a large part of the already mined gold which had previously been held by the smaller Central Banks

[1] G. D. H. Cole, *Gold, Credit, and Employment*, p. 32.

of the world to serve as the base for their currencies. As this base shrank in one country after another with the transfer of gold to France and the United States, where it was promptly "sterilized," the world's total supply of purchasing power shrank continuously and rapidly.

The fear of a steady fall in world prices, due to the failure of the production of new gold to keep pace with the increased need for it as production grows, has long been an economic nightmare. Here in the "sterilization" of the already existing supply the fear is being realized long before the niggardliness of Nature has produced any real deficiency in the supply of the metal. It is not owing to a failure of its production that gold has proved inadequate as a base for the currency systems of the world, but owing to a failure in its distribution.

Sir Henry Strakosch (Supplement to the *Economist*, London, July 5, 1930) has suggested a way of computing the degree to which this sterilization has deprived the rest of the world of the supply of gold necessary for the maintenance of stable conditions. Assuming that an annual increase of 3 per cent in gold reserves is necessary for the creation of new money to take care of the annual increase of 3 per cent which is generally supposed to be the natural rate of growth of production, he calculates the amount of new gold which is needed annually by the Central Banks of the world for this purpose. This figure he estimates at £68 million for 1929. Taking the figure for the production of new gold each year, he subtracts from it the amount sterilized, i.e. not used as the basis for any new emission of credit, by the United States, France and Argentina together. The result he compares with his estimate of the legitimate requirements of other Central Banks. On the basis of this computation he finds that in 1929, instead of new gold being available to other Central Banks to the extent of £68 million, the sterilization policy of the above three countries actually absorbed the whole of the new supply together with £14 million of the gold already held by other Banks. He finds that during the period 1924–29 there was no year in which the available supply of new gold was as great as the estimated requirements of the Central Banks of the world, the deficiency varying from 13·4 per cent in 1928 to 121·0 per cent in 1929 of the amount actually required. He also notes that there is a certain correlation between these annual deficiencies and the fall in prices as revealed by the *Economist's* wholesale price index. This computation illustrates the way in which extraneous forces, such as the pursuit of a sterilization policy by other Central Banks, may so drastically affect the supply of gold available to any individual Bank, and so threaten its existing reserves, as virtually to dominate all the other factors which it wishes to consider in the determination of its domestic credit policy.

But the diagnosis of maldistribution of gold as an important cause of the present economic troubles of the world does not in itself bring relief, and it must be admitted that no very effective remedy for the trouble has been put into operation as yet, nor does any single device promise to gain widespread popularity in the immediate future. The argument of the revolutionaries that it would be more profitable for economists, governments, and Central Banks to abandon the gold fetish and concentrate their efforts upon the perfection of a paper standard, which would at least secure internal stability, is therefore plausible.

§ 2. We saw in chapter i that the primary object of the international gold standard was the furnishing of a measuring rod whereby the currencies of all countries on the standard might be compared in value, and the rates of exchange between them maintained at parity. This, whatever its many shortcomings, the gold standard does inevitably achieve. The "managed currency" system or paper standard, advocated by the revolutionaries, on the other hand, inevitably involves fluctuating exchange rates, since the value of any currency in terms of any other is determined simply by the conditions of supply and demand between them. As against this, the revolutionaries promise internal stability in the value of the currency, i.e. a stable price-level. This they maintain, with some justification, is of greater importance to a country than stability of foreign exchange rates[1]; every individual making or receiving payments in the national currency is affected by changes in its value, and in particular a rise or fall in the price-level deranges the distribution of wealth as between receivers of fixed, and receivers of fluctuating, money-incomes; but fluctuations in foreign exchange rates only affect in the first instance that part of the community which is making or receiving payments in foreign currencies.

Before the cogency of the argument of the revolutionaries is admitted, however, it is necessary to investigate the strength of their claim that once the attempt to maintain stability of foreign exchanges has been abandoned they will be able to substitute their vaunted internal stability. It would be a sad disillusionment for a country to desert the gold standard in order to embark upon the quest for internal stability unhampered, only to find that this end was unapproachable.

Now, during the years 1923–31, the United States enjoyed almost complete independence of outside influences in the regulation of its currency, owing to the heavy inflow of gold which it experienced in the post-War period. At only one time

[1] This contention is, however, challenged by some authorities. L. J. A. Trip, formerly Governor of the Bank of Java and Treasurer-General of the Netherlands, in an article on *International Price-Level Adjustments* published by the League of Nations (*Selected Documents*, p. 86) in 1930, writes, "I should like to stress the great importance of maintaining the gold standard for the certainty it furnishes as to the extent to which the rates of exchange may rise or fall. This certainty, as borne out by experience, is one of the first and outstanding needs of international traffic. If one had to choose between the preservation of this certainty with a fluctuating price-level and a stable price-level without it, it would undoubtedly be in the interest of commerce and trade and of an adequate adaptation of national price-levels to choose the former."

during this period was there any serious possibility of its gold reserves being subjected to an intolerable drain from abroad, namely, during the autumn and winter of 1931–32, when the outflow of gold to a panic-stricken Europe, coupled with an outbreak of hoarding, diminished the "free gold" of the Federal Reserve System to a point which necessitated the temporary suspension of the easy-money policy which the System was at the time attempting to pursue. At all other times the System's gold holdings were amply sufficient for it to regard with unconcern the reactions of its monetary policy upon the foreign exchange rates. At the same time, the Reserve Banks were throughout this period committed to the new philosophy of governing their credit policy in accordance with domestic requirements and independently of its effects upon the foreign exchanges. Much may therefore be learnt from the experience of the Federal Reserve System during this decade as to the degree to which stability of the internal value of any currency is likely to be achieved by a Central Bank liberated from the necessity of considering the international repercussions of its domestic credit policy.

For this purpose a statistical examination of the history of the United States during this period has been carried out. Statistics, however, do not make light reading. In order to spare the reader a headache, therefore, the actual discussion of the data has been compressed into an appendix, illustrated by charts, which will be found at the end of the book. Here the conclusions reached as a result of this statistical study will merely be stated with only the barest minimum of the facts upon which they are based. This will inevitably give a dogmatic flavour to what is said here in the text. It is hoped, however, that the reader will remember that these conclusions are not merely the result of "wishful thinking" on the part of the writer, but that they represent his honest deductions from the evidence given in the appendix.

We saw earlier (ch. i, §§ 4–5) the reasoning which gives rise to the confidence of many experts in the power of a judicious operation of the two instruments of Bank rate and open-market operations to control the internal value of a currency. To recapitulate briefly: "The value of the monetary unit depends upon the action of the banks in creating credit. . . . If the Central Bank raises the rate of interest or Bank rate, imprudent banks will find their additional lendings unprofitable, unless they charge as much in turn to their customers. A rise in Bank rate is quickly reflected in a rise in the market rates for loans and discounts, and thus deters traders from borrowing. The creation of credit is thereby damped down, and the value of the money unit in commodities is raised. Similarly, the Central Bank by lending freely can increase the cash reserves of the other banks and stimulate them in turn to lend, and the value of the monetary unit is then lowered."[1] If the market or the banks fail to respond to this treatment, further pressure can be brought to bear upon them through the medium of open-market operations, whereby the size of the reserve base, upon which the credit structure of the country is built, can be directly expanded or contracted.

Briefly, there are three steps to this argument. (1) The Central Bank may control interest rates in its own country. (2) Interest rates determine the volume of the community's borrowings, and hence the total amount of currency outstanding. (3) The amount of currency in existence determines the value of each unit, i.e. the price-level. These steps will now be considered in turn.

§ 3. The phrase, "the rate of interest," is commonly subjected to unjustifiably loose and vague usage. At any moment there are numerous different interest rates in any one country, and the only one to which as a rule greater prestige is attached than to any other is the one which is probably

[1] R. G. Hawtrey, *Gold Standard in Theory and Practice*, pp. 25–6.

practically inoperative, namely, the Bank rate. Of no single rate could it be accurately said that it represented "the rate of interest" for the country. The existence of so many different rates is a matter of importance with respect to the ability of the Central Bank to control "interest rates."

Besides the recognized distinction between long- and short-term interest rates, there exists a further important distinction which often passes unnoticed, the distinction between open-market short-term rates and customers' short-term rates. It is usual to treat the open-market commercial paper rate or the bankers' acceptance rate as if they were the typical market rates of interest, but the fallacy of this procedure becomes obvious when it is realized that only an insignificant percentage of the short-term loans in most countries consist of these types of loan.[1] By far the greater part of short-term loans are contracted "over the counter" in the banks of the country between the local banker and a client whose character and occupation are familiar to him.

Now the outstanding characteristic of all customers' loans is the rigidity of the interest rates charged upon them. This rigidity arises chiefly out of the personal nature of the loans. An understanding has been built up between the client and the banker based upon years of mutual dealings, and this understanding is of real value to the client who would be unable to obtain accommodation so readily from any banker who was unacquainted with his affairs. At the same time, it is of importance to the small banker to retain his clientèle of local borrowers, since loans to the latter constitute the most lucrative part of his earning assets. As a result, the clients are willing to pay a rate above open-market rates rather than go in search of a new banker, while the banker for his part is willing to see

[1] On December 31, 1932, the loans of all member banks of the Federal Reserve System to customers amounted to $13,874,000,000, as against total open-market loans (acceptances, commercial paper, and loans to brokers) of $855,000,000. Cf. also figures given in the appendix.

that the rate that he charges shall not fluctuate with every movement in open-market rates.

Thus the numerically most important interest rate in the country, the customers' loan rate, remains to a great extent inelastic in the face of fluctuations in open-market rates. Yet it is only upon the latter that the policy of the Central Bank makes its influence directly felt. Customers' loan rates lie near the fringe of the sphere of influence of the Central Bank's operations. Indeed, their customary inelasticity is such that they do not readily respond even to the Central Bank's shortening or lengthening of the reserve base of the banking system through open-market operations.

As regards long-term rates, the most direct method whereby the Central Bank can exert its influence is through the purchase of securities. By a vigorous pursuit of this policy as a means of cheapening money in a time of business depression, the central institution may hope so to raise the price of long-term securities or bonds as to make the bond market receptive to new issues through an increase in demand relative to the already outstanding supply. Central Banks, of course, are only able to deal in the highest grade of securities, but it is generally hoped that if the purchases of this class of bonds are followed with determination the return which they afford will gradually dwindle to so low a level that they will become an unattractive investment for the more adventurous class of holders. The latter should then take advantage of the rising price of high-grade securities to sell out and reinvest the proceeds in bonds of a lower grade. The prices of the lower grades of bonds will then rise also, and a price rise initiated in government bonds by the Central Bank's purchases will gradually be diffused through the whole bond market. On a rising market, receptive to new issues, municipalities, public utilities, and corporations will be encouraged to come forward with flotations for the financing of capital improvements, replacements, etc., a certain amount of which they are ready at almost all times to undertake.

New money for these productive purposes will then be drawn out into circulation. Similarly, by heavy sales of its security holdings, the Central Bank may at other times reinforce a deflationary policy by reducing bond prices and so making the market unreceptive to new issues.

As a logical argument this reasoning appears unimpeachable. The trouble, however, is that prices are not so easily diffused through the different classes of bonds in the market as the argument assumes. Times of depression, when the Bank most wishes to drive investors from the market for governments into lower-grade bonds, are the times when investors are most chary of these municipal and corporation bonds. Business prospects are bad; bankruptcies may even be rife; municipalities are in difficulties as a result of declining revenue. The only class of securities which carries virtually no risk of capital loss is the government class. In such circumstances the cautious investor will prefer to hold government securities at a very low rate of return, or even to realize his gains on the rise in the price of government securities and leave the proceeds on deposit in the comparative safety of his bank, rather than to venture into the uncertain realm of second-class bonds. His resistance tends to increase as the depression proceeds, and therefore as the Central Bank pursues its policy with added vigour. In so far as this resistance is too strong to be overcome by the pressure of the Central Bank, the latter will fail of its purpose of raising prices, i.e. lowering interest rates, in the bond market as a whole.

In only one direction does the influence of the Central Bank upon interest rates appear undeniable, namely, in the case of open-market short-term rates. Here no personal relationship enters in to interfere with the free competition of the various lenders in the money market, and their lending capacity, which is easily susceptible to the Bank's policy, determines the keenness with which they bid against each other for the available business. The Bank's own rate, moreover, commonly sets an upper limit to the height to which these rates may at any time rise, though of course the regulations as to how widely the Bank rate may itself apply to the ordinary commercial securities dealt in in the open market vary from country to country.

The main significance of the Central Bank's power to influence these rates, however, is to be found in its effect upon exchange rates rather than upon domestic conditions. The volume of internal investment to which short-term open-market rates apply is insignificantly small in proportion to the total volume of loans. Funds invested abroad, on the other hand, are employed in the open market rather than in customers' loans. The rates prevailing in the various open markets, therefore, normally exert considerable influence over the flow of international liquid capital. For this reason the Bank rate is *par excellence* an instrument fitted for its time-honoured use of regulating movements in foreign exchange rates rather than for its new-found commission of aiming at internal stability.

§ 4. The contention that the volume of borrowings in any country responds automatically to variations in interest rates over-emphasizes the element of supply in the loan market at the expense of the element of demand. It is as true of credit as of commodities that the volume "produced" will depend upon the strength of demand as well as upon the cost of supply. There is a tendency for this fact to be overlooked and for too great confidence to be placed in the power of a rise or fall in interest rates to evince an immediate decrease or increase in the volume of loans outstanding.

Now the primary reason for raising a loan is found in the desire for profits. A man does not borrow for the fun of borrowing simply because interest rates are low; he borrows because he hopes to use the proceeds of the loan in such a way that he will reap a profit above the interest that he has to pay on the loan. Thus the main consideration which influences individuals to increase or reduce their borrowings is their estimation of the likelihood of their being able to earn a profit from their use. Interest rates only enter into the calculation in so far as they constitute one among the many necessary costs involved in the undertakings contemplated.

Here again the interest of the individual borrower will often lie in a direction contrary to the purpose of the Central Bank. The latter will wish to stimulate a demand for loan accommodation in times of depression and falling prices, and to check any further increase in loans when a price inflation is impending. The individual, on the other hand, will be anxious to increase his production or his holdings of commodity stocks or securities when prices are rising, since then it becomes profitable to hold commodities rather than money. At the same time, he will be discouraged from borrowing for similar purposes when prices are falling, since at such times the principal of his loan will increase in commodity values during its course, and will be correspondingly more burdensome to repay.

Now the degree of importance which will be attached to the rate of interest will vary as between short-term and long-term borrowers. It will admittedly be a matter of weight with the latter, to whom it will remain a fixed charge throughout the life of the loan, irrespective of the ups and downs which occur in the enterprise for which the money was raised. Moreover, the proceeds of a long-term loan are normally devoted to some increase or improvement in fixed capital, plant, machinery, etc. The goods and services which this fixed capital produces may be expected to vary constantly in price throughout the life of the loan, so that prospective receipts become less easy to forecast, and costs become proportionately more important a consideration. An increase or decrease in the flotation of new long-term loans may therefore be expected to result fairly readily from changes in the long-term interest rate.

To short-term entrepreneurs, on the other hand, the cost of borrowing is considerably less important. In the first place, their borrowings are usually spent on liquid capital, commodity stocks, raw material, increased pay-rolls, etc., which is being continually turned over, and which may therefore be reduced at short notice should the enterprise become unprofitable. Such a reduction would make possible a simultaneous reduction in borrowings, so that interest does not constitute as permanent and irrevocable an item in this case as with borrowers on long term. Secondly, on account of the rapidity of the turnover of the items on which the proceeds of these loans are spent, a more accurate estimate of probable returns on the enterprise is possible than in the case of long-term borrowings. Thus anticipation of the course of prices in the immediate future becomes a proportionately more urgent consideration, and interest payments become one of the (minor) costs.

Thus it would appear that the efficacy of changes in interest rates upon the volume of loans raised is greatest in the long-term market, where, as we have seen, the prevailing interest rates are to some degree outside the influence of the Central Bank, and least in the short-term market, in the open portion of which the Bank's influence is greatest.

Mr. R. G. Hawtrey has long championed the view that, however impervious manufacturers may be to changes in interest rates—owing to the comparative difficulty of adjusting rapidly the volume of their operations, which arises from the awkwardness and expense of recommissioning disused, or laying off operating, plant—merchants at least will respond readily to changes in the cost of money. Being mere middlemen between the retailer and the producer, their chief expense arises either from storage costs or from interest on the loans which they are bound to raise in order to be able to carry the goods which they purchase from the producer before they are relieved of them by the retailer. A rise in the cost of accommodation will, therefore, on this view impel the merchant to reduce his borrowings as far as possible. In order to do this, he allows a part of his stock to run off without replacing it. This not only reduces his own demands for credit, but also cuts his orders to producers, thereby leading them in turn to restrict their operations and possibly repay certain of their borrowings.[1] Similarly, as the cost of accommodation falls, the merchant will be less averse to borrowing and will be willing to increase his holdings of stock.

Now, although the importance of the contemporary rate of interest to the merchant as a cost item in the conduct of his business is palpable and undeniable, to elevate it to this determining position is an unjustifiable exaggeration. The matter of paramount concern to the merchant, as to all dealers in commodities, is that he shall be paid more for his wares than he himself has paid for them. In other words, the future course of prices is his first consideration, his estimates of which will have much greater influence than any other single factor over his decisions as to whether to expand, contract, or merely maintain, the volume of his stock. So long as prices are falling rapidly enough to wipe out or endanger the margin of profit which he reaps in normal times from the resale of his goods to the retailer, the wise merchant will refrain from increasing his holdings of commodities, however low the interest rate with which his banker may tantalize him. In the extreme case where the fall of prices is so drastic as to make his sales receipts lower than his buying costs, a negative rate of interest would be necessary to induce him to increase his borrowings for the purpose of adding to his stock. In comparison with price

[1] "Merchants are the class of traders most sensitive to credit conditions. A producer's working capital is dictated to him by his output, and no consideration of the rate of interest to be paid on bank advances will count for much against the paramount need to keep up output as near as possible to capacity. To a merchant, on the other hand, working capital means no more than his stock in trade for the time being. It can be varied without much inconvenience within wide limits, and the cost of borrowing is one of the principal factors determining the direction and extent of such variations."—R. G. Hawtrey, "London and the Trade Cycle," *American Economic Review* supplement, March 1929, p. 71.

movements, both present and anticipated, therefore, the rate of interest will be a matter of relative unconcern even to the merchant.

It is, therefore, fallacious to assume that the height of the rate of interest constitutes the only, or even the dominating, factor in the decisions of borrowers as to the volume of money that they will raise. To the extent that this factor is subordinated to other considerations in the minds of would-be borrowers, the control of the Central Bank over the volume of deposit currency outstanding will be diminished.

Here a special difficulty confronts the Central Bank owing to the fact that the efficacy of interest rates as encouragements or deterrents differs for different classes of borrowers at any one time. Borrowers fall broadly into two classes, productive borrowers and speculative borrowers (using the word "productive" in its widest sense to include those entrepreneurs who raise loans for the financing of distribution, storage, etc., as well as for actual manufacturing). Because the price of securities, the chief material for speculators, is more volatile than the price of commodities, the anticipation of profits or losses will normally rank higher in proportion to considerations of the rate of interest in the minds of speculators than in the minds of "productive" entrepreneurs. When the object of the Central Bank is to check a fall, or initiate a rise, in prices, this fact is perfectly healthy, since it would be unfortunate if every attempt of the central authority to make money easy for industry were fraught with the danger of inciting a stock exchange boom. When, on the other hand, the attempt is being made to check inflation, the greater susceptibility of entrepreneurs to a rise in interest rates proves a disadvantage, for production will tend to fall before rates have become high enough to discourage speculators in the heat of a bull security market.

Here we must again join issue with Mr. Hawtrey, who holds that "even a very high rate of interest for a short period is but a slight burden on a prosperous trader, but it deters people from borrowing in circumstances where borrowing is not really necessary."[1] This statement would appear to be the exact reverse of the facts. If the period of the high rates is very short it may, of course, fail to deter any borrowers, but that is contrary to the hypothesis that it has been induced by the Central Bank for the purpose of checking an inflation of some sort. So long as it lasts long enough to make its presence felt anywhere, the tight-money period will react first upon traders, while the borrowings of the speculator, which are not "really necessary," will continue unabated so long as the bull market continues.

§ 5. There yet remains to be considered the further question of how far changes in the volume of deposit currency influence or initiate changes in the value of money, that is, in the price-level.

Now this link in the chain of orthodox reasoning is based upon the assumption that the value of the monetary unit depends upon the quantity of currency and credit outstanding. This is the bald quantity theory of money, and of course "other things being equal" and "in the long run" it is hard to deny the truth of the assumption. In actual practice, however, and over short periods, it is palpably not true. In times of depression, for instance, the velocity of circulation tends to slow down considerably with the slackness of business. If at such times new credit is pumped out into the banking system, the lack of demand for it, and the absence of incentive for entrepreneurs or speculators of one sort or another to make quick use of it, profits being hard to find, may result in its being absorbed by a further diminution in the velocity of circulation with no effect upon prices whatsoever. At such times it will often be more profitable to hold liquid funds than to employ them in the purchase of goods, whether for further

[1] R. G. Hawtrey, *The Gold Standard in Theory and Practice*, p. 54.

manufacture or for stock, since goods will tend to depreciate on the hands of the holder. There will, therefore, be a natural tendency for every individual to postpone his purchases and to hold money, thus reducing the rate of turnover. This unwillingness to turn over the currency may, if the period is one of extreme uncertainty, be carried to the extent of hoarding, which is the equivalent of reducing the velocity of circulation of a part of the currency to zero.

A combination of some such factors appears to have been in operation in France, for instance, during the winter of 1931–32. A cable to the *New York Times* from Paris on March 11, 1932, said, "It is recognized in good financial quarters that something of monetary inflation exists in France as a result of large gold imports and the expansion of the bank note circulation, but it seems to have had absolutely no effect upon prices. This is taken to prove that the quantity theory of money, if not erroneous, is at least not working as rigorously as some had expected. It is now considered that prices should rise in response to such changes in the money supply only if those possessing the new money were to make purchases proportionate to the quantity of money possessed by them—which is not the case. Furthermore, the point is made that the new money is not distributed with any equality and that during a crisis such as now exists some holders have more than they care to spend while others have not enough to justify increased expenditure." In exactly the same way, when times are good and profits plentiful, the increase in the velocity of circulation due to the anxiety of all holders of funds to spend them quickly either to take advantage of the soaring profits offered to entrepreneurs or to lay in stocks of goods before prices go still higher, will do much to frustrate the efforts of the Central Bank, which tries to dampen the boom by reducing the reserve base of the banking system.[1]

[1] "It must be remembered that the same cash reserve will suffice to cover very different liabilities according as its rate of circulation is

But it is not only through a decrease in the velocity of circulation that the effect of an increase of currency upon the commodity price-level might be negatived. We saw earlier (ch. iii, § 4) that it is impossible to expect that the recipients of the new currency will distribute their new purchases evenly over all classes of commodities. In proportion as they concentrate them upon certain classes, the rise in the price-level will be confined, in the first instance at least, to a rise in the prices of these commodities. Now there are four ways in which the recipients of the new purchasing power can spend it; they may buy consumption goods, they may buy investment goods (plant, machinery, raw material, etc.), they may buy securities, or they may increase their bank deposits. If the period be one of depression, as it probably will be since the Central Bank is attempting to raise the price-level by an emission of currency, borrowers will not be readily forthcoming to avail themselves of the new credit, since neither new enterprises nor the holding of securities, the two purposes for which borrowing is normally made, will be likely to be profitable when prices are falling.

It must be remembered that the only means by which the Central Bank can put new currency into circulation is either by encouraging the private banks and other borrowers to increase their borrowings or by purchasing securities. If private borrowers are not forthcoming, the private banks themselves

more or less rapid. There is no absolute limit to the credit that may be granted against a given reserve unless its rate of circulation is uniform. Recent research in this connection has demonstrated that the rate of circulation of bank credits in particular is governed by a slow and steady increase, due to the more widespread use of instruments of payment necessitating no movement of coin, and also by a periodical variation closely linked with business cycles. There are examples on record of the rate of circulation trebling within the same period. This shows that the supply of credit is not strictly limited by the amount of the cash reserve, but that the latter only operates as a check when, for temporary reasons, circulation remains stationary."—Jacques Rueff, *Undue Fluctuation of the Purchasing Power of Gold*, League of Nations, *Selected Documents*, p. 49.

are unlikely to wish to increase their borrowings, and the Central Bank will be obliged to resort to open-market purchases of securities or bills in order to force the new credit out into circulation. For the same reason, the secondary expansion, which is likely to ensue when, as a result of these operations, the private banks find their reserve balances at the Central Bank increased, will also tend to be concentrated in the purchase of securities[1] or the repayment of indebtedness by the private banks. Thus the new credit will pass in the first instance to the holders of the type of investments that banks customarily hold, i.e. gilt-edged bonds. Although it cannot be permanently held up in the bond market, much of the new money is then likely to go simply to increase the deposits of the sellers of the bonds, either while they wait to purchase other securities, or because, at a time of falling prices, they prefer to hold bank deposits rather than securities. Another part is likely to go to repay loans which had been raised in more promising times. At least the sellers of the bonds are unlikely to increase their purchases of either consumption goods or investment goods to any marked extent with the proceeds of their sales, since they will not belong to the class who are so hard hit by the depression that they have just been waiting for funds in order to purchase for themselves the necessities of life, in the same way as the wage-earner might.

On the other hand, if, as the result of an easy-money policy on the part of the Central Bank, prices have begun to rise, and optimistic reports have fostered a stock exchange boom, a number of the recipients of the new credit, or of the secondary expansion of bank credit based thereon, may prefer to purchase securities rather than consumption goods. The Central Bank may then become reluctant to pursue its policy of plentiful money, which would, in the ordinary course of events, be

[1] Commercial bills, the other form of investment open to banks, will tend to be too scarce in times of business stagnation to afford an appreciable outlet for the banking system's surplus funds.

necessary to finance the purchase of the increased contemporary production at the existing price-level, for fear of encouraging speculation. Thus the preference of the community for securities may increase the volume of bank credit "held up" in financing stock transactions at the expense of that part of the community's money which is going to the purchase of consumption goods. The price-level of securities will then rise while the price-level of consumption goods falls, as actually occurred in the United States during the summer of 1929.

"The effect of the introduction of additional purchasing power into any highly organized economic community will depend, therefore, not only on the action of the body responsible for its introduction, but also on the behaviour of the aggregate of individuals who go to make up the community's power of spending, of saving, and of investment. That behaviour may modify the velocity of circulation and hence the amount of purchases which a given volume of money may effect in a defined period. In such circumstances it is clear that neither the effect of an influx or efflux of gold upon the total media of payment, nor the effect of changes in that total upon prices, is automatic or inevitable."[1]

Thus, while, over long periods, movements in the general price-level tend to correspond with movements in the total volume of currency outstanding, allowance being made for a secular increase to take care of a normal increase in production, over short periods other factors are capable of completely upsetting this relationship. All that can safely be said, therefore, is that the volume of any currency outstanding is one among many factors determining the value of each unit.

While orthodox economists, particularly of Anglo-Saxon countries, have tended to assume a more emphatic relationship than this between the two factors, volume of currency and the general price-level, it is noteworthy that many French authori-

[1] League of Nations, *Second Interim Report of the Gold Delegation of the Financial Committee*, Geneva, 1931, p. 11.

ties, notably Charles Rist, former deputy-governor of the Bank of France, have been content with this more cautious conclusion. A report from Paris to the *New York Times* of May 17, 1932, says, "In surveying the controversies which are carried on in various countries, financial Paris feels that the idea which seems to be spreading that multiplication of credits and currency tokens might cure the world depression is a crazy dream. The conviction is positive that monetary inflation would not be sufficient in the present state of markets to send world prices up. The example of France itself is cited, where both superabundance of currency and a large supply of idle capital exists, yet where prices do not recover." The experience of France during this period seems but to support the above moral drawn from statistical evidence from the United States.

Dr. L. J. A. Trip, the Dutch economist, is another prominent critic of the theory that Central Banks are able to exercise any considerable degree of control over the general price-level. It is worth while to quote in full his opinion as expressed by him in an article published by the Gold Delegation of the Financial Committee of the League of Nations in 1930.[1]

"The task of the banks of issue is confined to maintaining and restoring the fixed ratio of value between the national monetary unit and gold, as laid down in the monetary regulations. This task differs in principle from that which some people would like to see allotted to banks of issue, which consists in the maintenance of a stable level of prices with the aid of the index numbers of wholesale prices. Having performed the first task satisfactorily—apart from wholly abnormal circumstances—it should not be inferred that the banks of issue could fulfil the other task likewise. They keep the purchasing power of the medium of exchange at a par with that of gold, but they do not control the purchasing power of gold. The banks of issue cannot perform the second of these tasks.

"As to cyclical price fluctuations, it would have to be made

[1] League of Nations, *Selected Documents*, pp. 60–61.

a condition that the bank of issue should have complete control from the beginning of the whole credit business in its country, including all credit granted by private banks. It will need no comment that the fulfilment of this condition cannot be thought of and that at all events it lies outside the sphere of practical politics. From this it follows that the banks of issue cannot prevent these fluctuations and can intervene only when the rising movement is already in progress. The beginning of such a movement will by no means always be evident from a change in the price-level. The problem of business cycles is the subject of many and widely varying opinions, which is sufficient proof that prescribing a line of conduct to the banks of issue in this respect is out of the question. Notwithstanding this variety of opinions, however, it is quite generally recognized that, not only on account of the independent credit business of the private banks, but also owing to insufficient knowledge of, and experience with regard to, the problem of business cycles, the time for making definite recommendations has not yet arrived.

"As to long-period price trends, these may be the outcome of changes in the financial and economic positions of the individual countries. It is evident that the banks of issue will never have the power to prevent or control such changes. These changes must inevitably lead to a modification of the price-level in the respective countries. Such modification is necessary and beneficial and can in no way be avoided. For this reason, it would not only be impossible, but also detrimental and contrary to the general interest if the banks of issue were required to protect the stability of the index numbers of wholesale prices calculated for their respective countries. As long as trade exists and as long as all the factors which determine the financial and economic position of the different countries cannot be controlled, these index numbers can never be kept at the same level. If the position of a country is influenced adversely to any extent, this will inevitably be evidenced by a decline in the index number prevailing in that country."

While these sentiments are tinged by an unswerving loyalty to the international gold standard, much of the argument is equally applicable to the case of Central Bank policies in countries where the standard is inoperative. If valid, it casts further doubt as to the ability of Central Banks to control the value of monetary units.

§ 6. The above conclusions cannot be said to justify sanguine expectations that anything approaching price stability will be attainable by any Central Bank, even though it should abandon the international gold standard in an effort to gain a free hand for the attainment of that end. This being so, the arguments of the "revolutionaries" lose much of their strength. In place of the internal stability which they tend too easily to assume will follow upon the intelligent management of a currency divorced from gold, they can now only offer the somewhat vague promise of a greater freedom under which the goal of internal stability may be pursued.

As against this vague advantage there are certain further disadvantages to be set. In the first place, the prices of imported goods will vary continually with the constant oscillations which must admittedly occur in the foreign exchange rates. In any country, such as Great Britain, where the proportion of the value of imports to the total national income is high, these price changes will be diffused through much of the commodity market. Thus will be induced those very changes in internal prices which it is the object of the abandonment of the gold standard to obviate. The frequent changes which will ensue in the prices of raw materials, wool, cotton, rubber, and the rest, for instance, will constantly be reflecting themselves in price changes in the hundred and one commodities of which they form ingredients. It would be a wellnigh impossible task for any Central Bank to attempt to counteract these rapid changes in prices.

Secondly, export industries will be subjected to a considerable handicap. It is true that markets in forward exchange may be developed for all currencies, so that exporters may be able at all times to estimate the proceeds of their contracts in terms of their own currencies. The quotations for forward exchange, however, will themselves change from day to day, so that the individual exporter will be unable to foretell what will be the international price of his particular commodity by the end of the week. For a few weeks on end the exchanges may so favour him that he could undersell all foreign competitors if he were only able to make immediate contact with would-be foreign purchasers and to speed up his production to take care of all the orders. By the time that he has made contact, however, and set his plant to work to fill his orders, the exchanges may have turned against him. If he has committed himself to contracts expressed in foreign currencies, probably the only form of contracts which the foreign purchasers have been willing to enter into, the business may then suddenly become unprofitable. Export industries will, therefore, tend to suffer extreme irregularity, working to the full extent of their capacity for short periods while the exchanges make their sales abroad profitable, and stagnating at other periods when a rise in the value of the domestic currency has placed their wares at a disadvantage in the international market.

Thirdly, perhaps more important than the commodity export trade, the capital export trade will be brought to a virtual standstill. Some part of international commodity trade may continue with the help of well-organized forward exchange market, since these markets will extend far enough into the future to assure the exporter of a definite exchange rate on the proceeds of his sales at the settlement of the contract. No forward exchange market, however, will deal far enough into the future to assure a trustworthy exchange rate to a foreign lender on any but the shortest account. Lenders will therefore be unable to calculate beforehand what the principal of their loan will be worth in their own currencies at the time of repayment, quite apart from the difficulty of estimating the value of the intervening interest payments. Few borrowers will be willing to raise loans in a foreign currency, since they will be uncertain what their eventual cost will be in terms of their own currency, while the same doubts will restrain all but reckless lenders from making loans in any currency but their own. The whole of international financing will become one vast speculation. We have already seen how grave may be the effects of a breakdown in the mechanism of international lending.

Fourthly, the task of attempting to regulate the value of a currency requires not only prodigious insight and foresight, but also detailed information such as is nowhere obtainable except perhaps in the United States. Unfortunately, all production does not increase uniformly and smoothly at a fixed rate of so much per cent per annum requiring a similar increase in the volume of credit. We have already quoted the list of indices which the directors of the Federal Reserve Bank of New York study in formulating their credit policies, and it is probable that this list is still inadequate and the significance of much of its data misunderstood. The very end towards which currency management is commonly directed, the stability of the value of the currency unit, is itself nebulous. The value of any currency unit can only be measured by an index number of the amount of various things that it will purchase, and the inadequacy of any single index number is apparent when it is remembered how much of the national income and expenditure is composed of services, securities, labour, etc.[1]

[1] "In the execution of a stabilization problem, appropriate means of measuring the course of prices must be employed. That any single index number will serve all purposes seems doubtful. To measure secular trends and cyclical fluctuations, a wholesale price index which includes many commodities, such as that of the (United States) Bureau of Labour, seems inadequate. A general purpose index, such as that which has been constructed at the Federal Reserve Bank of New York, does not appear to be sufficiently sensitive, while basic commodity indices are apparently unduly so. For the particular problem presented by price changes required to maintain exchange

Even where it is possible to obtain accurate data of the prices of all these various items of expenditure, one composite price-index constructed on the basis of all available data is practically meaningless. A wholesale index number does at least attempt to measure only the price-level of a homogeneous group of commodities, just as a cost-of-living index attempts to measure the cost of a typical family budget. A composite index, on the other hand, which set out to combine the salary of a high-school teacher in Nebraska, the cost of a bus ticket in Oregon, the wages of a factory hand in North Carolina, and the price of spaghetti at a store in Worcester, Massachusetts, in an attempt to compare the value of the dollar at different dates, would be a nonsensical quantity. Yet is anything short of such an index a true measure of the value of a currency? Cassel has blandly remarked, "We are accustomed to measure the purchasing power of our money by the aid of wholesale price-index figures. . . . In reality, however, there are also other prices to be taken account of, particularly wages and the cost of living. . . . A stabilization should, therefore, always take account of wages and of cost of living as well as of the level of wholesale prices and should try to find for the currency a value to which all these levels can be adjusted with the least possible disturbance."[1] He wisely remains silent as to the difficulties which may arise when movements in these indices are discrepant or out of

equilibrium a special index is required, an index which in some way measures general changes in unit money costs of production. Perhaps such an index might be based upon a selection of those commodities which are neither exported nor imported. An index of this character would roughly measure the changes in money costs that may be required to maintain the equilibrium of payments with other countries."—O. M. W. Sprague, *American Economic Review*, March 1929. Such an index would, however, be practically impossible to construct accurately owing to discrepant movements in production costs in different industries and in different localities. Costs of labour, transportation, raw material, local taxation, rent, etc., vary from one place to another within a country as well as between nations.

[1] Gustav Cassel, *Post-War Monetary Stabilisation*, pp. 12–13.

proportion, as they frequently are, wholesale prices being considerably more sensitive as a rule than either of the other two.

Even though a satisfactory index number could be constructed which would reflect accurately the value of the currency unit at any moment of time, fluctuations may occur in it which may be due entirely to a small number of its components which have been temporarily disturbed. If the Central Bank then uses its influence to correct the fluctuations and restore the currency to its normal value, it will subject a number of perfectly stable components to the same constraint as the few recalcitrants. Suppose, for instance, that a wholesale commodity price-index were chosen, and that as a result of an adverse movement in exchange rates the prices of all imports rose. The index would then immediately reflect this rise in the price of the imports themselves and of their various derivatives, while prices in a number of sheltered industries remained completely unaltered. The instruments which the Central Bank would bring into operation for the maintenance of the value of the currency unit, however, would tend to apply with equal force to all alike, to the sober and inoffensive as well as to the fluctuating and culpable prices which initiated the disequilibrium.[1]

§ 7. Out of the foregoing survey it is now possible to formulate certain conclusions concerning the dilemma which the financial world is facing. After desperate efforts to preserve the international gold standard, efforts which contributed to one of the most severe and widespread deflations of prices that the world has ever seen, one country after another has been

[1] The fact that we have seen that it is unlikely that the prices of all commodities will be affected equally or in the same direction by the credit policy of the Central Bank does not weaken the argument here. Granted that the incidence of credit conditions will fall differently upon the prices of different commodities, there is no reason to suppose that those prices which have caused the disequilibrium will be precisely those most affected, while stable prices continue unaffected.

forced to remove its currency from a gold basis until only a handful of nations retain the interchangeability of their currencies with gold in an unrestricted form. In other words, contemporary circumstances have rendered the universal employment of the international gold standard impracticable.

In the face of an unquestioning assumption on the part of many that the abandonment of the gold standard is a purely temporary necessity, and that all countries of international significance will endeavour to return to a gold basis as soon as occasion offers, certain revolutionaries, despairing of any country ever being able to keep its currency linked to gold without subjecting its value to fluctuations imposed upon it by external influences, have advocated the complete abandonment of a metallic standard once and for all. They maintain that by scientific management internal stability of the purchasing power of the currency unit can be achieved, but only at the cost of fluctuations in foreign exchange rates due to the operation of uncontrollable world forces. Better, they aver, to recognize the uncontrollability of these world forces and to concentrate upon the attainable end of internal stability than to lay the purchasing power of the currency open to the influence of every world-price disturbance by attaching it to the international yardstick, gold.

Now if the revolutionaries' promised stability were realizable their case would be a strong one. Both theoretically and practically (cf. the appendix), however, there are serious reasons for doubting whether currency management is as potentially effectual as its proponents claim. The experience of the United States during a period when the country was virtually independent of outside influences in the pursuit of its financial policies indicates that the maintenance of a stable purchasing power for a national currency is no easy matter. There is therefore a danger that the plan of the revolutionaries might involve the abandonment of the very real advantages of steady exchange rates for the distinctly nebulous advantages of endowing the Central Bank with a freer hand for the pursuit of an ultimately unattainable, though eminently desirable, end, the maintenance of the internal value of the currency.

Thus there is much reason for the persistent hesitancy of the powers that be to embark upon the strange and untried path of non-metallic managed currencies. The gold standard has worked well in the past, even though the exigencies of the present emergency have upset its smoothness of operation, and its advantages in the form of stable foreign exchange rates are undeniable. To renounce such proven advantages in pursuit of the uncertain claims of the champions of managed currencies is a radical, if not a desperate, step. The loyalty of orthodox economists to the international gold standard is not based simply on blind conservatism but on an appreciation of its tested utility.

The strength of this loyalty is well illustrated by the following quotation from the *Proceedings of the American Academy of Political Science* in January 1930, when a decade of painful reconstruction had restored all the important currencies of the world to a gold basis.

"The gold standard has emerged triumphantly from the welter of disordered currencies of the World War period and gold has now become more universally than ever before the foundation of the structure of credit throughout the world. This return to the haven of familiar monetary practice is significant of the widespread conviction that the gold standard is an essential factor in the maintenance of a reasonable measure of international financial stability, for which there is no promising or practicable substitute. Aside from the defect, perhaps not incurable, of long-time secular price trends, the gold standard worked well during the half century preceding the War and the public is hopeful of not less satisfactory results in the future. That these hopes can be realized I am firmly convinced, but, under present and prospective conditions, they can be realized only through a greater measure of co-operation and conscious effort than was required under the conditions that obtained in the pre-War period."[1]

The last sentence of this quotation opens the door to the most likely escape from the dilemma. At one extreme, the post-War gold standard, working on the rankly individualistic basis of each Central Bank's pursuing its own independent policy, has failed, and will continue to be impracticable so long as the factors surveyed in the preceding chapters of this book exercise their malign influence. At the other extreme, the complete abandonment of gold offers certain losses and only uncertain gains. Is there no hope of retaining some form of the gold standard which will continue to yield the advantage of steady foreign exchange rates, and yet from which international co-operation may remove, or at least modify, not only the factors which destroyed the post-War international gold standard but also the fluctuations in world prices which have exercised so disturbing an effect upon the internal values of gold currencies?

In the remainder of this book some attempt will be made to answer this question.

[1] O. M. W. Sprague, "Working of the Gold Standard under Present Conditions," *Proceedings of the American Academy of Political Science*, January 1930.

CHAPTER VII

TOWARDS A WORKABLE GOLD STANDARD

§ 1. The world is at the present time less a conglomeration of independent economic units than at any previous period in its history. The increased speed and facility of international communications and transport, the growth of the "division of labour," the internationalization of finance through the organization of open money markets and stock exchanges, international debtor-creditor relationships, the ever-increasing importance of international commerce to each individual nation, all combine to make it continually more difficult for any country to keep the even tenor of its way without constant reference to the progress of events outside its own boundaries.

In the matter of finance the world is perhaps more closely knit than in any other sphere. Money, purchasing power, is not only the concern of every nation but of every rational man. The health of the rubber industry is of importance to all the vast multitude of people who make use of rubber products of one sort or another, but the supply of rubber is of direct interest to only a small minority. The size of the wheat crop may affect the poorest classes who will have to reduce their consumpion of bread if the price of a loaf rises during the winter after a small crop, but it will leave the large majority of the world's citizens unmoved. The supply and the value of money, on the other hand, touches everyone.

"Oh, ain't it funny
The dif-fer-ence that money
Makes to you,"

ran a popular song of a few years ago. The writer would have had difficulty in finding another word which could be substituted for the word "money" in the context in apposition to the impersonal "you." Only if the object of his serenade had been a farmer, miller, or grain operator, could he reasonably have inserted the word "wheat."

Yet, although money is of intense interest to all citizens and therefore to all enlightened governments, the viewpoint from which the individual approaches the topic is different from that which an enlightened government must needs take. The individual, except in unusual cases, is always anxious to increase his holdings of money; yet if this were made possible for all citizens simultaneously, the value of each unit of money would decline roughly in proportion. The object of the enlightened government, or central controlling agency, therefore, must be to guarantee such a supply of monetary units as shall maintain a fixed value for each.

This goal has obtained such wide recognition that it is surprising that, in view of the equally widely admitted financial interdependence of nations, more headway has not been made in the direction of international co-operation towards its attainment. Such a suggestion might have been scorned as impracticable twenty years ago, but now not only the machinery but also the will to co-operate has appeared. Nations now continually take counsel together for devising methods for the prevention of war, realizing that the safety of each cannot be guaranteed without the security of the whole. The League of Nations, regarded by many simply as an instrument for furthering world peace, has accomplished its most fruitful work in other spheres in which collaboration between nations is indispensable. The Bank for International Settlements, though its *casus originis* was the problem of the transfer of reparations payments, affords a meeting-place where the financial authorities of the world may assemble in conference over their mutual problems. It is no longer necessary, therefore, for monetary theorists to approach their problems as though every effort of a domestic authority were going to involve international repercussions which must be accepted in a spirit of resigned pessimism. It is their duty rather to show how co-operation may obviate, and even turn to good effect, the results of the close interrelationships of all financial systems.

The call to a common international effort has been sounded with increasing frequency in the economic camp of recent years, and with it have come dire warnings of the consequences if the nations of the world fail to "get together" before they are very much older. Broadcasting from his office in Basle on the evening of May 11, 1932, Gates McGarrah, president of the Bank for International Settlements, said, "No such widespread results as followed the tidal wave of apprehension which originated in Austria in the summer of 1931 could have occurred except for the already existing conditions of monetary systems and financial and economic relations which, like international broadcasting, transcend political and geographic frontiers. All the information available at the Bank for International Settlements leans to the conclusion that any hope that a single country can achieve prosperity apart from the rest of the world is indeed based on insecure foundation."

According to the *New York Times* of May 8, 1932, "Great Britain's recent experience (of an attempt to arrest the fall of her domestic price-level in the face of a world-wide decline), in the view of some observers, tends to prove that in present conditions an individual country can do little by itself to arrest the world-wide sweep of falling prices. . . . It has been suggested by the National City Bank and others that world co-operation in this effort should be sought, and something close to Central Bank co-operation is going on, although there is no formal engagement among banks to act in concert."

The British Committee on Finance and Industry[1] closes Part I of its report in the following significant words. "It is necessary in any policy, whether of expansion or contraction, which is adopted by a particular Central Bank that due attention should be paid to the relation of this policy to the policies which are being pursued by the other Central Banks. It is

[1] *Macmillan Report*, p. 105.

a condition of adherence to an international standard that a Central Bank must not get much out of step with the average movements of other Central Banks, under penalty of provoking large movements of gold. It is for this reason that we lay so much emphasis in what follows on the importance of international co-operation."

"The absolute necessity of international co-operation on broad lines," says Gustav Cassel, "for the stabilization of the value of gold is most clearly seen if we only for a moment reflect on the alternative to such co-operation. This would obviously be a general and ruthless competition for gold, a consequent continual rise in the value of gold, and a corresponding world-wide economic depression for an unlimited future."[1]

It should, therefore, be clear that, if we are going seriously to champion the cause of a continuance of an international gold standard, we must posit an ever closer degree of inter-governmental, or inter-Central Bank, co-operation. Nor, in doing so, shall we be overstepping the bounds of probability, for, although no *ad hoc* body exists officially as yet, the above quotations, together with what has already been said concerning the spread of internationalism and the essential unity of purpose of all nations, indicate that something in the nature of orgnaized international effort is on its way.

It is not necessary here to discuss in detail the lines along which an international financial organization should be constituted, nor whether it should be a permanent institution or rather consist of a series of conferences similar to the disarmament or reparations conferences or the World Economic Conference of 1933. It need only be assumed that Central Bankers and Treasury officials should "graduate" from their present practice of hasty transatlantic telephone calls and occasional "goodwill tours" to the more systematic method of periodical meetings around a table at which all important

[1] *Post-War Monetary Stabilisation*, pp. 98–100.

countries may be represented simultaneously. It is not even necessary that any one place or institution, such as the Bank for International Settlements, should be selected as the permanent rendezvous for the Conference. The world has become accustomed to the practice of individual governments sending out invitations to their neighbours to come and consult with them over some specific issue. If that method were more easily handled than a permanent institution, it might be equally effective for enacting the most essential measures, though, as we shall see in the next chapter, a standing institution is to be preferred if more than the absolute minimum is to be achieved.

Even assuming that constant international co-operation becomes a possibility, however, it is essential to keep clearly in mind the end towards which that co-operation is to be directed. Much loose talk on the subject is due to the fact that the ultimate object of an international standard is lost sight of. Now, we have seen that the primary advantage of an international standard is the stability that it gives to the foreign exchanges of all countries whose currencies are linked to it. This enables sums of money expressed in terms of one currency to be at any time translated into an equivalent quantity of every other currency, at a practically constant ratio, thereby greatly facilitating both international commerce and international lending. Such an achievement, however, does not constitute the *summum bonum* of financial organization so long as the value of the standard itself may vary, for then every national currency will be unavoidably subjected to similar variations in value. There is thus a double purpose at which Central Banks, pledged to co-operate in making the international gold standard a workable proposition, must aim; the assurance to the individual banks of a sufficient quantity of gold to enable them to guarantee the gold value of their currency without threatening their own internal stability; and the assurance to all Banks collectively of a sufficient quantity of gold to enable them as a group to emit or contract credit at will in an attempt to fit the supply of currency to the demand and so maintain its value, and therefore a stable level of world prices.

It will be seen that for the pursuit of both of these objectives an abundant supply of gold is necessary. Unfortunately, according to the now generally familiar predictions of experts, the world is faced with the prospect of a steadily declining production of new gold. Mr. Kitchin, for instance, estimates[1] that even as early as 1940 the amount of new gold available annually for Central Banks and Treasuries, after making due allowance for non-monetary demand, will have fallen to a bare 1·5 per cent of the already existing holdings. Accepting Cassel's estimate that world production normally increases at a rate of some 3 per cent per annum, it appears inevitable that the supply of new gold must prove inadequate to take care of the new production at a stable price-level. Some means must therefore be found for effecting economies in the use of the present monetary gold stock of the world, so as to create in it a surplus above present needs which may be drawn upon in the future to make good the deficiency between the supply of and the demand for new monetary gold.

§ 2. We have already seen that there is at present considerably more gold in the Central Banks and Treasuries of the world than is needed to take care of current needs. There is, therefore, no physical impossibility contained in the statement that a surplus should be created from the already existing stock to be drawn on in case of a shortage at a later date. The trouble at present is not that the existing supply is physically inadequate but that it is so badly distributed between the nations of the world that a large part of it lies sterilized in the vaults of Banks which are prevented by fears of inflation from making use of it, while other Banks all over the world are starved of the precious metal.

[1] Memorandum submitted to Macmillan Committee in 1929.

But, passing over for the moment the question of maldistribution, the world is guilty in another way of not making full use of its present gold supply, namely, in maintaining an antiquated body of legal regulations, which no longer have any factual justification, as to the minimum amount of gold which the various Central Banks must hold. In most countries these legal requirements are expressed as a function of the note issue, either as a fixed percentage or as a hundred-per-cent backing for every note issued above a certain maximum fiduciary figure. This is a historical accident which has grown up from the days when the chief purpose of gold reserves was to assure the convertibility of the national currency. In those days the most important danger against which the Central Bank had to guard was the possibility of domestic panic, leading to the withdrawal from banks of deposits not only in the form of notes but also, and perhaps still more, of gold.

While a domestic drain of gold was still a possibility, it was at least rational to maintain some form of relation between the note issue and the volume of the Central Bank's gold holdings, in order to avoid arousing public suspicion as to the soundness of the domestic note currency. Now that gold coin has been generally withdrawn from circulation, however, an internal demand cannot arise. It is therefore foolish that the volume of gold which any Central Bank is required by law to hold should be regulated in some fixed relation to the note issue, or conversely that the volume of notes which an issuing Bank may put out should be restricted by the size of its gold holdings.

In actual fact, in countries where the cheque system has developed the volume of the note issue is no longer even an indication of the potential internal demand for gold. The volume of deposit currency has long since taken its place as the numerically important part of the total currency, and therefore as constituting the item which would induce the greatest internal drain of gold in case of a panic causing the public to rush to convert their assets into gold. In these countries the note issue is no longer an active factor causing inflation or deflation of prices, but simply responds passively to the demand of the public (cf. ch. iii, § 2). The volume of notes in circulation, therefore, is customarily one of the last financial indices in these countries to reflect any tendency towards a monetary dislocation, so that it is even more irrational for countries with well-developed chequing systems, such as Great Britain and the United States, to relate their gold holdings and the volume of their note issues than it is for countries, such as France, where currency notes still constitute a large and active portion of the total currency.

But now that gold is no longer held as a safeguard against an internal drain, it is not necessary to link the minimum gold holdings of any country for that purpose either to the note issue or to the deposit currency outstanding. Instead the chief *raison d'être* of gold reserves has now become the provision of a means of balancing international payments when a temporary disequilibrium has led to a depreciation of the national currency to the "gold export point." In other words, the purpose of a gold reserve is now to meet an external rather than an internal drain, and to guarantee to each gold-standard country enough of the metal to enable it to maintain its currency from falling below the gold export point with relation to other currencies, i.e. to keep its currency on the gold standard.

The Macmillan Committee go so far as to say that "now that gold coin has been withdrawn from circulation . . . the sole practical use of a gold reserve is to serve as a medium of meeting a deficit on the balance of international payments, until steps are taken to bring it again to equilibrium."[1] For such a purpose there should be no legal minimum, since all such minima lock up a portion of the gold reserve and withdraw it forever from use. Moreover, being lower limits, these

[1] *Macmillan Report*, p. 67.

minima only become operative when the gold reserve has already shrunk considerably below its accustomed size, exactly at the time, that is, when the extra amount of gold locked up in the irreducible minimum would be of the greatest value to the Central Bank concerned. It may, of course, be advisable for each Central Bank to decide for itself a figure which it will consider its own absolute minimum for safety, and below which it will not allow its gold holdings to fall without making vigorous efforts to restore them to at least that level. This minimum figure, however, so far from being incorporated in the laws of the country as a legal minimum, should not even be made public, since in that case attention would be attracted by any Bank whose reserves fell even temporarily below their accepted minimum. Foreign suspicion and distrust might then ensue to make even more arduous the Bank's task of attempting to replenish its gold holdings.

The Macmillan Committee, however, overstate the case in the above quotation. Even though there is no longer any danger of internal drains of gold, confidence has to be maintained in the currency of any country on the gold standard so long as the possibility of an external drain exists. It is doubtful whether at present foreign confidence could be maintained in any currency for which no minimum gold reserve were prescribed by law. Here much can be accomplished by international co-operation. If any one country abolished, or even appreciably reduced, its legal reserve requirements there would very probably develop a "flight" from the currency of that country. In the present state of international nervousness nations are only too ready to see signs of instability in one another's financial structures, and no country could afford to attempt a downward revision of its reserve requirements alone. The Glass-Steagall Act, passed by the Congress of the United States in February 1932, to allow the Federal Reserve Banks to use government securities as part of the reserve against their notes, was a veiled method of reducing the legal minimum gold backing of American currency, and even so mild and avowedly temporary a measure caused a flight from the dollar which might have proved embarrassing to a financially weaker country.

If international co-operation could be secured, on the other hand, for a universal reduction in legal reserve requirements, no "flights" from any currency would be possible, since all currencies would be equally implicated. It would probably be impossible at the present stage to obtain universal agreement for the total abolition of legal requirements, and until national institutions have become more experienced at monetary management so drastic a step might be undesirable. There is little doubt, however, that international agreement could be secured for some reduction of present legal minima.[1] It is palpably absurd that the major portion of the gold holdings of all gold-standard countries should be constantly rendered unavailable for export, the main purpose for which it is held. It is only rational that this portion should be steadily reduced in favour of the portion which may be used for redressing disequilibria in international balances of payments.

An international conference on this subject at an early date would be desirable. To exactly what point reserve requirements should be reduced it should be the business of the conference to decide. It seems desirable however, that legal requirements should be fixed with reference to the total volume of the Central Bank's liabilities, deposit as well as note, in each country.[2] This plan would have various advantages. It

[1] "We need an edict by the arbiters of fashion, who are none other than the Central Banks themselves (and their governments) acting in agreement, that legal reserves may now be fixed lower."—J. M. Keynes, *Treatise on Money*, vol. ii, p. 311.

[2] In countries where, as in Great Britain, private individuals as well as private banks hold deposits at the Central Bank, allowance must be made for this fact in the computation of the legal minimum reserve. Only those deposits which belong to other banks should be reckoned in for this purpose, since it is these which form the basis of the country's supply of deposit currency. There is no reason why

would continue to link the volume of gold holdings to the foreign demand likely to arise. For this demand is likely to vary with the total amount of each country's currency outstanding, as each country's purchases abroad tend to rise and fall with the increase and decrease in its supply of money, and those of the Central Bank's deposits which belong to private banks roughly determine the country's supply of deposit currency. It would impose a check, similar to that imposed in a more clumsy and irrational way by present requirements, upon the issue of currency as a whole. It would comprehend both countries where deposit currency and countries where the note issue account for the major part of the monetary supply.

It is often observed, for instance, that in countries, such as France, where the major part of the nation's business is transacted by means of currency notes, an anomalously large amount of gold is demobilized in comparison to countries where chequing is common. A reserve requirement of, say, 40 per cent against the note issue is a much severer restriction upon the supply of money in such countries than it is in countries where the note issue only constitutes perhaps one-fifth of the total currency, the remainder being furnished by bank deposits. This difficulty would be obviated if the legal minimum in all countries were reduced to some percentage, varying in each country if need be, of currency notes plus the reserve balances of private banks.

Whether, if this plan were accepted, it would be preferable to fix the new minima as a percentage of Central Bank liabilities or to adopt the method of a fiduciary issue with every unit of currency above a fixed maximum backed by gold is a point which must be settled in Conference, as is also the question of the figure at which either the percentage or the fiduciary maximum should be fixed. Since the object of working out

a particular gold reserve should be held against private deposits held at the Central Bank rather than against private deposits held at any other bank.

legal minima is simply to arrive at the lowest minimum which will satisfy a suspicious world, no specific numerical recommendations can be made until it is seen how strongly the wind of mutual trust is blowing. What can be safely said is that under existing arrangements an unjustifiably large amount of the world's monetary gold is tied up as backing for currency notes, which are no longer likely to be presented in quantities for payment in gold; that the primary object of a gold reserve is now to afford a means of redressing a lack of balance in foreign payments, and the secondary object to assure public confidence in the soundness of the currency; and that, in view of a probable future shortage of newly-mined gold, the stock of metal available for the primary purpose should be fortified by a universal agreement to mobilize part of the gold at present held for the secondary object.

§ 3. Apart from the economies in the use of the existing stock of gold that could be achieved through international agreement, there are also various measures which it is within the power of individual countries to adopt for the conservation of the world's present supply of the metal. In the first place, the experience of the last eighteen years has conclusively proved that countries can safely and comfortably dispense with gold as a part of their circulating medium. Gold disappeared from circulation in most of the belligerent countries during the war, and the citizenry began positively to prefer easily handled paper money to the more clumsy and bulky coin. There is no longer any difficulty in persuading individuals to place as much confidence in the stability of currency notes as in the stability of gold coin itself, so that the danger that part of the circulating medium may stand at a discount with reference to other parts is non-existent.

It is, therefore, an anomaly that in so enlightened and highly developed a country as the United States gold coin and gold certificates, which for the purpose of reserve requirements are the equivalent of gold coin, should continue in active circulation. That function could just as easily, and far more economically, be performed by ordinary Federal Reserve notes. Since a reserve of only 40 per cent is at present required in the United States against Federal Reserve notes, 60 per cent of the gold at present in circulation, or immobilized as backing for gold certificates, would be added to the stock of gold available for other purposes if gold were entirely withdrawn from circulation in that country.[1]

At the same time France is now legally empowered to return to a gold circulation if the fancy should take her. There have been rumours that the recent heavy inflow of gold into France, though not of course brought about in order to enable the country to restore gold to hand-to-hand circulation, may encourage the Bank of France to take that step, if only to weaken the charge that the gold imported is serving no active purpose but is being sterilized in the vaults of the Bank. Such action would be in the nature of a major disaster for the whole gold-standard world. It would divert gold from sterilization in the Bank's vaults to a more thorough and permanent sterilization in the unnecessary function of supplanting perfectly satisfactory notes from circulation and from furnishing the peasant with a store of value in his proverbial sock. It is earnestly to be hoped that, should such a step be seriously proposed in France, the other important financial nations of the world would exert the strongest persuasion possible to discourage it. The arguments of the United States in such a

[1] Since these words were written, (*a*) the reserve requirements of the Federal Reserve Banks have been somewhat modified by the emergency measures of President Roosevelt's Government (*vide* § 43 of the Act of May 12, 1933), and (*b*) a considerable amount of gold coin and gold certificates have returned from circulation as a result of the campaign against gold hoarding. By the end of May 1933, gold coin and certificates officially recorded as outside the Treasury and the Reserve Banks were reduced to $605,000,000, the lowest amount since 1922. It is to be hoped that this process may continue.

case would be considerably strengthened if she herself had previously withdrawn gold and gold certificates from circulation within her own borders.

Almost as a corollary to these recommendations for the withdrawal of gold from circulation, it is to be hoped that countries at present operating on the gold specie standard may go over to the gold bullion standard.[1] The latter works quite as efficiently as a means of keeping the currency linked to the international standard, as the experience of Great Britain showed between 1925 and 1931. Gold bullion has as world-wide a value as gold coin, so that, so long as countries guarantee to deal in the former at a fixed price, their currencies cannot depart from par by more than the interval between the gold points. At the same time, the gold bullion standard affords a further discouragement to internal demand for the metal. The obligation of a Bank to redeem its notes in the coin of the country not only encourages creatures of whim to cash their notes into gold "just to see what gold looks like" and so on, but also increases the physical quantity of gold which the Bank must hold by laying special emphasis on the necessity of holding adequate reserves of this particular form of the metal. The gold bullion standard, on the other hand, economises gold first, by discouraging internal demand, since few citizens are likely to buy bullion at the Central Bank except for purposes of export so long as the open market continues

[1] "More and more monetary experience has demonstrated that the true use of gold in the modern world is to serve as a medium of international payment when the exchanges or the international balances are adverse; if the international gold standard is to be reconstituted, as it must be, practice should take account of this lesson and Central Banks should combat any conception that gold is properly employable as a store of wealth, or that its primary object is to ensure convertibility of notes so that all who will may hoard gold coin on demand, to the detriment of the public good and the general economic welfare. In this connection a more general employment of the gold bullion standard would appear desirable."—*Third Annual Report of the Bank for International Settlements*, 1932–33.

to satisfy the demands of the trade; and secondly, by rendering all types of gold available for all types of demand, instead of making that part of the reserves that consist of bullion ineligible for purposes for which the buyer demands coin.

A further economy in the use of gold might be effected in certain countries by depriving private banks of the right to reckon till-money as part of their reserve balances. This suggestion implies, of course, some form of legal control over the size of these reserve balances, an implication to which we shall return later (§ 5). Supposing for the moment that such legal control existed (even in countries, such as Great Britain, where no specific reserve ratio is prescribed by law, we have seen that a fixed percentage tends to be quite closely adhered to), an incentive would be offered to private banks to hold no unnecessary cash in hand beyond their normal requirements if their till-money were excluded from computation in their reserve balances. Under the present British system, for instance, private bank reserves consist of "cash in hand and at the Bank of England." It is a matter of unconcern to the banks, therefore, whether they carry more or less cash in their tills and less or more at the Bank of England. The reserves earn no interest in either case, and, being more readily available if held in the tills, the major part of the reserve money tends to be held in this form rather than at the Central Bank. This constitutes a form of money-hoarding, since the cash so held is not only withdrawn from active circulation but is also rendered unavailable to the central institution for use as a reserve against its own liabilities or for other purposes.

If the private banks were in all countries required by law to maintain a fixed ratio of reserves to deposits, and if, at the same time, till-money were excluded from computation in reserves, this form of hoarding would be reduced to a minimum. The Central Banks would then be relieved of the necessity of immobilizing a portion of their gold holdings as reserves against this unjustifiably large part of "notes in circulation." At the same time, no additional risk would be laid upon the financial structure. The Central Banks would be no more likely than at present to be subjected to heavy demands for gold in exchange for their notes, gold being no longer used for domestic monetary purposes; while, if the private banks, after yielding to the temptation to reduce their till-money to an injudiciously low level, were subjected to a "run," they would be able to draw notes from the central institutions as easily as under the present system.

Before the autumn of 1931 a further recommendation towards a feasible economizing of gold might have been found in the wider adoption of the gold exchange standard as against either the gold specie or the gold bullion standard. This method of pooling gold reserves, whereby the Central Banks of smaller countries were enabled to reckon holdings of foreign exchange in other gold-standard countries as part of their own gold reserves, found great favour in the decade of post-War reconstruction. European funds had found their way in considerable volume to America during the uncertainties of the period following the armistice. So long as the United States remained on an unrestricted gold standard these balances were convertible into gold as readily as if they had been held in gold form at the various European Central Banks, allowance being made for the cost and the time entailed in repatriating them in gold. Moreover, whereas any actual gold acquired by the Central Banks and retained in their vaults earned no return, balances held in other gold-standard countries could be loaned out in the open market. In this way Central Bank reserves became an earning asset in a way hitherto unknown. The gold exchange standard, therefore, received approbation not only from the point of view of world economy but also from the individual Central Banks.

An irreparable blow was dealt to the system with the suspension of gold payments by the Bank of England in September 1931. At that time the Bank of France alone held huge sterling balances, whose value fell some 30 per cent almost overnight. The example shook the confidence of all Central Banks who had been in the habit of holding large balances abroad. The ensuing outflow of gold from the United States was largely due to the repatriation of dollar balances by European Banks, notably by the central institutions of France, Holland, Belgium, and Switzerland, who began to fear lest the United States should also suspend gold payments and leave their reserves correspondingly diminished in value.[1]

In the circumstances, it seems impracticable to urge the revival of the gold exchange standard in its previous form. What prospect there might be of reintroducing the system with the establishment of a world Central Bank will be discussed in the last chapter (ch. ix, § 5).

§ 4. Such are the various means whereby the Central Banks and governments of the world, independently or in concert, can achieve economies in the existing monetary gold stock, and thereby enlarge the surplus available in case of a falling-off in gold production, while increasing the margin of gold holdings which will be at their free disposal in the execution of their policies of monetary management. We must now direct our attention to the problem of avoiding in the future a recurrence of the maldistribution of the available gold supply which has marked the workings of the international gold standard during recent years.

The first reform to be suggested in this connection again revolves around the question of international co-operation. The inevitable penalty which the linking of a nation's currency to an international standard involves is that that currency is laid open to repercussions which may arise from fluctuations in the value of other currencies linked to the same standard. If, as a result of changes in either the prices of commodities

[1] Since these words were written, this fear has, of course, been realized.

or in the price of money, i.e. in interest rates, abroad, the value of money becomes greater or less in some country or countries than in others, there will be a tendency towards disequilibrium in foreign exchange rates which will involve all members of the international system alike, and which may lead to heavy gold movements. This tendency will be strong or weak according as international confidence is strong or weak. We have seen in earlier chapters that the tendency is nothing like so automatic as has commonly been supposed by orthodox theorists. Yet in the long run, particularly if international co-operation succeeds in reviving the optimism of the financial world, it will be impossible for any member of the gold-standard system to remain long "out of step" with the other members without occasioning disequilibrium in foreign exchange rates, accompanied probably by a considerable flow of gold.

According to Hawtrey,[1] "International gold movements arise when different countries do not exactly keep pace with one another in the expansion or contraction of credit," rather than when imports and exports fail by chance to balance. While it is no longer automatically and universally true that gold flows are governed by the relative credit policies of Central Banks in view of the factors discussed in earlier chapters, yet as a general principle this statement remains unimpeachable. It will, moreover, become increasingly true as such obstacles to the smooth working of the gold standard as tariff barriers and international distrust are removed. In particular, the relative positions of interest rates in various gold centres will always exert some influence upon international gold movements, even though this influence may for certain periods of time be outweighed by other considerations. It is therefore of vital importance to the whole question of the practicability of the gold standard for the future that from now onwards the individual policies of Central Banks should be co-ordinated

[1] R. G. Hawtrey, *The Gold Standard*, p. 96.

and to some degree governed with regard to their reactions upon the international system as a whole.

Here again there is no need to despair of the possibility of achieving agreement to the principle of international co-operation. If there were ever any doubt as to the question, the experience of the last few years has proved pretty conclusively the utter impossibility of the international standard functioning satisfactorily so long as individual countries pursue their own financial ends without any reference to their reactions upon the rest of the gold-using world. Moreover, those financially powerful countries, whose support for any far-reaching co-operative plan is indispensable, are the very countries most interested in rendering the gold standard a practicable objective. If gold were permanently abandoned by a large section of the world, their losses through the consequent depreciation in the value of their gold holdings would be very considerable. If co-operation is necessary to make the gold standard a possibility for the world at large, therefore, they of all nations should be the champions of the cause of financial internationalism.

When it comes to a question of specific recommendations as to the form that international co-ordination of credit policies should take once agreement to the principle has been secured, concrete suggestions are again difficult. It is palpably impossible to recommend, for instance, that Bank rates should be kept always at the same level in all countries. Even if it were conceivable that assent might be given to so radical a proposal, it is easy to imagine a state of affairs in which interest rates were only one among many factors, or in which it might be healthy for the whole system that they should be raised in certain countries relative to others.

Inability to predicate concrete recommendations does not, however, indicate any inherent weakness in the argument for international co-ordination of policies, but is due rather to the multiplicity of the eventualities in which such co-ordination should be employed. As a minimum the consortium of bankers, recommended in § 1, should be given power and opportunity to discuss plans for a concerted credit policy throughout the gold-standard world. If this were done, many advantages would accrue through the airing of the proposed policies which individual Banks were intending to follow. Pressure might be brought to bear upon any Bank which, inadvertently or purposely, was countenancing financial developments within its sphere of influence which were militating against the general interest. For instance, the Central Bank of any country which was enjoying a prolonged inflow of gold might be induced to avoid the necessity of sterilizing much of the imports by embarking upon a policy of mild commodity-price inflation, or by stimulating an export of capital through an easing of money rates or through increasing its own holdings of foreign balances. Similarly, if it were decided that it would be to the advantage of the whole system if gold prices were raised or lowered, each individual Bank could embark upon the desired policy of inflation or deflation without fear of becoming involved in the international complications which might have arisen if it had attempted to pioneer the path alone.

To take a concrete instance. In the spring of 1932 the Federal Reserve System of the United States was committed to a policy of resuscitating the commodity price-level in terms of dollars. Such had been the openly avowed policy of the Reserve Banks for some time, and that with the approval of the economic world, where it has long been realized that the drastic fall of world prices must be checked if possible. Yet the sight of the United States Congress attempting to speed the Reserve Banks on their way towards a price inflation, or "reflation" to use the euphemism coined by Representative Patman from Texas, shocked foreign confidence and hastened an outflow of gold. Apart from the somewhat inane Goldsborough bill, which commanded the Federal Reserve Banks to accomplish the rise in prices for which they had long been striving, the inflationary spirit of Congress had shown itself also in a reluctance to balance the budget. Leaving aside the political arguments against the experiment of indulging in an unbalanced budget, the economic advantages to the world as a whole which might have followed from the United States finding the funds necessary to meet their current outgoings at that time by an increase in the national debt might have been considerable. The country's national debt had been appreciably reduced since the War, so that it was ridiculous to talk as though its increase to the extent of the necessary two billion dollars would prove an intolerable burden upon the productive capacity of the country, an argument which might carry weight in the case of poorer countries in a similar situation. The raising of the necessary funds by a government loan or by increased short-term borrowings, on the other hand, might have proved an ideal way of initiating in the country best fortified to withstand the outflow of gold, which might result, that upturn in prices for which the whole world was hoping. A feature of the situation in the United States at the time was the scarcity of sound borrowers willing to make use of the abundance of idle funds awaiting employment (cf. Appendix, § 4). The government, in raising money already spent or required for future expenditure, would have been mobilizing these funds, and putting them to a productive use in a way which private entrepreneurs were proving reluctant to do.

The chief argument adduced against balancing the Federal budget of the United States by increased borrowing was based upon fear of the reactions of such conduct upon foreign observers. If the suggested international consortium of Central Banks had then been in operation, the possibility of unfavourable reactions abroad to an inflationary policy by the Federal Reserve System or by Congress might have been negatived by a public announcement by other Central Banks that they approved of the "reflationary" steps in the United States, and that they intended to abet them by pursuing a similar policy in their own countries so far as might be necessary in order to keep their credit policies in line with that of the United States. By such means, any policy, whether of inflation or of deflation, once agreed upon as desirable, might be pursued by concerted action without any individual Bank running the risk of upsetting the equilibrium of its foreign exchange rates by attempting to pioneer the way alone.

Agreement as to the most desirable policy to pursue may, of course, be difficult always to obtain. This fact, however, must not be allowed to discourage the experiment of the international consortium. In the first place, there will often be extreme cases, such as the present case of depressed world prices, in which fairly complete unanimity may be expected. Secondly, it will frequently be possible for a compromise to be worked out; it is hard to imagine, for instance, that the Federal Reserve Board of the United States always experience that "sweet and pleasant thing, the dwelling together in unity," yet the policy of the Federal Reserve System as a whole bears an outward semblance of pretty thorough consistency at any one time. Thirdly, universal agreement will not always be necessary; so long as the most powerful members of the consortium are in agreement, their adoption of one policy may either enforce its adoption by dissenting weaker members or may at least enable them to dispense with the co-operation of the dissenters. Fourthly, as time goes on, the principles which should govern the concerted credit policies of the various Banks will become clearer with experience, so that, although disagreement may at first be the rule rather than the exception, this state of affairs may be regarded as a necessary evil in the transition towards a happier condition at a later date.

§ 5. Having given the feasibility of an international coordination of the credit policies of Central Banks, however, the fight against maldistribution is still far from won. Although the right conduct of this policy of credit co-ordination might go far as a substitute for the old hoped-for automatic self-distribution of the gold supply, which we have seen to have disappeared under the evolution of the new philosophy of Central Bank management, the other three obstacles still remain, to wit, the breakdown of international lending, tariff barriers, and the inability of Central Banks to exercise anything like complete control over the value of their domestic currencies. While it would be optimistic indeed to hope to be able to recommend measures which would remove these barriers, certain suggestions may be made for the amelioration of the present situation. To these suggestions we must now turn our attention.

First as to the question of internal control. One of the main conclusions which emerged from the discussion of chapter vi, based on the statistical evidence given in the appendix, was that the demand for credit in any country lies to a great extent outside the control of the central institution. It is possible under such financial constitutions as obtain in Great Britain and the United States for Central Banks to exercise great influence over the supply of money through the instruments of Bank rate and open-market operations, whereby they act upon the private banks of the country, who are in turn the purveyors of credit. Beyond offering inducements to borrowers through manipulation of interest rates to increase or reduce their use of currency, however, the banking system has little control over the volume of currency in use.

This impotence is due to the frequent divergence of interest between the users of credit individually and the community as a whole. In times of stock or commodity speculation, for instance, the point at which further increase of credit outstanding becomes undesirable in the interest of the country almost always antedates the point at which borrowers, with an eye to private gain from the employment of money in existing prosperous conditions, are prepared to restrict or halt their demand for accommodation. In times of depression, on the other hand, the liquidation of credit commonly far exceeds the socially desirable limit before individuals can be induced to increase the volume and velocity of circulation of currency in use.

These facts point directly to one moral which has so far been almost entirely overlooked. The government and/or the Central Bank, as curators of the public welfare often in opposition to the particularized motives of individuals, must enter upon the demand side of the credit equation as well as upon the supply side. It has long been recognized to be within the just and right province of one or both of these institutions to impinge upon private enterprise, and particularly upon the conduct of private banks, with regard to the supply of money. It is now high time that they were endowed with the right, and even the obligation, to throw in their influence on the side of demand as well.

Now in a capitalistic society it is not easy for a central authority either to force private entrepreneurs to borrow money for projects which they are unwilling to undertake or autocratically to deny them accommodation for purposes for which a private bank is willing to finance them. In order to affect the demand side of the credit equation, therefore, it will be necessary for the central authority itself to employ the credit which it is desired to pump out into the monetary system of a country in a period of depression; and, on the other hand, to soak up credit for the liquidation of indebtedness when it is desired to lessen the aggregate demand for money.

These operations it is particularly within the scope of a national government to perform, in the one case by a programme of public works, and in the other by reduction of the national debt through increased taxation. The case for the incorporation of a consistent programme of public works into the ordinary machinery of currency management is therefore strong, though it has not as yet been accorded its due place. Public works have for some years been mooted from time to time by politicians in a number of countries as an emergency method of relieving unemployment, but their potential utility as a regular factor in credit policy has never been fully appreciated.

At the same time, there appears to be a growing body of economic sentiment in their favour, though most of it is tinged with an air of tolerant acquiescence in a temporary emergency expedient rather than a realization of their possibilities as a permanent factor. P. W. Martin, in his exhaustive study of *The Problem of Maintaining Purchasing Power*,[1] voices the most definite appraisal of these possibilities. "There are," he says, "four instruments of monetary adjustment to cope with the four types of monetary stability. The Central Bank rate of discount would be the chief means of protecting the gold reserve, thereby safeguarding the gold standard and guaranteeing exchange stability; international agreement to maintain purchasing power to the utmost extent possible, short of price inflation, would secure an approximately horizontal trend of commodity prices; open-market operations would furnish the principal means of control over the money and security markets; finally, the special financing of public works, by making possible the maintenance of purchasing power upon the commodity market, would furnish the essential basis of business stability."[2] Here a planned public works policy stands where it should by right in apposition to the other recognized means of controlling the value of money. Other authorities are inclined to confine themselves in the main to stressing the value of a policy of public works as an emergency measure in times of pronounced depression.[3]

[1] London (King), 1931.
[2] Op. cit., p. 234.
[3] Cf. *Unemployment and Public Works*, International Labour Office, Geneva, 1931, p. 26; "Relation of Home Investment to Unemployment,"

The defect of treating public works purely as an unregulated emergency measure to which resort may be had in a somewhat haphazard way if a depression becomes unusually severe lies in the fact that such an approach ignores the utility of the twin process of restricting the use of money in an incipient or progressing boom by means of increased taxation. This process, while useful in itself as enforcing a diminution of purchasing power at a time when the latter shows signs of becoming redundant, is also useful in facilitating the embarkation upon public works when it is desirable to increase purchasing power.

The proposal of a public works programme in times of acute depression is always apt to encounter some opposition on the grounds that it will result either in heavier taxation then and there when the country is in need of all the relief that it can obtain, or, if the projects are to be financed by means of a loan, that further borrowings at a time when the Treasury is already distressed by falling revenues will tend to impair the national credit. If public works were embodied in the regular credit policy of the country, these objections would be met. There would be no question of increasing taxes at the time of embarking upon the projects, since the whole object of the plan would be to set to work idle funds by means of a loan rather than to deprive the country of part of its already reduced purchasing power through heavier taxation. Indeed, if confidence in the soundness of the plan were once firmly established by experience, taxation might actually be lowered at such times, the extra funds required to balance the budget being obtained by the raising of a loan to be repaid in more prosperous times. There would also be no question of impairing the credit of the nation through the floating of the necessary

R. F. Kahn, *Economic Journal*, June 1931, p. 182; *Macmillan Report*, p. 204; *World-Unemployment and its Problems*, Karl Pribram, Norman Wait Harris Memorial Foundation speech at Chicago University, June 1931; *Post-War Unemployment Problem*, Henry Clay, London, 1929.

loan once the sincerity of the government had been proved by its prompt repayal of public works loans out of an increase in taxation with the return of prosperity.

As to the exact method of financing the public works, it seems preferable that loans for the purpose should not be raised through the ordinary channel of the open market. It is true that, at the times when public works should be undertaken, there commonly exists a quantity of idle funds awaiting an outlet for investment in just such securities as the new government borrowings would offer, and that to that extent these idle funds would be mobilized and set to a productive use. There are, however, two good reasons for preferring an alternative method of financing the plan, namely, by direct borrowing from the Central Bank on the security of government bonds issued *ad hoc*.

First, even though the quantity of idle funds awaiting investment were large at such times, any loan which borrows already outstanding purchasing power for the purpose of putting it to productive use merely transfers that money from the possession of one section of the community, the rentiers who buy the bonds issued, to another section of the community, the factors of production who are put to work with the proceeds of the loan. In so far as the money thus borrowed might have continued to lie idle, "hoarded" in the form of surplus bank deposits by the would-be lenders, this procedure does, of course, "vitalize" a portion of the community's purchasing power which was previously "sterilized." Nevertheless, we have seen (ch. vi, § 3, and appendix, § 3) that the success of the Central Bank's efforts to resuscitate the bond market at such times by its purchases of open-market securities depends on its winning the waiting game which it plays with the most cautious class of rentiers who are unwilling to invest in any but the highest-grade securities until the yield on the latter becomes practically unremunerative. Any increase in the supply of government bonds at such a time would weaken the Central

Bank's efforts on behalf of the market for lower-grade bonds by increasing the opportunity for the timid investor to acquire government obligations, and by tending to raise the return on all classes of government bonds. It would be useless for the Central Bank to hope to stimulate the general bond market by its purchases of securities if the government were flooding the market with new issues as fast as the Central Bank acquired part of the old.

Secondly, just as the flotation of a bond issue for the purpose of financing public works merely transfers funds from temporary idleness in the investment market to active employment in the consumption market in the hands of the newly employed factors of production, so the retirement of the bond issue by heavier taxation in prosperous times merely transfers funds from the consumption market in the hands of the taxpayer to the investment market in the hands of the rentier from whom the bonds are redeemed. In both cases the process is undoubtedly a healthy one, since the Central Bank will at the one time be anxious to stimulate, and at the other time to restrict, an inflation in commodity prices. The transfer of funds between the investment and consumption markets will therefore further its ends in both cases. This method, however, will not be as effective as the issue (or cancellation) of completely new money, which can be pumped into (or withdrawn from) circulation directly and absolutely if the requisite amount is raised by the direct sale of special bonds to the Central Bank (or liquidated by means of heavier taxation).[1]

The objection will no doubt be made that this method of raising money is so delightfully simple that it will afford governments who adopt it an insidious encouragement to undertake luxurious and unnecessary public works at unjustifiable moments, while the unpopularity of higher taxation,

[1] This suggestion presupposes, of course, that the Central Bank has sufficient surplus reserves at its disposal to accommodate the government without hampering its own credit operations.

even in times of plenty, will tempt them to put off the evil day of repayment. While the existence of this danger cannot be denied, a safeguard may be looked for in the publicity which would inevitably accompany all such operations. In order that the plan may be put into operation at all, some form of preliminary international sanction or recognition would be desirable if not essential, since, without it, there would be a risk that any government which raised funds in this way might precipitate a flight from its national currency as retribution for so radical a departure. If the plan were only put into operation after receiving international sanction, its course would always be closely watched in any country where it was being used. Any suspicion that the plan were being abused in any country, therefore, would bring upon the offender the disapprobation of its fellows in the form of a withdrawal of foreign balances.

Such a Damoclean sword should go far to discourage ill-advised use of the plan, always supposing that international pressure had not already done so. It is, after all, possible to distinguish rank and unjustifiable inflation from the projection of justifiable public works at an opportune moment. In order both to reassure public confidence in the case of a worthy application of the plan and to discourage its abuse, it might be advisable for any government intending to raise funds in this way to submit its proposals to the already mentioned international consortium for their endorsement. In order that their dignity should not be outraged by having their proposals publicly denounced by a non-sovereign body, governments would in this case probably take the added precaution of discussing their proposed plans privately with members of the consortium before officially submitting them for the inspection of the international body. This would afford a further check upon would-be profligates.

Thus it is to be hoped that, again under the aegis of international co-operation, the instrument of planned public works may become incorporated in the recognized armoury of Central Banks for the pursuit of their credit policies.

§ 6. A further expedient which should be adopted for the purpose of strengthening internal credit control may be found in the extension to countries where it is not already enforced of the legal regulation of the minimum reserves to be held by the private banks at the central institution. Unlike the legal reserves of the Central Bank itself, member bank reserves are not immobilized, since they form the greater part of the material whereby the Central Bank can carry out its credit policies. We have already seen that in countries where no such requirements exist it is immaterial to the private banks how much of their reserves they retain in their tills and how much they hold with the Central Bank. As a natural result of the preference of banks for ready cash rather than claims on the Central Bank, this leads to an unnecessary expansion of the note issue, part of which is constantly idle in the tills of private banks. If the private banks were required by law to hold a certain percentage, roughly equal to their accustomed reserve ratio, of their liabilities at the Central Bank, they would be impelled to reduce their till-money to the minimum necessary for safety.

In proportion as the private banks transferred funds from their tills to their deposit accounts with the Central Bank, the latter's liabilities on note account would be reduced and its liabilities on deposit account increased. Under the system at present generally in force, whereby Central Banks are required to carry a larger reserve against the note issue than against their deposit liabilities, this adjustment would reduce the total reserves which the Central Bank must hold. The surplus funds available for the conduct of its open-market operations or for export would be correspondingly increased.

There is a further reason for considering the desirability of legislation upon the reserve holdings of private banks. The success of the international gold standard will tend to become increasingly dependent upon the degree of credit control exercised by Central Banks, operating in concert for the smoothing-out of international irregularities and singly for the attainment of internal stability. It will, therefore, be essential that the Central Banks shall be adequately supplied with "ammunition," i.e. with surplus funds in excess of their minimum legal reserves, for the execution of their policies. The supply of this ammunition is largely influenced by the size of the deposits which private banks keep at the central institution. It may, therefore, be socially desirable that these deposits be maintained by law at a slightly higher level than the private banks would adopt if left to their own inclinations.

In view of these considerations, the Macmillan Committee avers, "In a modern banking system, where member banks are in a position to hold earning assets which can be quickly turned into cash at the Central Institution, indirectly as in Great Britain or directly as in most other countries, the amount of reserves which they require strictly for their own safety and convenience may be extremely small. Since their reserves earn no interest, there will, therefore, be a tendency to whittle them down gradually by one means or another to the lowest figure which will not disturb public opinion. Moreover, the main reason for expecting the banks to keep reserves above the minimum needed for daily convenience is no longer primarily the safety and solvency of the banks themselves, as it was in former times, but the necessity of providing the Central Institution with adequate resources wherewith to manage the monetary system and safely furnish the member institutions with precisely those conveniences for rapidly liquidating earning assets, upon which the latter depend when determining the amount of their cash reserves. Thus the appropriate amount of the reserves of the member banks cannot now be left to their own individual self-interest but must be governed by the proper requirements of the system as a whole."[1]

The force of this recommendation hangs upon the emphasis which must be increasingly placed upon the relative importance of the welfare of Central Banks for the smooth working of the international system as against the convenience of individual banks and their clients. The size of the minimum legal requirements to be imposed upon member banks should, of course, not be fixed above the normal reserve ratios at present adhered to, if that can conveniently be avoided, since such a step would induce credit stringency by compelling the banking system to increase its reserves suddenly and/or reduce its deposits. Indeed, in countries where till-money is at present included in reserves for the computation of reserve ratios, due allowance must be made for the fact that private banks will always be obliged to retain a certain amount of cash in their tills. The reserve percentage which they are to be required to carry at the Central Bank should accordingly be fixed below their present reserve ratios. The fixing of a legal minimum reserve for member banks would, however, at least ensure that reserve ratios should not be whittled down any further, and would at the same time give the Central Bank greater certainty as to the probable future size of one item in its supply of ammunition.

This whole recommendation would become unnecessary if the previous suggestion of fixing the legal reserve requirements of the Central Banks themselves as a percentage of their total note-cum-deposit liabilities were adopted. In that event, if the proportion which Central Banks were obliged to hold were the same against notes as against deposits, these institutions would gain no advantage by an increase of their deposit liabilities as against their liabilities on note account. The question of an increase in the supply of ammunition from this step would then not arise.

[1] *Macmillan Report*, p. 158.

§ 7. Even after the incorporation of the above recommendations into the recognized armoury of monetary management, it is impossible, in view of the conclusions of chapter vi, to hope that Central Banks will be able to exercise so complete a control over domestic conditions that all countries operating upon the international gold standard will be able to keep exactly in step. Disequilibria, leading to gold movements, must inevitably occur from time to time. "On account of the multiplicity of factors with which a policy of price stabilization has to contend, deviations in the relative price-levels and changes in the balances of payments between countries are certain to take place even when each is striving for price stability."[1] Before turning our attention to the specifically international problems connected with these disequilibria, viz. international loans and tariffs, there is one further recommendation applicable to national financial structures which should serve to reduce the volume of international gold flows.

Under the international gold standard various factors combine to afford foreign exchange rates between the various members of the international system a fluctuation range within the so-called "gold-points." Seignorage charges, interest charges incurred while bullion sold to the Central Bank is being minted, and other regulations which vary from country to country, all serve to raise the price at which Central Banks will sell gold a little above the price at which they will buy it. Meanwhile, since gold is normally only bought from the Central Bank for export, and since it will only fetch the same money upon arrival at its destination as it costs in the centre where it is purchased if the exchanges stand at par, the cost of shipping and insuring it in transit between one gold centre and another must be reckoned in.

Thus gold will only be shipped from country A to country B if A's currency stands at such a discount in terms of B's

[1] W. A. Brown, *England and the New Gold Standard*, Yale University Press, 1929, p. 301.

that the gold, upon arrival in B, will fetch enough of B's currency to cover both its cost price in A and the costs of shipping, insurance, etc. The points in the exchange rates at which it will become profitable to buy gold in A and ship it to B, or to buy it in B and sell it in A, all these costs being taken into consideration, are known as the gold points. So long as the exchange rates remain within these points, the shipment of gold between the two countries will involve a net loss, so that gold will only flow in response to those relatively uncommon transactions which are undertaken for special non-commercial purposes.

Now it is desirable from the point of view both of the various money markets and of the Central Banks that the position of these gold points should be known accurately, so that gold movements should not occur unexpectedly.[1] It is also desirable that the interval between them should not be greatly narrowed down, for then gold would tend to be constantly in motion between the various gold-standard countries, with a consequent increase in the "unproductive" expense of shipping it and an imposition of an unnecessary strain upon gold reserves in all countries.

The present trend, on the other hand, is working both towards uncertainty as to the exact position of the gold points and towards a diminution of the interval separating them. The ever-increasing speed of communications tends to reduce the loss of interest incurred by the shipper of gold while the metal is in transit, thereby reducing the cost of the operation and raising the gold export point, while continual changes in freight charges and insurance rates involve frequent fluctuations in the expense of transferring gold from one centre to another, each of which is reflected in movements of the gold points themselves. Moreover, even when the gold points are not actively fluctuating, they are commonly separated by only

[1] Cf. P. Einzig, "Gold Points and Central Banks," *Economic Journal*, September 1929.

a very small interval in the case of countries which lie near each other geographically, on account of the greater ease, speed, and safety of transhipments of gold between them.

It is, however, anomalous that a smaller fluctuation in Anglo-French exchange rates should cause gold to flow between the two countries than would be necessary to prompt a movement of gold between either of the countries and the United States. No particular advantage accrues to either England or France to counterbalance the disadvantage of their respective gold reserves being more susceptible to a foreign drain than are the gold reserves of the United States. The slightly greater fluctuation which may occur in the sterling-dollar than in the sterling-franc exchange constitutes no encumbrance to either England or the United States. If then the larger interval between the gold points of the sterling-dollar exchange at the same time affords useful protection to the gold reserves of both England and the United States, there is no logical reason why the gold reserves of France and England should be denied similar protection with respect to each other.

We have seen that the primary advantage of an international standard is the stability with which it endows foreign exchange rates, while the advantage of a paper standard is the internal stability which it enables the Central Bank to pursue, unhampered by external considerations. If the interval between the gold points were widened to a fixed difference of, say, 2 per cent, i.e. if the gold export point were fixed at a discount of 1 per cent from par, and the gold import point at a premium of 1 per cent, a kind of compromise between these two desiderata would be achieved. Stability of foreign exchanges would be guaranteed within a range of 2 per cent, which is probably not so wide a range of fluctuation as to discourage foreign lending or to inconvenience traders, while a greater degree of independence of external events would be given to the Central Bank from the fact that the world value of the national currency could oscillate within a 2 per cent range before the disadvantages of membership of an international system made themselves felt. At the same time, if the gold points were fiexd at this, or some other, definite interval, and that interval were made applicable to all the foreign exchange rates between any country and the outside world, the disadvantages of the uncertainty which prevails at present as to the exact level at which gold will be exported or imported would disappear. For all these reasons, therefore, it would be advantageous if the position of gold points were immovably fixed in all countries and for all exchanges.

Stabilization can be simply effected by individual Central Banks, though, of course, international sanction would strengthen the project. All that is necessary is that the Central Banks should announce that their buying prices for gold should stand at ½ per cent below the par value of their currency and their selling prices at ½ per cent above. In order that exchange rates on more distant countries should not be subject to wider fluctuations than exchange rates on neighbouring countries owing to the fact that the shipper's expense over and above the Central Bank's selling price would be greater in the former than in the latter case, the Central Bank should in each case undertake to bear the cost of conveying the gold to the centre in which the shipper desired to sell it. This cost the Central Bank could defray out of its profits arising from the 1 per cent difference between its buying and selling prices for gold. Gold could then be bought in any centre for ½ per cent above its par value and sold in any other centre at ½ per cent below its par value, all other charges being removed from the care of the shipper. It would, therefore, always be profitable to ship gold from any country when, and only when, its currency stood at a discount of at least 1 per cent relative to some other currency. Thus the foreign exchange rates would be allowed a fluctuation range of 1 per cent on either side of par, i.e. a total maximum fluctuation of 2 per cent.

Since the chief object of this recommendation is to give

some protection to gold reserves against exposure to too easy drains for foreign account, it is debatable whether a maximum fluctuation of 2 per cent would prove sufficient for the purpose. Much transfer of gold would probably be obviated if the gold points were so fixed as to allow a fluctuation of, say, 4 per cent, which would follow if the Central Banks' buying and selling prices were fixed at 1 per cent below and above par. As against this advantage, however, there must be considered the fact that a possible loss of 4 per cent on exchange transactions might be sufficient to discourage international lending, particularly on short term, since such a loss might more than wipe out the interest received on the loan. While it is obviously unlikely that the full maximum 4 per cent loss would ever be incurred on any loan, the fact that such a possibility exists might in itself suffice to put a damper on the volume of foreign loans—and nothing should be done to injure the already ailing mechanism of international lending.

It is therefore desirable that the buying and selling prices of all Central Banks operating the gold standard should be fixed at ½ per cent on either side of par. If this measure were adopted, it would not only obviate unnecessary gold movements between countries that are so close together as to make shipments of gold profitable almost as soon as exchange rates deviate from par, but it would also make the exact time of gold exports or imports more certain than at present.

It should be noted that the recommendation of ½ per cent on either side of par as the appropriate position for the buying and selling prices of Central Banks presupposes that all Central Banks will have adopted the same system. Until international agreement to this end has been achieved, it might be necessary for any Central Bank pioneering the way to set its gold points wider apart, particularly if it adopted the suggestion that it should itself be responsible for the costs of shipping the gold to the desired centre. Otherwise, if the Central Bank in the centre to which the gold was to be consigned were still buying and selling gold at par, the pioneering Bank might be narrowing the gold points rather than widening them, since the total cost to the shipper of the operation would in this case be the $\frac{1}{2}$ per cent premium charged by the pioneering Bank on its sale of the gold.

We may now proceed to a consideration of ameliorative measures of a more purely international nature, for which continuous co-operation between nations is essential.

CHAPTER VIII

THE THREE EVIL GENII AGAIN

§ 1. In chapter v the part played by tariffs, War-debts, and reparations in the current problems of international economics was strongly emphasized. Something must now be said as to the possibility of removing the malign influence of these factors. It must be admitted at the outset, however, that none of the world's contemporary economic difficulties is less susceptible of scientific treatment by economists than the maladies caused by these three evil genii. Born of the minds of politicians, they continue to draw ample nourishment from the same source. Their end can therefore only be compassed by international co-operation in the political sphere, a more difficult end to achieve than international economic co-operation.

We saw in chapter v that there were only three ways in which a country with an adverse balance of international payments could rectify the situation. It might increase its net import of capital, it might increase its net export of commodities, or it might export gold. Similarly there are only three ways in which countries with a steadily favourable balance may make sure of receiving payment; by a net export of capital, by a net import of commodities, or by an import of gold. But there is a limit to the extent to which gold can be used to redress balances of payments, a limit fixed by the amount of gold which debtor countries will be willing to release before suspending the gold standard. Thus no country will be able to maintain a favourable balance of payments for a prolonged period unless it is prepared either to keep up an annual net export of capital or to allow its net commodity export balance to dwindle or its net commodity import to increase.

It was largely the refusal of two of the world's largest creditor nations to face this issue that occasioned the breakdown of the international gold standard in 1931–32 by placing upon the movement of gold an unduly large part of the strain of effecting a balance in international payments. Until these and other creditor nations modify their stand as nations upon the question of tariffs and their attitude as individuals towards foreign loans, there is little hope that the international gold standard will be able to function freely again.

At present four out of the world's seven important creditor nations still adhere to the gold standard, namely, France, Holland, Switzerland, and Belgium, while all of them hold sufficient stores of gold to view with apprehension the fall in the value of the metal which would inevitably ensue from its universal demonetization. Even though the United States and Great Britain have now left this polite society, their vast golden hoards and their creditor position still form a bond of sympathy between them and the company of the faithful. The maintenance of gold as an international standard and the payment of money owed to them, therefore, constitute two aims for the attainment of which the financially powerful nations of the world are unanimously desirous. It is to be hoped that unanimity of aim may eventually bring unanimity of action.

§ 2. The first problem to which unanimous action by the creditor nations must be addressed is the problem of tariffs. Only by being readily receptive of the goods of debtor nations can the creditors hope to be paid all the money due to them from abroad on commodity, interest, and capital account. The alternative method of effecting a balance in their international payments by lending abroad the excess due to them each year is at best only a makeshift. While it is true that the amount of international indebtedness can safely increase each year, just as the total volume of international borrowings by corporations and individuals may continue to increase indefinitely, so long as it is justified by increased production, yet there is a tendency for every debtor country to become gradually more and more mature and therefore less and less dependent upon foreign capital. As this tendency develops, amortization payments will overtake and eventually surpass the volume of net new capital borrowed abroad by the debtor countries. Meanwhile, cumulative interest payments will have been mounting, so that, as the erstwhile debtors supply more and more of their own needs for new capital, the net capital and interest movements will tend to be away from the debtor countries and back to their original creditors. These repayments of capital and interest will only be receivable by the latter in the form of commodities. While, therefore, capital movements are invaluable for effecting a temporary balance in international payments, and also for the development of countries which are still unable to supply their own needs for capital, they cannot be relied upon permanently to redress the balances.

In the case of tariffs, it is again hard to prescribe concrete recommendations. The economist can say of the tariff in the abstract, as the Irish priest said of sin, that "he's agin it." The practical shape which this antagonism should take is not so easy to formulate.

The logical objective, of course, must be world free trade. The extent to which trade barriers have helped to strangle international commerce, and therefore to reduce the aggregate wealth of the world, has already been amply stressed (ch. v). The case for free trade as stated above can be most strongly pressed against those nations who enjoy a favourable balance of payments on both commodity and interest account. Nations whose balance of payments on commodity and/or interest account is adverse, on the other hand, may object to the above arguments that in their case a tariff is necessary in order to restrain their nationals from increasing their purchases of foreign, at the expense of domestic, goods, and so further aggravating the disequilibrium in their total balance of payments. On the other hand, unless the creditor nations receive some form of *quid pro quo* for any offers of tariff reduction that they may eventually be led to make, it is doubtful how far they will be willing to carry their offers into practice.

At the same time, it is hard to believe that the various exchange restrictions which have made their appearance in the last few years (cf. ch. v) are more than temporary emergency measures, so that it may confidently be expected that, with the relief to world currencies which would ensue from a lowering of tariff barriers by creditor nations, these restrictions would be withdrawn. This in itself would give the creditor nations a valuable return for their tardy liberality.

Once again, however, the working out of the actual details must be left to the governments of the nations. The work of the economist can only be to point out the end to be aimed at, the lowering of tariffs in those countries whose balance of payments on commodity and interest account is favourable. The execution of that end must be left to diplomats and politicians. It is to be hoped that the World Economic Conference, which foundered in July 1933 upon the rocky question of exchange stabilization, may soon be reconvened for a discussion of tariffs. To recommend that the delegates to this conference should pledge themselves to universal free trade would smack of the impractical, but it is at least within the limits of reasonable hope that, under the spur of a common aim, and in the face of the extreme seriousness of the present situation, some mutual agreement might there be worked out for the universal lowering of trade barriers by the creditor nations and for the withdrawal of exchange restrictions by the debtor nations.

Unless some agreement of this sort is reached by international co-operation, the outlook for the future of world commerce, on the prosperity of which the increase of wealth necessarily depends, is far from hopeful. Strangulation of the body of international trade is rapidly supervening as a result of the feverish measures of self-protection adopted by the nations severally. Only by the collective application of first aid can that body be restored to a state of healthy normalcy. A prolongation of the gloomy situation outlined in chapter v would slowly throttle world commerce to death, or at least into a state of suspended animation.

With the breakdown of the mechanism of foreign exchanges, there is no alternative to a removal of existing trade restrictions but a return to the primitive system of international barter. Movements for a revival of this system are already on foot in different parts of the world. In February 1932, the American Manufacturers' Foreign Credit Insurance Exchange set up a committee to consider methods for aiding foreign buyers whose governments were opposed to the shipment of gold to the United States; among the possibilities which the committee was ordered to consider was "the exchange of goods between this country and foreign countries based on valuations independent of a transfer of gold, and similar to old-fashioned barter."[1]

On April 18th, the International Commodity Clearing Company was formed in Bremen by one hundred merchants "to promote the exchange of goods between Germany and other countries, eliminating difficulties in the payment of foreign exchange. The company will approach prospective importers and exporters and try to exchange German exports for imports. While the clearing company, with a capital of $120,000, is relatively small, it reflects a movement which is rapidly gaining ground in Germany. Such clearing companies are believed by many to lead to State control of foreign trade."[2]

State control seems, indeed, to be the logical conclusion of the import quotas, restrictions on exchange transactions, etc., which are rapidly becoming the order of the day. So long as governments feel themselves obliged by the necessity of safeguarding their respective currencies to resort more and more to such measures, their interference with the free conduct of

[1] *New York Times*, February 2, 1932. [2] Ibid., April 19, 1932.

international commerce inevitably increases. If the trade of the world continues to dwindle until it reaches the point where nations experience difficulty in obtaining even necessities from foreign sources, governments may be compelled to take over international commerce in its entirety. The clumsiness inherent in the resulting system of international barter should supply further encouragement to the nations of the world to co-operate in the revival of a healthy commerce based upon the well-tried financial instruments which the international gold standard can supply.

§ 3. The case for a drastic reduction of War debts and reparations is equally easy to argue upon the premises of international economics, but equally difficult of political application. The presentation of the case in chapter v could hardly fail to convince a neutral observer that world commerce would be healthier were War obligations totally or partially renounced. Indeed, certain neutral powers have on occasions voiced their conviction on this point. It is, however, natural that creditor nations should instinctively see in such renunciation primarily a reduction in the incomes of their respective Treasuries. It is, therefore, impossible to hope for any considerable degree of relief until the politicians of the said countries are convinced that the share of the resulting increase in world prosperity which would fall to their respective electorates would more than counterbalance the loss incurred by their Treasuries.

In the hope of hastening this conviction, it is the duty of economists to keep constantly before politicians and electorates the fundamental issues involved. The strongest argument at their disposal to this end is to be found in the fact that, under present conditions, War obligations are not being, and cannot be, paid. The debtor nations are not able to command a sufficient volume of foreign exchange to meet their payments. The loud reiteration by creditor nations of their legal claims to payment is no more constructive than the clamouring of depositors around the doors of a closed bank. It would be infinitely more helpful if the claimants would recognize the *status quo*, and postpone, or partially write off, their claims in a constructive effort to hasten the rehabilitation of the debtors.

In the interests of this rehabilitation, it must further continually be stressed that perhaps the greatest difficulty that international finance is now facing is lack of confidence. So long as international mistrust persists, debtors will be unable to obtain that relief without which they cannot regain their solvency. In so far as the dead weight of War debts and reparations around their necks increases their instability, the task of convincing their creditors of their essential solvency will be the harder; lack of confidence will tend to be prolonged; and the very maintenance of the nominal principle that War obligations must be honoured will continue to make the collection of these obligations painful, if not impossible.

Some reduction, if not total renunciation, of War claims is, therefore, to be urgently advocated. It would be futile to suggest the form or degree which this should take, as such details will inevitably be settled in accordance with political rather than economic considerations. There is much to be said for drastic reduction rather than complete renunciation. The effect upon confidence of concerted reduction would be considerable, as great perhaps as the effect of renunciation. Moreover, the erstwhile debtors, having now adjusted their economy to a lower price, wage, and living standard than prevails in the creditor countries, might acquire an unjustifiable advantage over the erstwhile creditors if the burden of the War obligations were totally withdrawn, particularly as certain of those creditors have large internal debts contracted during the War. Also it is morally desirable that as much of the debts as can be collected without damage to the world's financial system should be paid.

Such details, however, are unimportant beside the principle, which must be constantly kept to the fore, that some permanent scaling-down of wartime obligations should be effected at the earliest possible moment.

These recommendations, tame though they seem after the fiery denunciations of the three evil genii in chapter v, constitute all that can safely be proposed on this subject. A wave of uncertainty as to the wisdom of tariffs and War obligations seems to be making its appearance among the creditor nations at this time. This doubt the economist must attempt to turn to conviction by placing squarely before the public the injurious effects of a prolongation of these institutions. Beyond such propaganda work, he is powerless. The practical adaptation of his propaganda must be left to his fellow-worker, the politician.

CHAPTER IX

THE WORLD BANK

§ 1. The recommendations which have been made in the last two chapters have included no suggestions which call for the setting up of machinery which is not already in existence, with the exception of the consortium of international bankers and Treasury officials which was advocated in chapter vii. A recommendation will now be considered which, if adopted, might prove fruitful of many beneficial results in the attack upon the present problems of international finance, namely, the foundation of a World Central Bank.

In all financially well-developed countries at the present time, the whole banking system revolves around the Central Bank. Here are consolidated all the reserves of the private banks with a resultant economy in the use of the available supply of cash (gold and notes) which the banks feel bound to hold as a reserve against their liabilities. If these reserves were not centralized, but if instead each private bank held in its own vaults the amount of cash reserves which it deemed prudent, or which it was obliged by law to hold, waste would ensue from the fact that each bank would tend to hold a little more than the minimum on account of the difficulty of obtaining additional cash in case of need. With its development as the repository of member bank reserves, however, the Central Bank has learnt to furnish, through its readiness to rediscount or to undertake open-market operations, means whereby the private banks may readily reinforce their reserves when necessary. Thus the question of reserves has now become something of a routine matter to the individual member banks. So long as they maintain a prudent or legal percentage of their total liabilities in reserve at the Central Bank, they are prepared to leave the question of the actual or prospective size of the country's total cash reserves to that institution.

The holding of all bank reserves at the Central Bank entails the further advantage that it obviates the movement of cash in the settlement of balances of indebtedness between the various member banks. If there were no Central Bank and each private bank held its reserves in its own vaults, at the end of each day or each week cash would have to be physically transferred from one bank to another in settlement of debts outstanding between them as a result of the cheque transactions of their clients. Under the present system, the size of these debts may be computed at the end of each day through the medium of the clearing house. The balances outstanding may then be easily settled by means of cheques transferring reserve balances held at the Central Bank from one member bank to another.

The Central Bank for its part, in return for accepting responsibility for the maintenance of an adequate cash reserve for the currency and credit structure of the country, attempts to govern the credit policy of the banking system with a view to the conservation of reserves and/or the stabilization of the internal value of the currency. This controlling function is not merely considered permissible to it by the private banks, but is actively encouraged, since the Central Bank alone is in a position to consolidate the credit policy of the country as a whole, and to direct it towards a unified aim.

Thus the chief advantages which accrue to a country from the possession of a Central Bank as the focal point of its banking system are (i) the economizing of reserves, (ii) the obviation of the constant movement of funds between private banks, and (iii) the unification of the credit policy of the system as a whole.

Now there is no inherent reason why these advantages should not be attained on an international scale by the foundation of a World Central Bank. All three of the advantages mentioned would be of value to the international financial structure, particularly the last. The necessity of an economical use of gold has already been stressed. The constant physical transference of gold from one Central Bank to another is only less obnoxious than the similar transference of gold from one private bank to another in the same country because less frequent; there can be little excuse for so clumsy a method of settling international balances of payments now that the world has become accustomed to the methods of the clearing house. As to the unification of the credit policies of individual Central Banks, not only is it impossible to hope that disequilibria in international balances of payments may be avoided without some form of co-operation to ensure that Central Bank credit policies shall be kept "in step," but also stability of the value of the international standard itself can only be aimed at if all-important Central Banks follow a co-ordinated credit policy.

It was probably the hope of the founders of the Bank for International Settlements that that institution might in time develop into just such a Central Bank of Central Banks. Indeed, various of its statutes seem to have been drawn up expressly to fit it for this purpose.[1] This Bank has functioned actively in facilitating the collection of reparations and in the conduct of certain international loans, and the value of the services which it has performed in these directions is undeniable. At the same time, largely through the prestige of its officers, it shows signs of becoming a focal organ for international discussions, formal and informal, of the world's contemporary financial problems. A discussion of the potentialities of a Central Bank of Central Banks, therefore, falls well within the realm of practical possibility.

§ 2. The first requirement for the successful functioning of the World Bank would be that Central Banks should entrust to it part, if not all, of their gold holdings. As in the case of a national Central Bank, this procedure would achieve an economy of reserve "cash" (in this case gold only) by pooling

[1] Cf. P. Einzig, *The Bank for International Settlements*, London, 1930.

all available reserves, while at the same time providing the central institution with the material for its operations (cf. § 3).

In order to meet the criticism that such a huge store of gold as would result from the pooling in one place of most of the monetary gold stock of the world would prove too tempting a prize in case of war, it may be noted that it is not necessary that the gold be actually transferred to the vaults of the World Bank. Exactly the same results would follow if the requisite amount of gold were set aside by each Central Bank in its own vaults under earmark for the World Bank, and a credit for it entered in the books of that Bank as a deposit by each of the participating Central Banks.

With the initial deposit of part of their gold reserves, the Central Banks would then open accounts at the World Bank. The establishment of these accounts would restore to the gold-using world a method of economizing gold which has been closed to them since the widespread abandonment of the gold exchange standard. We saw in the last chapter how the currencies of countries operating upon this type of standard were maintained at par by the Central Banks concerned buying and selling foreign exchange in the requisite quantities, and how the suspension of gold payments by Great Britain in September 1931 dealt the death-blow to the system by reminding its users of the ever-present possibility of the depreciation of their foreign balances. The establishment of a World Bank which commanded confidence would make possible the revival of a form of the gold exchange standard, since Central Banks could then assist in the maintenance of the stability of their respective exchange rates by buying and selling their claims to deposits at the World Bank, deposits which would not be exposed to the risk of sudden depreciation.

If this system were set up, deposits with the World Bank would naturally rank as the equivalent of gold in the accounts of the participating Central Banks. The need for independent gold reserves would then disappear. Such reserves, we have seen, are only necessary for the purposes (i) of inspiring confidence in the solvency of the Central Bank concerned and in the soundness of its currency unit, and (ii) of meeting an external demand for gold in settlement of a disequilibrium of foreign payments. Both these purposes would be equally well served by deposits with the World Bank. For the purpose of inspiring confidence, the Central Banks' official gold reserves would be undiminished so long as the World Bank continued on a gold basis. For the purpose of satisfying a foreign demand, deposits held at the World Bank could be sold as readily as gold itself.

Indeed, it is by using their balances held at the World Bank for the settlement of foreign indebtedness that Central Banks could obviate physical gold movements between their respective countries. For the most efficient working of the system, it would be advisable that participating Central Banks should renounce their obligation to sell gold for their own currency notes upon demand at a fixed price. Instead, they should continue to link their currencies to the international standard by making them convertible at a fixed price into drafts upon the World Bank. Thus when the exchange rate between country A and country B sank to the gold export point, that is, the point at which it becomes profitable under the present system to ship gold from A to B, instead of the Central Banks selling actual gold to those who wish to make a profit by exporting it to B, it should merely undertake to sell a draft on its deposits at the World Bank. So long as B were also a participant in the system, the draft could then be mailed to the payee in B, where it could be sold to the Central Bank for the same price as gold. If B were not a member of the system, the consigner would have to go to the additional expense of mailing or cabling the draft to an agent in the town where the World Bank was situated; the gold could then be withdrawn and shipped from there.

It may be seen how simply the recommendation in the last chapter dealing with the stabilization of gold points could be fitted into this system. In place of their obligations to buy and sell gold at a fixed price, the Central Banks should now substitute the obligation to sell gold drafts on the World Bank at ½ per cent above the par value of their currency and buy them at ½ per cent below par. If all Central Banks were members of the system, and if, at the same time, the World Bank were obliged to sell gold for drafts on itself at ½ per cent above par and buy gold with drafts at ½ per cent below par, the desideratum of stabilizing the gold points of all currencies at an interval of 2 per cent apart would be achieved (see ch. vii, § 7).

Drafts on the World Bank would then replace actual gold in the settlement of international balances of payments. At the same time, the object of the international gold standard would be achieved in the linking of all currencies to drafts on the World Bank, which would in turn keep these drafts interchangeable with gold.

For the purpose of all these transactions, simplification would result if all drafts on the World Bank were drawn in terms of the same currency unit, or perhaps in terms of a physical quantity of gold. Only so could the drafts sold by the Central Banks have an accurate meaning. Suppose, for instance, that an English firm wished to take advantage of the fact that the sterling-franc exchange rate stood at the gold export point. If the draft which they purchased at the Bank of England on the World Bank were drawn in terms of sterling, they would be unwilling to pay the necessary ½ per cent premium unless the draft represented the amount of gold that could be purchased with the stated amount of sterling at par. Otherwise the draft upon arrival in Paris would be translated into francs at the current rate, and sterling being, by hypothesis, depreciated, the consigner would thereby incur a further loss which would make the transaction unprofitable. Indeed, unless the Central Bank's draft were convertible into gold at the World Bank at, or within ½ per cent of, par, it would carry no more advantage than an ordinary bill of exchange.

If, then, all drafts upon the World Bank represented physical quantities of gold, it would be simpler if they were all expressed in terms of a weight of gold or, for abbreviation, in a new unit, which we may call the "aureal" (1 aureal = 1 centigram of pure gold). Central Banks would then carry their reserves in aureals at the World Bank, and link their currencies to the aureal by undertaking to buy and sell it at fixed prices in their own currencies. Drafts on the World Bank sold by the various Central Banks would then be cleared at the World Bank itself, and balances transferred from the account of one Central Bank to that of another, as the reserve balances of member banks are transferred through the medium of the national clearing house under the present system. The World Bank for its part would guarantee the gold value of the aureal.

Such are the recommendations which would endow the World Bank with the passive "clearing-house" functions of an ordinary Central Bank. If such a system were established, Central Banks would find in the World Bank an institution which would afford them two of the three chief facilities which, as we saw in the last section, they in turn afford to private banks in their countries, namely, the economizing of reserve cash through the pooling of reserves, and the obviation of the physical movement of gold. We may now pass to a consideration of measures which might go further and endow the World Bank with the active functions which might empower it to afford to the Central Banks the third and most important of the aforementioned facilities, the unification of the credit policy of the gold-standard world as a whole.

§ 3. To enable it to pursue an active policy for the control of world credit conditions, the World Bank should now be equipped with the powers usual to a Central Bank, that is to say, the right to discount eligible bills and to purchase certain classes of securities. In this way, the funds initially deposited by the Central Banks would be mobilized for the benefit of the financial world. Here a further advantage would be derived from the establishment of a special currency unit for the use of the World Bank. With the creation of the aureal, the World Bank's purchasing power would no longer be confined to the volume of gold deposited with it by the Central Banks. Just as a national Central Bank creates *ex nihilo* a certain quantity of deposit currency in terms of its national unit upon the basis of the gold which it holds on behalf of private banks, so the World Bank could create aureals in excess of its total gold holdings. Whether a fixed minimum ratio of gold reserves to aureal liabilities should be prescribed for it by law, or whether the governors of the Bank should be allowed a free hand in the matter, it must be left to the creators of the system to decide.

The World Bank could then function precisely as an ordinary Central Bank. Its assets would consist of gold, securities, and discounts, and its liabilities of the deposits of Central Banks. It would be both unnecessary and inexpedient for the World Bank to issue aureal notes. Its purpose being to serve Central Banks only, there would be no need of such notes for circulation, and the Bank's reserves should be wholly available against the claims of its depositors and not be wasted as backing for an unnecessary addition to the world's supply of currency in circulation. Cheques and drafts issued by the Bank in payment for securities or discounts would then be promptly redeposited with it, and its asset-liability condition would be at all times clearly ascertainable.

The duties of the Bank in the exercise of its positive function of credit control would then be twofold; to attempt to maintain a long-time stable value for the international standard, gold or, which is synonymous, the aureal; and to attempt to iron out short-period cyclical fluctuations in its value. While enough has already been said as to the efficacy of Central Bank policies for the maintenance of a stable value for currencies to cast doubt upon the ability of the Bank to achieve any considerable measure of success in either of these directions, something may be hoped from its use of ordinary Central Bank procedure, if this procedure receives concerted support from national Central Banks.

For its guidance in the pursuit of the first of these two aims, the World Bank will need an index number of world prices. The difficulty of discovering and compiling a suitable index will always remain great. In this case, however, the problem will be less complicated than in the case of a national Central Bank, since only wholesale prices need be considered, the cost of the service of retailers being a matter for national management. Probably the most serviceable index would be one based on the wholesale prices of a wide range of commodities which enter into international trade, each price (f.o.b. in the country in which the commodity is produced) being duly weighted in accordance with its estimated importance in world commerce. Such an index would reflect with fair accuracy fluctuations in the truly international value of the standard. Improvements in the computation of the index may be expected to follow with experience in its use.

With movements in the index number of world prices as its guide, the World Bank should aim at stability in the usual way by the use of its discount rate and its power to buy and sell securities. Here difficulty will arise from the natural desire of each Central Bank to retain autonomous control over credit conditions within its own sphere. The individual Central Banks are hardly likely to aid in the establishment of an international institution which will subsequently interfere with their own pursuit of their several internal policies. It is therefore probable that some reservation will be incorporated in the charter of the World Bank similar to that in the statutes of the Bank for International Settlements, which forbids that institution to operate in any national market without the permission of the Central Bank concerned.

Inasmuch, however, as only the reserve base of the Central Banks would be ultimately affected by the conduct of these operations, and inasmuch as the operations would only be undertaken after agreement among the Central Banks who are members of the World Bank, much may be hoped from the co-operation of the Central Banks to the end agreed upon through the medium of the World Bank. This hope will be particularly strong when the agreed aim is the raising of world prices. At such times there is little likelihood of opposition arising to the purchase of securities in various world markets by the World Bank for the extension of the reserve base of the Central Banks. In 1931, for instance, the Macmillan Committee[1] "concluded that a restoration of the international price-level should be a prime object of international statesmanship. . . . We see no great reason to doubt the feasibility of attaining this objective in due course, provided that the Central Banks of the leading creditor countries will work together with this end in view. No one would doubt the ability of a closed monetary system to bring about a rise in prices; in fact it is only too easy. The chief ground of hesitation is the difficulty of securing adequate co-operation among Central Banks, rather than any obstacle inherent in the nature of the problem." Once agreement as to the desirability of raising prices has been achieved, the power of the World Bank to increase the total reserve base of all Central Banks by an issue of aureals beyond the total quantity of its holdings would prove an instrument of considerable utility.

When a world contraction of credit appears advisable, however, the path of the World Bank is likely to become less smooth. Even if it is unanimously commissioned by its members to sell securities, national jealousies are likely to be aroused by the way in which it executes this commission. Each Central Bank will probably be experiencing some anxiety as to the adequacy of its own reserves in face of the inflation of credit, which will presumably be in progress. The World Bank is therefore likely to be bombarded with accusations that it is not

[1] *Macmillan Report*, p. 118.

pursuing its operations impartially, but is selling securities more rapidly in some markets than in others.

Since the reduction of the credit bases of the Central Banks will only take place upon their own agreement if, as is probable, the aforementioned stipulation is made that the World Bank may only operate in any market with the consent of the Central Bank concerned, it might be unnecessary for the Bank to engage in any selling operations at all. Instead, it might be left to the individual Central Banks to carry out at their own pace and in their own way the agreed degree of credit contraction. The World Bank might then merely execute its security sales after the various Central Banks had already fortified their reserves by their own contractions of credit. If the inflation, however, shows signs of developing into a dangerous world-wide boom, it will be advisable that, for the sake of preserving confidence, the World Bank should reinforce its reserves at an early stage by contracting the volume of its earning assets.

The success of the credit policies of the World Bank is bound to be largely dependent upon the degree of support which the Central Banks accord it. At the outset, this support is likely to be given grudgingly, since no Central Bank will be anxious to abrogate any part of its sovereignty over credit conditions within its private sphere. As the facilities which the World Bank will have to offer become more fully understood and appreciated, however, and as the Central Banks make increasing use of their power to build up their reserves by rediscounting at the World Bank, it may be hoped and expected that they will become reconciled to occupying in other respects also the relation to the World Bank that member banks in a national system occupy to the Central Bank. In particular, as the Central Banks, finding that they themselves no longer have any use for gold, grow accustomed to keeping the whole of their gold reserves with the World Bank, either actually in its vaults or under earmark in their own vaults, it may be hoped that they will gradually cede to the World Bank the ultimate authority in determining the total amount of Central Bank reserve money to be left outstanding. In proportion as this delegation of authority proceeds, the credit policies of the World Bank will gain in weight and efficacy.

§ 4. The task of the World Bank in attempting to obviate short-period credit cycles is likely to prove a considerably more difficult affair. We saw in chapter vi what a stumbling-block the credit cycle is likely always to prove even to the most sanely ordered national Central Banks. The task of the World Bank will certainly be no less complex.

Now the credit cycle commonly originates in one country and thence spreads as an infection to others. The problem of the World Bank attempting to dampen the cycle, therefore, raises the question of its relation to individual Central Banks as against its relation to Central Banks as a whole. While it is highly improbable that, for a considerable time after its foundation, the World Bank would be allowed in any way to dictate to any Central Bank the credit policy that it should follow, yet it may be hoped that, through the medium of the World Bank, international agreement might be reached as to the most expedient course to be pursued when a cyclical inflation or deflation of credit showed signs of developing in any country. The World Bank might then be empowered to govern its credit policy towards that country accordingly, with the assent of the Central Bank concerned.

For instance, suppose a credit inflation showed signs of breaking out in England. A meeting of the governors of the World Bank, presumably a widely cosmopolitan group, would be called to discuss the situation. The representative of the Bank of England, knowing the facts of the case better than the rest, would probably succeed in persuading the board of governors that the view of the Bank of England was correct, that an incipient inflation threatened, and that the Bank of England must raise its Bank rate, even at the danger of putting itself out of alignment with other Central Banks. In view of this situation, it might then be decreed that the World Bank should part with some of its holdings of sterling bills and securities. To this the Bank of England could scarcely fail to agree, having itself announced its intention of raising its rate. Moreover, if it were anxious that the reserve base of the English banking system should be contracted, it would evidently prefer that some other agent than itself should conduct the necessary soaking-up of funds, since this would leave its earning assets unimpaired, and at the same time would not deplete its supply of "ammunition" against further emergency developments.

If at any time the board of governors should decide that an incipient inflation of credit was appearing in any country, but should fail to obtain the permission of the Central Bank involved to conduct the desired security sales in the country's open market, it should at least be empowered to employ a discriminatory discount rate against the offending country. The power to vary its discount rate between different Central Banks would be a necessary, or at least a helpful, adjunct to the World Bank's execution of its credit policies, particularly in its relations with individual Central Banks. It is easy to conceive a situation in which it would be desirable to tighten credit conditions in one country where inflation threatened, and ease them in another where commercial loans were small. Unless the World Bank's rediscount rate could be varied towards the two Central Banks concerned, the attempt to bring about this desideratum could only be made through the medium of open-market operations, the instrument in the use of which the World Bank will probably be subject to the will of the Central Banks. The power to rediscount on its own terms should be kept as the spontaneous and active item in the World Bank's armoury, and, as an aid to its active use, the Bank should be permitted to apply varying rates to the several Central Banks.

Thus the procedure of the World Bank in its attempt to dampen cyclical credit fluctuations should be to conduct an impartial discussion of the situation through its board of governors, and thereupon to formulate a policy to be pursued. It should then lend its full support to the Central Bank concerned in the execution of the determined policy (or, if the Central Bank dissented from the verdict of the board, bring pressure to bear upon it to conform to that verdict) by the ordinary Central Bank methods of open-market operations and manipulation of the rediscount rate. Beyond this, there is little that it can do. It may be hoped, however, that the support that it could lend to any Central Bank in the pursuit of any end, once that end has been decided upon, might be a considerable asset to that Bank in the execution of its policy.

§ 5. We are now in a position to examine the extent to which the establishment of a World Bank might aid in resuscitating the normal flow of international capital. The most immediate way in which it might achieve this end is by a well-ordered conduct of the Bank's own open-market operations. By selling its holdings of securities in countries where capital is plentiful, and even, if necessary, raising its rediscount rate against the Central Banks of such countries, and by simultaneously reinvesting the proceeds of such sales in countries which are short of capital, and, if necessary, reducing its rediscount rate against the Central Banks of such countries, the World Bank could effect a considerable transference of capital from the former to the latter group.[1] Unfortunately, like any Central Bank, the World Bank could only influence the long-term

[1] Before undertaking such operations, the World Bank should, of course, satisfy itself that the capital-receiving country is really in need of its aid, and that the new funds, which will probably become available in that country as a result of the easier credit conditions, are likely to be applied to productive purposes. On no account must the credit standing of the World Bank be prejudiced by too liberal a policy towards borrowers of doubtful worth.

interest rates of any country through its purchase of the highest-grade securities outstanding in that country. However, just as Central Bank security purchases improve the reserve position of private banks and so encourage them to increase their investments in bonds of all types, so World Bank security purchases would strengthen the reserve position of the Central Bank concerned, and enable it to pursue an easy-money policy with a facility that might otherwise never have been possible.

It is to be hoped that the World Bank would be aided in the attainment of this end by the Central Banks of creditor countries. Mr. Hawtrey has observed that "Central Banks have ready to hand a device which would enable them absolutely to guard against imports of gold at any time. If a Central Bank chooses to make a regular practice of buying foreign exchange at rates just within the gold import point, it need never import gold at all."[1] Under the present system, the natural deterrent which prevents Central Banks from following so broadminded a course is the fear that the currencies that they buy may depreciate by reason of the countries concerned abandoning the gold standard. So long as the World Bank received sufficiently powerful support to guarantee its solvency, this fear might now be allayed. Any Central Bank which found its currency approaching the gold import point with reference to some other currency could purchase a sufficient quantity of the latter exchange to prevent an import of gold, or a transference of aureal deposits, and could then deposit the exchange thus acquired at the World Bank, where it would be placed to its credit in terms of aureals.

Suppose, for instance, that the franc-mark exchange rate were rapidly approaching the point at which the Reichsbank would be compelled to sell aureals which would subsequently be deposited to the credit of the Bank of France. Just before this "gold point" were reached, the Bank of France might purchase a quantity of marks and so prevent the "export" of

[1] *The International Gold Problem*, p. 122.

aureals from Germany. If it were willing to run the risk of depreciation, the Bank of France could then hold these marks in the form of foreign balances in Berlin, where they would then earn interest. If, on the other hand, the Bank of France preferred to safeguard itself against the possibility of depreciation, it could deposit these marks at the World Bank, where they would be credited to its account in aureals at the usual rate. The deposits would, of course, earn no interest (unless it had been found possible for the World Bank to pay interest on its deposits). They would, however, rank as part of the gold reserves of the Bank of France, for which no interest is normally expected. Meanwhile, the World Bank would be drawing interest by investing in Berlin the marks sold to it by the Bank of France. This interest would represent a kind of commission paid to it for guaranteeing the ready convertibility of the French Bank's aureal holdings. The net result of the whole transaction would then be that the Bank of France had transferred a certain volume of its own reserves, or of the credit which it was able to create on the basis of those reserves, to the World Bank, whereby the latter had been enabled to increase its holdings of German securities, that is, its loans to Germany. By a steady repetition of such transactions, the creditor countries could make a quantity of their surplus capital available to debtor countries through the medium of the World Bank, which would act as a kind of guarantor of the liquidity of the capital transferred.

If the exchanges of any country remained consistently adverse, and if the other countries continued to pursue the policy here suggested, there might of course ensue the amassing of an excessive quantity of one particular currency in the hands of the World Bank. For instance, in the case above cited it is possible that, if the mark were low on all foreign exchanges, and if all countries were co-operating to prevent an outflow of aureals from Germany, the World Bank might find itself becoming overstocked with marks to the credit of other Central

Banks than the Reichsbank. If the causes of the mark's depreciation were more than temporary, this would be a dangerous situation if allowed to continue. It would, therefore, be expedient in such circumstances for the World Bank to advise other Central Banks to desist from further purchases of marks. The World Bank would then be free to attempt to persuade the Reichsbank to adopt a deflationary policy which might serve to rectify the disequilibrium in its exchanges.

The performance of the function of guarantor suggests a further way in which the World Bank might, if sufficiently strongly supported, aid in the revival of the flow of capital from the creditor to the debtor nations. We have seen the impasse into which the whole of international indebtedness has drifted, largely through the unwillingness of the creditor countries to continue to extend to the debtors the regular supply of new capital which is necessary to the latter if they are to remain solvent (cf. ch. iv). We saw that the main reason for this unwillingness was the fear of impending insolvency, which inhibits the normal lenders from undertaking the risk involved in all foreign loans in the uncertainties of the present period. This unwillingness, however, leads to a vicious circle, for the more reluctant creditors become to lend, the nearer the debtors approach to insolvency. At the same time, it is unreasonable to expect any individual private bank or corporation in any creditor country, or even any creditor Central Bank, to embark alone on the task of aiding debtor nations by a long-sighted extension of credit. The revival of the solvency of debtor nations is one of the problems which cannot be tackled by any bank, or even by any country, acting alone. The concerted strength of the most powerful creditor nations is necessary for the task.

If the World Bank could be built up into a true international focus for the combined policy of the Central Banks of the world, it might be able to perform the functions of a much-needed international investment corporation for the direction of capital to those countries where it is most needed, but whither its owners are unwilling to send it without some more secure guarantee of its safety than is at present available. The various expedients which were adopted in the United States during the autumn and winter of 1931–32 afford examples of the way in which idle credit may be mobilized through the medium of some well-supported corporation, and made available for uses to which it would not have been devoted without the intermediary guarantee of the corporation. Although these American corporations met with only a modified measure of success, it is undeniable that they supplied loans to deserving borrowers who were unable to raise the necessary funds in the ordinary way. Moreover, they did at least prove the willingness with which banks and other holders of capital may be expected to provide funds for a corporation of recognized soundness, even when that corporation avowedly intends to apply the funds thus collected to the very purposes for which the holders individually were unwilling to lend them. A clearer example could not be required of the way in which collective effort may restore that elusive confidence which may have entirely disappeared from a financial world of unco-ordinated individuals.

The transference of a large part, or all, of the gold reserves of the most powerful Central Banks of the world to the World Bank would constitute an overwhelmingly strong guarantee of the latter's solvency. Provided the Bank were then conservatively managed, and provided it did not attempt to guarantee foreign loans too extensively or on any but the most palpably justifiable grounds, it might command just such confidence as would be necessary for an international investment corporation. Loans similar to the Austrian Reconstruction Loan, which was itself sponsored by the Bank for International Settlements, might then be floated under the ægis of the World Bank for the benefit of debtor nations. Such loans need not always be restricted to use by governments; upon due investigation by the World Bank, it is quite conceivable that railroads or acceptance brokers and other finance houses might be deemed worthy, and in need, of loans which could most easily be raised through the medium of the Bank. Not only would credit thus be made available for the loan-starved debtor nations by this procedure, but it would also cost the debtors less than any credit which might be raised under the present system, a very important consideration in view of the seriousness of the transfer problem.

The size of the capital movements from creditor to debtor countries which the World Bank could induce in its capacity as guarantor of loans of this type would be considerably greater than the movements which it could bring about by means of its own open-market operations. In the latter case, the volume would be limited by that portion of its assets which it could afford to dedicate to this purpose; in the former case, the Bank would merely act as the channel through which the volume of funds standing idle or commanding a negligible return in creditor countries could be induced to flow to those debtor countries where they were so badly needed.

The function of guaranteeing international loans is, of course, a dangerous one for any organization to perform. It is not, therefore, suggested that the Bank should embark immediately upon a lavish and undiscriminating programme of loans to all comers. It may, indeed, be optimistic to hope that in the near future a cosmopolitan body governing the World Bank would be willing to sponsor any such advances. It may be hoped, however, that with the exercise of discrimination the Bank may be able to float certain justifiable loans among the creditor countries, which the latter would not have been prepared to undertake singly, but to which they may be willing to subscribe collectively owing to the consequent distribution of the risk.

We saw in chapter iv how essential to the smooth working of an international standard a steady flow of foreign capital may be. International lending does not constitute as permanent a way of settling international balances of payments as the net export of goods. It does, however, tide over a temporary disequilibrium, and, in so far as it aids the borrower to increase her productivity, it hastens the coming of the time when she may hope to be able to balance her international payments without recourse to new borrowing. If the World Bank could restore something of the normal international flow of capital, it would by that accomplishment alone justify its creation many times over.

§ 6. From what has been said in the foregoing sections, it will be seen what advantages to the working of an international standard might result from the creation of a World Central Bank. Economy of gold reserves, obviation of gold movements, stabilization of gold points, co-ordination of national credit policies (i) for the maintenance of a stable long-time value for the standard and (ii) for the dampening of cyclical credit fluctuations, and co-operative direction of the flow of international capital, all would be facilitated by the establishment of such an institution.

There is a further forceful argument in favour of the creation of a World Bank. The alternative to a closer degree of international co-operation in the management of the gold standard is the permanent desertion of gold in favour of fiduciary national standards. If the transition to such standards were forced upon the world by the breakdown of the old gold standard before nations had become accustomed to a co-operative control of money, international co-operation might never be secured; the need for it would be much less urgently felt under an aggregation of national fiduciary standards.

Not only the breakdown of the old gold standard, but also a future shortage of gold may eventually force the abandonment of gold as the international yardstick. The creation of a centralized world organ for the co-ordinated management of monetary systems at this time, when the necessity for world co-operation is palpably necessary for the preservation of any form of the international gold standard, would teach the world the principles of that monetary co-operation without which confusion will always be present to some degree in the mechanism of international finance.

More than that. The establishment of some such international system as that outlined in this chapter would pave the way to a peaceful and unobjectionable abandonment of gold, or any other commodity, as the standard to whose value all currencies must at present be linked if they are to be assured a stable international valuation. The transition from an aureal standard based on gold, as outlined above, to an international fiduciary aureal standard could be painlessly achieved without causing any of the chaos in foreign exchange rates which would result if nations were to abandon the gold standard separately and without co-operation in the subsequent management of their currencies.

While, for the sake of securing public confidence, the World Bank should be founded originally upon a gold basis provided by the transfer of gold from Central Bank reserves, it will easily be seen that, once the system has operated well enough to secure wide international support, the possession of gold will no longer be necessary either to Central Banks or to the World Bank itself. The power to create aureals in excess of the actual quantity of gold held will constitute the first step towards the divorce of the total quantity of the world's reserves from the outstanding quantity of mined gold. Thereafter, if, as is to be hoped, the system be managed in the interest of stable world prices, the volume of aureals created should tend to bear less and less relation to the World Bank's gold holdings, until finally it is realized that the part played by gold in the system is an artificial and unnecessary one. The supply of aureals, judiciously controlled by the World Bank, but not limited by niggardly Nature, would have supplanted the metal as the basis of the world's currency supplies.

This realization has gradually been growing upon monetary authorities even under the present system, where gold is still used in international transfers for the settlement of balances of payments. It is much more likely to grow under the system proposed, whereby gold would never be physically used for any purpose, but would lie fallow in the vaults of the World Bank or under earmark in the vaults of Central Banks. In either case it would never see the light of day, and the system would be in no way affected if it were suddenly discovered one morning that some sorcerer had spirited away the entire world's stock overnight.

In such circumstances, if King Gold ever showed signs of again becoming a tyrannous monarch, even after he had been safely locked up behind the bars in the various Banks, he could be quietly deposed by mutual agreement of his ministers, the Central Banks, without his subjects, the money-using public, noticing the difference in the regime under which they were living. Thus the fear of a future gold shortage, a traditional bugbear of monetary theory, would be scotched for ever.

So ends the series of practical recommendations which it seems possible to offer at the present time. The political difficulties in the way of the adoption of many of these recommendations will perhaps be great, yet none of them can justly be held to be outside the bounds of practical possibility. They are here offered in the belief that, whatever the institutional obstacles that lie in the way of their adoption, the duty of economists is to formulate the theoretical, but at the same time attainable, ideals to be aimed at, and to thrust these aggressively before the public and our other masters. To the politician must be left the details of the means whereby these ideals are to be pursued, but sound progress can scarcely be hoped for unless the ideals pursued are themselves sound. It is only in proportion as economists are prepared to scrap old hypotheses in the light of new historical facts, and to examine all theories, however revered, in the searching light of statistical and factual evidence, that they will be entitled to attempt to guide politicians in their well-intentioned endeavours for the public good. "For if the blind lead the blind . . ."

APPENDIX

A STATISTICAL EXAMINATION OF THE DEGREE TO WHICH CENTRAL BANKS MAY ACHIEVE INTERNAL STABILITY

§ 1. The object of this book is to examine theories in the light of contemporary fact. The presumption that Central Banks may by scientific management of their credit policies control the internal value of their currencies is one of the most commonly accepted dicta of present-day monetary theory. As the argument of those who advocate managed fiduciary standards in preference to continued adherence to the international gold standard derives most of its force from this hypothesis, it is important to discover as far as possible from history past and present what justification there is in fact behind this optimistic contention.

While no important nation has in the recent past permanently deserted the gold standard in order to be free to apply its endeavours to the achievement of internal stability of the value of the domestic currency through scientific management, the United States was during the years 1923–31 in the fortunate position of being virtually independent of external influences in the pursuit of her credit policy on account of the exceptional strength of her gold reserves. At the same time, it was the avowed aim of the Federal Reserve System during this period to maintain a stable level of prices in the United States. In the attempted execution of this aim, the Reserve Banks were guided by more complete statistical information than lies at the disposal of any other Central Bank. In proportion as they failed to achieve their end the arguments of those who urge that internal stability would be within the grasp of any Central Bank that would rid itself of outside influences by an abandonment of the international standard will be weakened. This appendix constitutes an attempt to evaluate statistically the success which crowned the efforts of the Federal Reserve Banks to realize this prophecy.

It should be noted at the outset that if this were a book on statistics the material here used for the construction of the various charts would have to be treated for the smoothing out of secular and seasonal trends. Graphs which have been so smoothed, however, are apt to convey a misleading impression to the ordinary reader. Inasmuch as this book is intended for others besides statisticians, it has been thought best to plot the raw data in all cases. Where it is necessary to make allowances for regular trends, the attention of the reader will be called to this fact.

The investigation falls into three parts, corresponding to the three steps in the argument of the "revolutionaries" as enunciated in chapter vi. First will be examined the degree to which the Federal Reserve Banks have influenced the course of interest rates short- and long-term; secondly, the degree to which interest rates have affected total borrowings and therefore the volume of deposit currency outstanding; thirdly, the degree to which movements in total deposits have determined the price-level.

§ **2.** It is clear that the Federal Reserve Banks have exercised very considerable control over open-market interest rates during the period under review. In this they have, of course, been very much aided by the use of their bill-buying rates, in addition to their rediscount rates. The former is the rate at which the Reserve Banks stand ready to buy eligible bankers' acceptances from private individuals as well as from member banks, while the latter is the rate at which they will rediscount eligible paper for member banks only. While the Banks' bill-buying rates are commonly below their rediscount rates, they are only applicable to prime bankers' acceptances, whereas the higher rediscount rate applies to a wider variety of commercial paper.

It is evident that by the use of their bill-buying rates the Reserve Banks can set an upper limit to the market rate for prime bankers' acceptances, since no private bank or other lender would be offered any such bills if they attempted to charge a higher rate of discount on them than was being contemporaneously charged by the Reserve Banks. On the other hand, the Banks can do much to raise an open-market rate which has fallen considerably below their own buying rate by the usual process of selling on the open market some of their holdings of securities, and thus narrowing the reserve base of the member banks and forcing them either to increase their borrowings or to contract their loans, either of which alternatives would serve to tighten open-market rates.

The bankers' acceptance rate and the commercial paper rate are the two open-market rates which apply to the accommodation of business as against the call-loan rate which applies chiefly to speculative loans. Commercial paper, being simply paper that has not received the guarantee of the name of some well-known financial institution in addition to the name of the issuer, normally carries an interest rate which stands a little above the rate on bankers' acceptances. The two rates, however, naturally move in very close conjunction, the differential between them being approximately equivalent to the cost of securing the endorsement of an "acceptor." Control of the bankers' acceptance rate, therefore, implies equal control of the rate on commercial paper. In actual fact, the latter has now become a matter of little significance as compared with the former, for bankers' acceptances have almost completely supplanted commercial paper in the New York market, the latter having dropped to $100 million in total volume in January 1932, while the former still amounted to a value of little less than $1,000 million. The bankers' acceptance rate may, therefore, be taken as the standard open-market rate for commercial borrowing.

Chart IV illustrates the close relationship in which the

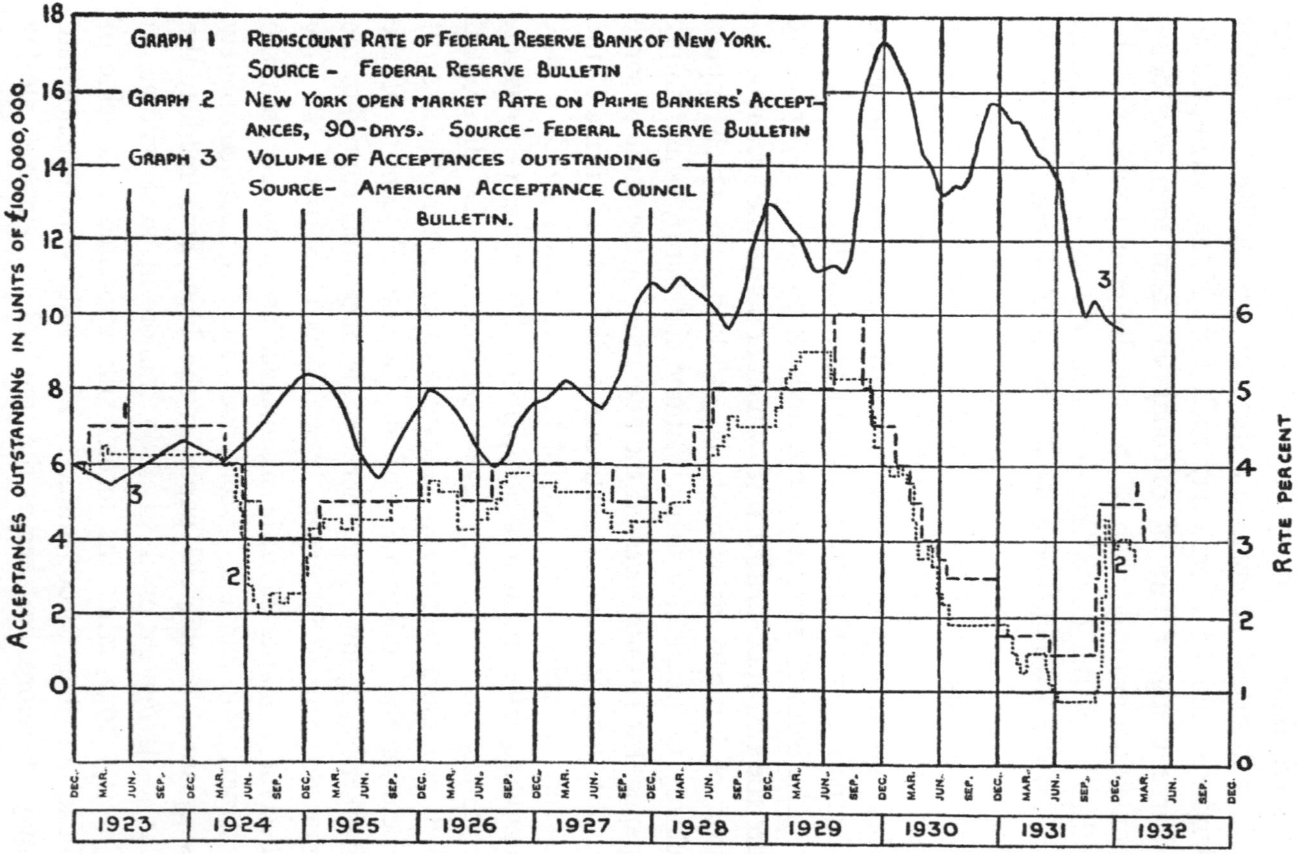
Graph 1 Rediscount Rate of Federal Reserve Bank of New York.
Source - Federal Reserve Bulletin
Graph 2 New York open market Rate on Prime Bankers' Acceptances, 90-days. Source - Federal Reserve Bulletin
Graph 3 Volume of Acceptances outstanding
Source - American Acceptance Council Bulletin.
Acceptances outstanding in units of £100,000,000.
Rate percent
1923
1924
1925
1926
1927
1928
1929
1930
1931
1932

CHART IV

rediscount rate of the Federal Reserve Bank of New York and the rate on 90-day prime bankers' acceptances in that market have moved during the last decade. It will be seen that the latter commonly stands a trifle below the former in the same way as the open-market rates in London commonly stand below the Bank rate. This is, of course, the natural state of affairs in any market where the private banks and other lenders are expected to take care of the needs of private borrowers, who are not supposed in normal times themselves to have recourse to the Central Bank for accommodation, the latter's funds being reserved for the use of the banking system itself. The state of affairs portrayed on the chart in the spring of 1929, when the open-market acceptance rate and the Reserve Bank's own bill-buying rate stood above the rediscount rate for a period of five months, was a totally illogical one. It is probably to be explained by the fact that the Reserve Bank of New York was at that time anxious to raise its rediscount rate but was unable to obtain the leave of the Federal Reserve Board for the move. Having autonomous power over its bill-buying rate, it may have hoped to force the hand of the Reserve Board by putting this rate above its rediscount rate.

An interesting feature which the chart also brings out is the differential which commonly exists between the two rates during the autumn. This differential is due to the action of the Reserve Bank of New York in cutting its bill-buying rate during this season in order to facilitate the movements of crops and other produce which are financed largely through the medium of bankers' acceptances, while not giving encouragement to the private banks to increase their borrowings for undesirable purposes by reducing the rediscount rate.

An example of the way in which open-market rates may also be influenced by the Central Bank's open-market operations without necessarily the accompaniment of a change in the rediscount rate is shown in Chart V. Here the "free reserves" of the member banks of the Federal Reserve System (cf.

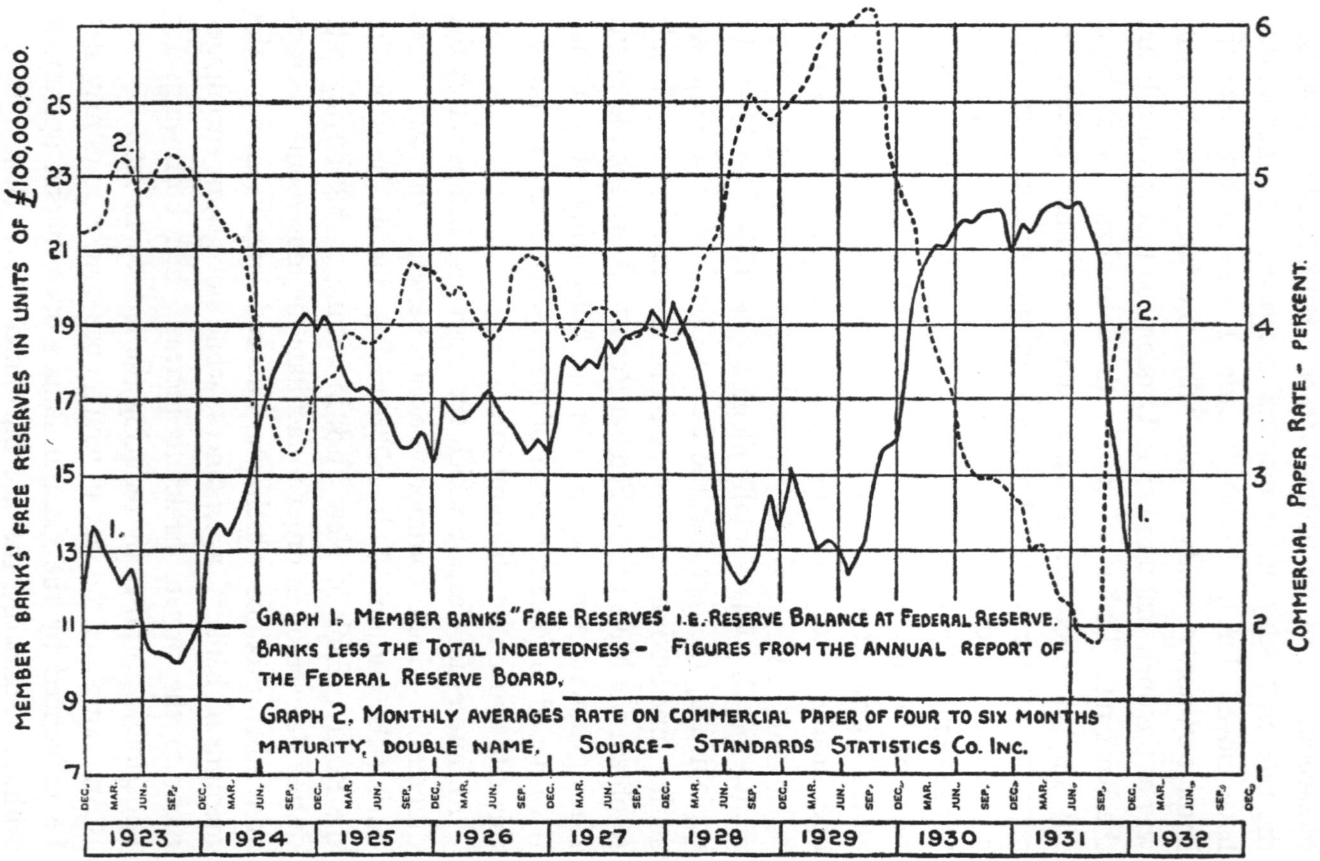

MEMBER BANKS' FREE RESERVES IN UNITS OF £100,000,000.
COMMERCIAL PAPER RATE - PERCENT.
GRAPH 1. MEMBER BANKS "FREE RESERVES" I.E. RESERVE BALANCE AT FEDERAL RESERVE. BANKS LESS THE TOTAL INDEBTEDNESS - FIGURES FROM THE ANNUAL REPORT OF THE FEDERAL RESERVE BOARD.
GRAPH 2. MONTHLY AVERAGES RATE ON COMMERCIAL PAPER OF FOUR TO SIX MONTHS MATURITY, DOUBLE NAME. SOURCE- STANDARDS STATISTICS CO. INC.
1923
1924
1925
1926
1927
1928
1929
1930
1931
1932

ch. ii, § 2) are compared with the New York open-market rate on prime commercial paper. This chart exhibits a remarkable degree of symmetry, the commercial paper rate rising as the free reserves fall and vice versa. The symmetry is frequently broken during the last month of the year, but this is explicable by the fact that there always occurs at this season an outflow of currency into circulation, which reduces the free reserves of the member banks, but which does not alter the commercial paper rate, since it is purely a temporary phenomenon caused mainly by the seasonal demands of the public and the banks. The chart would appear to establish a fairly close connection between the volume of member bank discounts and the interest rates prevailing in the open market, and thus to indicate that the Reserve Banks can exert considerable influence in the direction of firming these rates, when it wishes to counteract an inflationary tendency, simply by the sale of open-market holdings.

There is, however, another type of interest rate charged for the accommodation of business entrepreneurs, namely, the rate charged on so-called "customers' loans." This rate has been called "the characteristic and typical 'bank rate' of the country,"[1] and, although little attention is customarily paid to it in discussions of interest rates in general, its claim to such a title is amply justified by the volume of the loans to which it applies. The following table, published in the *Federal Reserve Bulletin* of March 1928, brings out the constancy with which this type of loan continues over long periods to be numerically of infinitely greater importance than any other class of loan.

This table shows that both in 1922 and in 1927 customers' loans accounted for over 60 per cent of total loans and investments in the United States as against the 6 per cent of all types of open-market loans combined. It would seem, therefore, that open-market rates are of quite trivial importance

[1] Carl Snyder, "Interest Rates and the Business Cycle," *American Economic Review*, December 1925.

APPROXIMATE DISTRIBUTION OF LOANS AND INVESTMENTS OF ALL KINDS IN THE UNITED STATES ON JUNE 30, 1922, AND JUNE 30, 1927

(*Amounts in millions of dollars*)

	1922	1927	Increase or Decrease (−)	Percentage Distribution of Total	
				1922	1927
Total loans and investments	40,105	54,372	14,242	100	100
Loans to customers	25,228	33,912	8,659	63	62
Open-market portfolios, total	14,877	20,460	5,583	37	38
Investments	12,525	17,217	4,692	31	32
Loans to brokers in New York City ..	1,328*	2,275	947	3	4
Acceptances purchased*	229	389	160	1	1
Commercial paper purchased*	795	579	−216	2	1

* Estimated.

in comparison with rates on customers' loans where it is a question of the Central Bank attempting to expand or contract the outstanding volume of deposit currency through monetary ease or stringency. The alteration in the amount of credit in use which is likely to ensue from changes in open-market rates is evidently insignificant compared to the already existing volume of deposit currency based on customers' loans. Unless the changes are reflected in the rates charged for this type ot loan, they are hardly likely by themselves to accomplish the purpose of the Central Bank.[1]

Until recently it has been difficult to obtain accurate information as to this type of loan even in the United States, where banking statistics are generally more readily available than in any other country. Since 1918, however, the Federal Reserve Board has conducted a regular reporting service to supply information on customers' loan rates from certain selected cities where Federal Reserve Banks or branches are located. On the basis of this information three composite rates are now published regularly in the *Federal Reserve Bulletin* for New York City, for eight other northern and eastern cities, and for twenty-seven southern and western cities respectively. These composite figures are based on the three types of customers' loans—commercial loans and demand and time loans on securities. The method of computing the averages takes into account (*a*) the relative importance of each of these three types of loans, and (*b*) the relative importance of each reporting bank, as measured by its total loans. Unfortunately, these figures are only available since the beginning of 1927. Mr. Carl Snyder, of the Federal Reserve Bank of New York, however, has very kindly supplied similar figures prior to that date compiled by his Bank for (1) New York City, and (2) the other thirty-five cities. From these data, Chart VI has been

[1] The question of the power of the Central Bank to affect long-term interest rates, and hence the pace of investment, will be discussed later (§ 3).

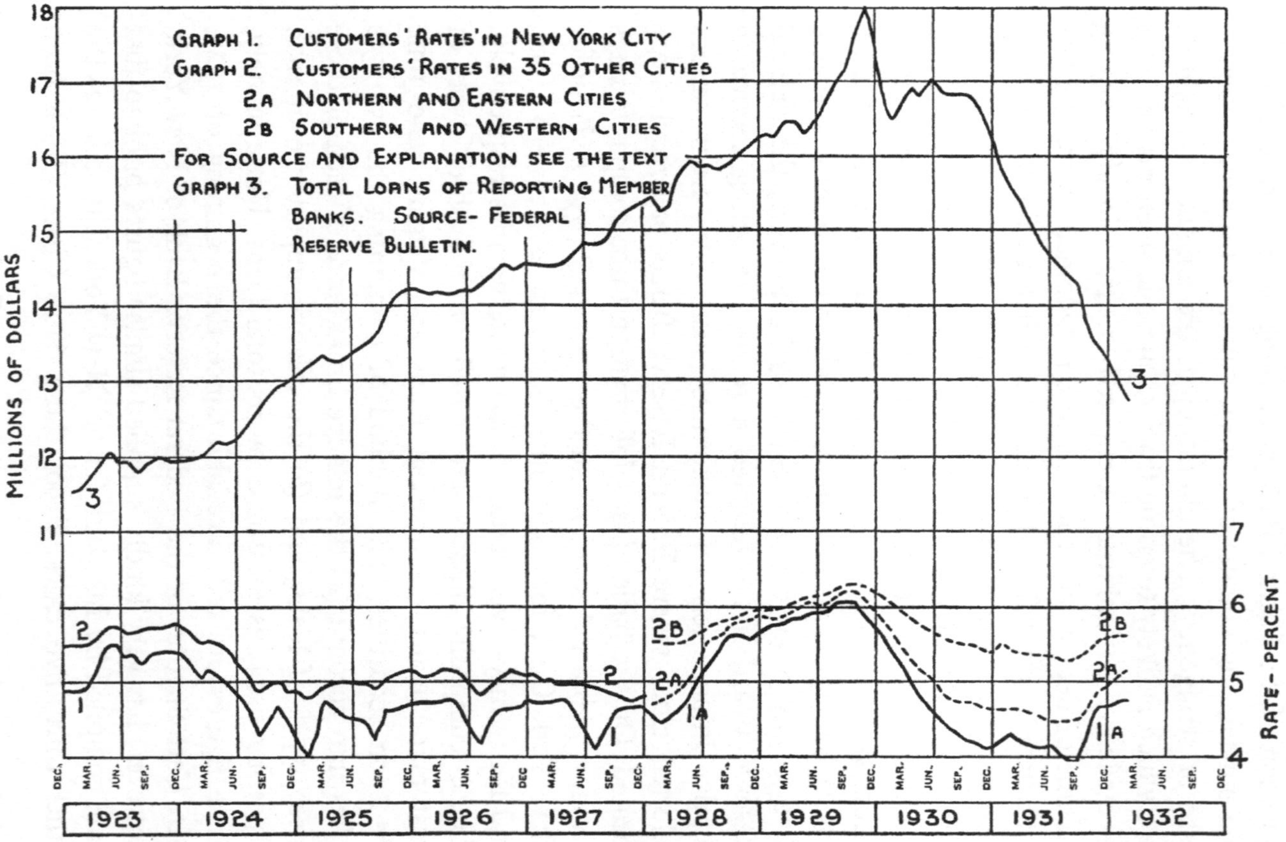
GRAPH I. CUSTOMERS' RATES IN NEW YORK CITY
GRAPH 2. CUSTOMERS' RATES IN 35 OTHER CITIES
2A NORTHERN AND EASTERN CITIES
2B SOUTHERN AND WESTERN CITIES
FOR SOURCE AND EXPLANATION SEE THE TEXT
GRAPH 3. TOTAL LOANS OF REPORTING MEMBER BANKS. SOURCE- FEDERAL RESERVE BULLETIN.
MILLIONS OF DOLLARS
RATE - PERCENT
1923
1924
1925
1926
1927
1928
1929
1930
1931
1932

CHART VI

constructed, Mr. Snyder's figures being used prior to 1928 and those of the *Federal Reserve Bulletin* thereafter.

The immediately striking fact which this chart brings out is the relative steadiness of these rates in comparison with open-market rates. Curve 2, the curve for customers' rates in thirty-five cities, lies throughout its course within a range of 1 per cent, and the New York rates over the same period, i.e. 1923–27, within a range of 1½ per cent, while contemporary open-market rates covered a range of 2¼ per cent. Even more striking, however, is the testimony of the troubled period from January 1928 to December 1931, when the two open-market rates fluctuated through a range of 4¾ per cent; during the whole of this time customers' rates in New York City only moved within a range of 2⅛ per cent, while the corresponding figure for the eight other northern and eastern cities was 1·8 per cent, and for the twenty-seven southern and western cities exactly 1 per cent. In the year 1931 alone, while both the open-market rates dropped exactly 1 per cent between January and August, the corresponding drop for the three classes of customers' loans was less than 0·2 per cent in each case, while in the subsequent hardening of rates in the autumn of the same year, which brought both open-market rates up over 2¼ per cent in some six weeks, the three customers' rates only registered rises of 0·7 per cent, 0·4 per cent, and 0.2 per cent respectively. It is to be noted, moreover, that the figures from which the chart was constructed include rates for loans on securities. This type of loan carries a more variable rate than pure commercial loans, as is borne out by the figures for the different classes of loans published regularly in the *Federal Reserve Bulletin*. When due allowance is made for this fact, rates on customers' "all other loans" will be found to fluctuate even less.

The reason for this relative stolidity in customers' rates is to be found in the personal relationship which they involve between borrower and lender; this relationship constitutes by far the most important characteristic of such loans. The main business of the ordinary country or small-town bank is derived from financing the industry of the locality. The small bank manager is the friend and patron of the local farmer or retailer, conversant with their financial affairs, the prospects of their occupations, their current needs. Without his assistance their original purchase of stock and equipment would have been impossible, and if his aid were suddenly withdrawn their plight would be sorry indeed.

The small banker, for his part, realizes that on the success of these clients depends his largest source of income. The open money market means little to him. The major part of his earning assets, and certainly the most profitable part, is composed of just such customers' loans, together with the local real estate mortgages, which are, after all, simply a form of long-term customers' loans. Thus to the small banker two policies are essential, to retain his customers by accommodating them to their satisfaction, and to avoid harassing them with inopportune demands for repayment for fear of killing the goose that lays the golden egg by forcing them into bankruptcy. The first of these policies will demand as a corollary that the banker does not vary his interest charge with every fluctuation in open-market rates, while the second necessitates his refraining from calling in his loans at will. To compensate himself for these two concessions he will, of course, charge a considerably higher rate than that obtaining in the open market, but once the rate is established it will tend to be adhered to constantly through all the short-time fluctuations in other interest rates.

Be the reason for this stolidity what it may, however, the important fact is that the stolidity itself is very real. To the extent that it persists, the control which the Central Bank is able to exercise over customers' loans, which, as we have seen, constitute so large a proportion of the total loans and advances, and therefore of the total deposit currency, of the country, will be small. The experience of the United States seems to indicate that in point of fact control over short-term rates is limited to the open-market rates on bankers' acceptances and commercial paper, which together constitute a completely insignificant percentage of total loans.

§ 3. So far we have only discussed the influence which Central Bank policies may have upon short-term interest rates. While it is, of course, in the short-term loan markets that such inducements as the Central Bank is able to offer to borrowers in the shape of higher or lower interest rates will be likely to take effect, both on account of the greater adjustability of short-term than of long-term rates, and because of the greater rapidity with which short-term loans are contracted, changes in short-term rates may be passed on to the long-term money market with important consequences.

The earning assets of the banking system fall into two classes, loans and investments. Into these two classes each individual bank must divide the credit which it is able to create on the basis of its reserves. We have seen that all banks tend to keep themselves "loaned up" to the maximum limit which their reserves will allow, so that any falling-off or over-expansion in either of the classes of their earning assets tends to be soon compensated by a corresponding increase or decrease in the other class. But whereas, in the case of investments, a bank may buy or sell at will without the necessity of consulting the seller or buyer who constitutes the other party to the transaction, since willing sellers and buyers will always be forthcoming at the current price in the stock market, in the case of its loans a bank is not the only deciding party in any individual transaction. Should a bank decide that its loans should be increased, it must first find the necessary borrowers, and these cannot always be found even though they be offered the temptation of lower interest rates (cf. § 4); while similarly, a bank will not always be able to contract its loans by the expedient of charging a higher price for its accommodation.

Thus the adjustment which a bank may be impelled by a change in the volume of its reserves to make in its earning assets cannot always be made at will in the volume of its loans. The volume of its investment holdings, depending as it does upon the will of the bank alone, constitutes the adjustable item in its earning assets, and will often be called upon to take up the slack caused by discrepant movements in the volume of its reserves and the volume of its loans.

Such discrepant movements are most likely to occur when a country is experiencing an extreme depression or extreme business activity and speculation. When prices are falling steadily, for example, borrowers will be discouraged from raising loans for any purpose, while the Central Bank in its efforts to check the depression will be exerting its influence to build up the reserves of the banking system as a means to inducing easy money rates. The private banks then, finding their reserves mounting, will attempt to increase their earning assets correspondingly. Since private borrowers are scarce, they will be forced to seek an outlet for the new credit which they wish to create in the open investment market. Prudence will normally send them into the bond market rather than the stock market. If their purchases continue for any length of time the prices of bonds may rise to the point where the market will become receptive to new issues; the demand for bonds will have begun to exceed the existing supply.

Now the considerations which determine the time at which it is profitable to borrow money on long term are profoundly different from those which lead to the raising of short-term loans. In the first place, the rate at which funds can be obtained will be of considerably greater importance in the former case than in the latter, since interest on bonds remains a fixed and immutable cost to the borrower throughout the life of the issue. A short-term borrower raises a loan for a period during which he feels sure that conditions will enable him to make a profit even after paying the rate of interest demanded, and, if in the subsequent period conditions do not appear to justify a similar expectation, he is under no obligation to renew the loan. The floater of bonds, on the other hand, accepts an obligation to pay a fixed sum in interest regularly over a long period, fair weather or foul.

Secondly, bonds are usually raised for capital improvements rather than for the immediate production of saleable consumption goods. Municipalities, public utilities, and railroads, which together constitute a large percentage of the bond-floaters in any market, have at all times a waiting list of capital improvements to be undertaken at an auspicious moment.[1] Inasmuch as these improvements will not be sold direct to the public, but will be used rather to produce goods and services for sale over a long period of time, the contemporary trend of commodity prices will not profoundly affect the expectation of the receipts which will ensue from these undertakings. Even though the decline in commodity prices spread over into the prices of the services which the new capital improvements are intended to purvey, the new plant may reasonably be expected to outlive the contemporary fall in prices and to continue to produce goods or services in subsequent and more prosperous periods. Thus, in the absence of calculations of immediate receipts, costs become the consideration of paramount importance. Here the contemporary fall in prices will provide an added inducement to embark on the enterprises at this time, for raw material, labour, and money will all be cheaper in times of business pessimism than at other times.

If, therefore, at a time of business recession the Central Bank

[1] "American railroads, public utilities and industrial corporations, although borrowing conservatively, will require many hundreds of millions of dollars this year. For the present their most pressing requirements must be financed by means of bank loans. Obviously there is a limit to which this type of financing can be pursued, so that new bond financing will be done just as fast as the market can readily absorb it."—*New York Times*, January 31, 1932.

can so increase the reserve base of the banking system as to drive the banks into the bond market in search of new earning assets, the resultant increase in the receptivity of the bond market to new issues may provide just the necessary inducement to a number of corporations to come forward and raise new funds for capital improvements. This done, pay-rolls may start to swell, the construction industry, which is particularly closely connected with the bond market, may revive, orders for steel and other important commodities needed for construction may increase, and the enhanced activity will then be diffused throughout the entire industrial structure.

Chart VII comparing the flotations of domestic bonds with contemporary bond prices lends considerable force to the argument that there is always a mass of new long-term financing awaiting a favourable market for flotations. From a low point in the unfavourable market of 1923, flotations rose rapidly during 1924, continued a slight upward movement throughout 1925 and 1926, and increased sharply with the rise in bond prices in 1927. A moderate decline occurred in 1928 despite record prices early in the year; apparently long-term needs were sated as a result of the heavy financing of 1927. With the decline in bond prices from April 1928 to October 1929, flotations decreased rapidly, only to burst forth again with renewed vigour with the rise in bond prices early in 1930. The almost complete failure of new issues to respond to the favourable price-level of bonds, exhibited by curve 1 in the chart, during the first half of 1931, is significant. It is conceivable that this lack of response was in part due to the fact that the heavy flotations of the previous year had satisfied all needs for the immediate future. It seems more likely, however, that the lack of correspondence between curves 1 and 3 at this time arose from the contemporary failure of lower-grade bonds, as brought out in Chart VIII below, to keep pace with the price gains of the higher grades, thereby discouraging the flotation of new issues of the former class.

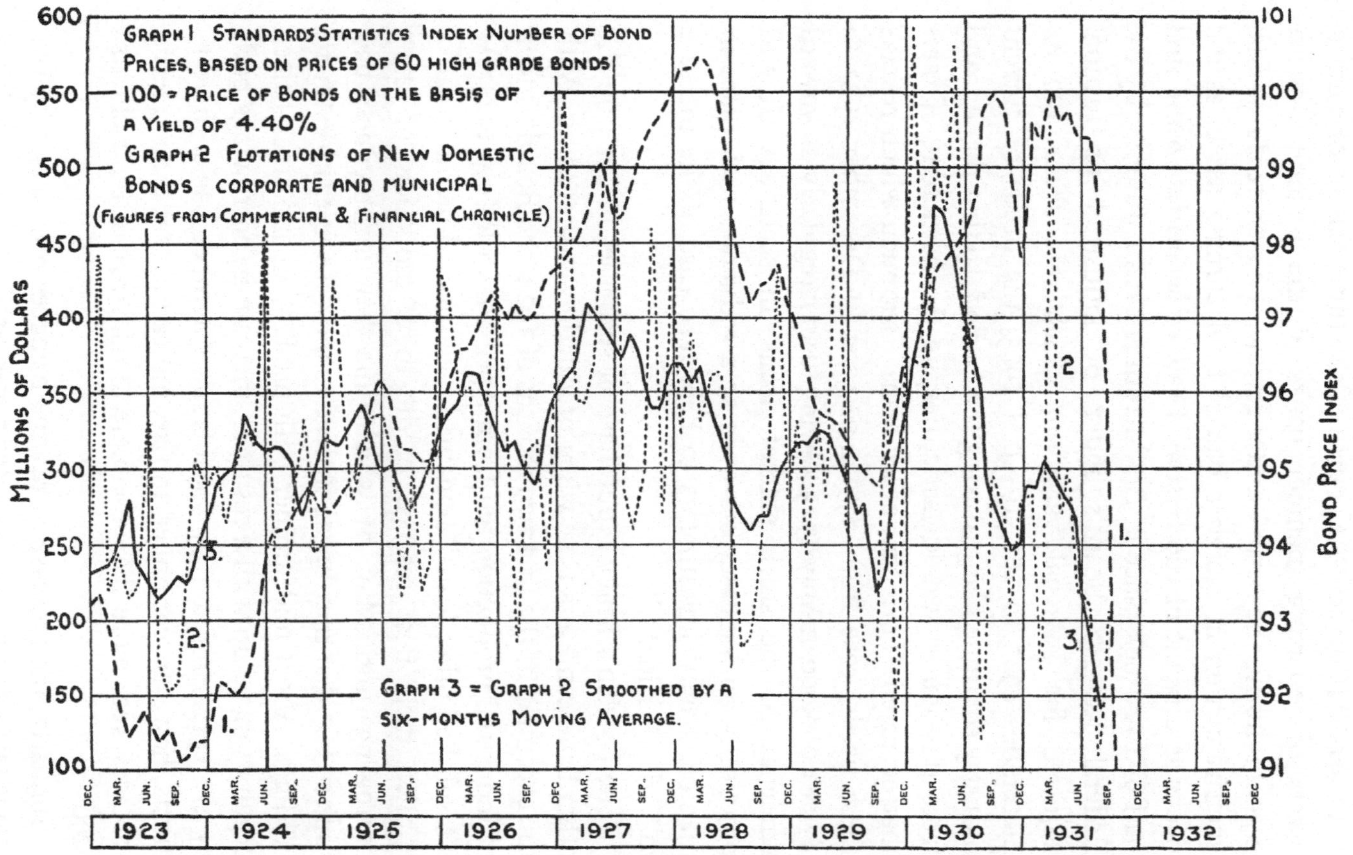

Graph 1 Standards Statistics Index Number of Bond Prices, based on prices of 60 high grade bonds
100 = Price of Bonds on the basis of a Yield of 4.40%
Graph 2 Flotations of New Domestic Bonds corporate and municipal
(Figures from Commercial & Financial Chronicle)
Graph 3 = Graph 2 Smoothed by a six-months Moving Average.
Millions of Dollars
Bond Price Index
600
550
500
450
400
350
300
250
200
150
100
101
100
99
98
97
96
95
94
93
92
91
1.
2.
3.
Dec. Mar. Jun. Sep.
1923
1924
1925
1926
1927
1928
1929
1930
1931
1932

CHART VII

Chart VIII depicts the course of the three classes of earning assets of reporting member banks of the Federal Reserve System during the period under review. This chart shows that such reduction in member banks' total earning assets as did occur as a result of the System's sale of securities in the first half of 1923 took place in the investment item. Judging by the Federal Reserve Board's index of industrial production, adjusted for seasonal variation, which rose from 100 in. December 1922 to 107 in April 1923, the needs of current industry continued large during this period, so that the demand from this source was inelastic, despite the hardening of rates that occurred. Thus "all other loans," the item which reflects these needs, rose from \$7,322,000,000 in December 1922 to \$7,781,000,000 in May 1923. Owing to an irregularly downward tendency in the stock market, loans on securities showed practically no increase, but even so a reduction took place in member banks' investments to help take care of the increase in "all other loans."

The System's heavy repurchase of securities in 1924 on the other hand came at a time when production was receding. With the exception of the first two months of 1924, the Board's index of industrial production fell from April 1923 till July 1924. As a result "all other loans" remained inelastic and member banks applied their new reserve credit to a reduction of their borrowings until May, by which time their indebtedness had sunk so low that they began instead to increase their investment holdings. About midsummer both production and stock prices began to move up with a resultant increase in borrowings both by entrepreneurs and by speculators. Member banks' investments, however, continued to rise, indicating that their reserve balances were more than adequate to take care of their clients' needs.

Similarly, the increase in reserve balances occasioned by the heavy security purchases of 1927 was used almost entirely to carry new investments and loans on securities in view of a

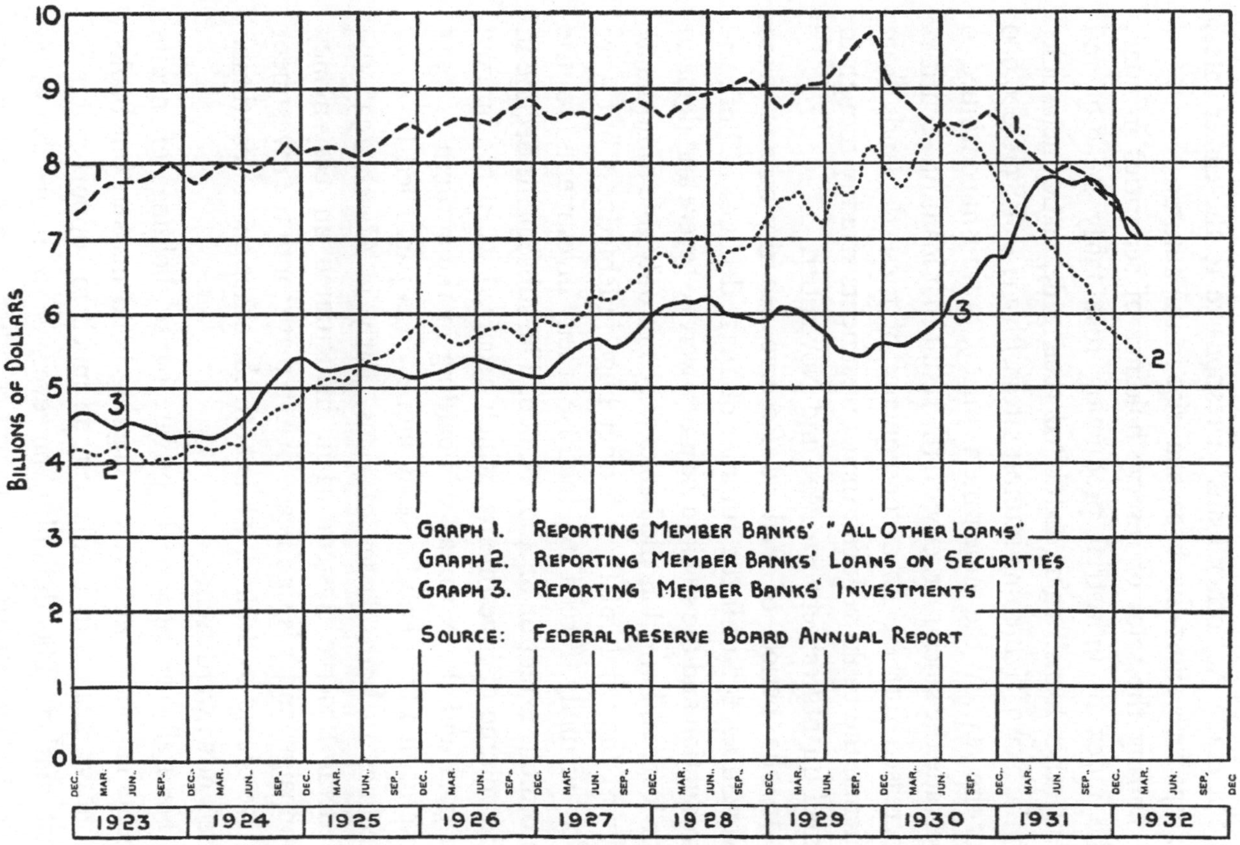
Billions of Dollars
10
9
8
7
6
5
4
3
2
1
0
1
2
3
Graph 1. Reporting Member Banks' "All Other Loans"
Graph 2. Reporting Member Banks' Loans on Securities
Graph 3. Reporting Member Banks' Investments
Source: Federal Reserve Board Annual Report
Dec. Mar. Jun. Sep.
1923
1924
1925
1926
1927
1928
1929
1930
1931
1932

CHART VIII

28-point rise over the year in the Standard Statistics index of the price of 404 common stocks. A decline in the production index made "all other loans" irresponsive to the easier rates, except for a short-lived seasonal rise in the autumn.

During the sales of reserve holdings of securities in 1928, the index of industrial production rose fairly steadily and "all other loans" again exhibited their phlegmatic inelasticity in the face of tightening interest rates with a rise of $340,000,000 for the year. At the same time a spirit of optimism continued to pervade the stock market with the result that loans on securities increased further. As a consequence of these demands from clients, the banks reduced their investments steadily though in small quantities between May and November.

In the period of Federal Reserve security-buying from November 1929 till the summer of 1931, declines in both the production and the stock price index were so severe and demand for loans so light that the banks were not only able to liquidate almost the whole of their former huge indebtedness but were also virtually forced to increase their investments to the enormous extent of $2,400,000,000. The subsequent decline in the volume of investments, which occurred when the outflow of gold and the outbreak of hoarding in the autumn of 1931 interrupted the period of easy money, was paralleled by equal declines in both classes of loans. Early in March 1932 the Federal Reserve System again inaugurated an easy-money campaign, and it is significant that in that month the investment curve ceased to decline, while both the other curves continued their downward trend.

Naturally an increase in private banks' holdings of investments cannot alone revive a flagging bond market, but banks, as heavy dealers in bonds, can do much to support prices in that market. The difficulty, however, is to induce banks to increase their portfolio of securities other than governments, which latter will already be well enough supported by the purchases of the Central Bank. In this connection the following table showing the distribution of the investments of reporting member banks of the Federal Reserve System between government securities and other securities during 1931 is interesting:

REPORTING MEMBER BANKS' HOLDINGS OF INVESTMENTS DURING 1931

(Millions of Dollars)

	Government Securities	Other Securities
January	3,163	3,603
February	3,385	3,717
March	3,638	3,749
April	3,913	3,832
May	3,957	3,865
June	4,048	3,768
July	4,121	3,677
August	4,074	3,639
September	4,154	3,641
October	4,171	3,604
November	4,072	3,506
December	4,127	3,418

This table shows that by far the larger part of the expansion in banks' holdings of investments, which took place in the first six months of the year as a result of the heavy purchases of securities made by the Reserve Banks, occurred in government securities even in face of the fact that the yield on such securities fell to a discouragingly low ebb at this time. The fall in the value of other securities held by the banks during the latter part of the year is probably due very largely to the contemporary fall in bond prices, but at least the table hardly justifies any hope that even during the early part of the year the bond market as a whole was receiving any appreciable support from the banking system. Indeed, it is not easy to expect the banks to invest on a lavish scale in so uncertain a bond market as existed throughout the latter part of 1931. Better to hold government securities at a yield of 1 per cent or less, or even to allow idle excess reserves to accumulate, than to venture into a persistently bearish bond market where holdings depreciate steadily as they lie in the portfolio.

Chart IX illustrates the comparative impotence of the Federal Reserve System to diffuse its influence on long-term interest rates at all evenly over all classes of bonds in the open market. This chart was constructed from data supplied by Standard Statistics Company of New York, and shows the fluctuations in the yields of six grades of bonds (excluding foreign securities) classified according to their security rating, approximate prices being computed by converting the average monthly yield into a $4\frac{1}{2}$ per cent bond maturing in twenty years. It will be seen that the strength of the bond market following the collapse of the stock market in the autumn of 1929 was only general during the first five months of 1930, after which it was restricted to the A classes of bonds, which include only government and municipal securities. The divergency between the movements of the A-1 bonds and the B bonds, consisting of railroads, public utilities, industrials, etc., is particularly marked during the first eight months of 1931 when the Reserve System was conducting a steady drive for easier credit conditions through its purchases of securities. Throughout this period, no class of securities outside the government class was free from the pessimistic doubts that pervaded the investing community. As Chart VIII shows, fluctuations were occurring during this period in the prices of the two lowest classes of bonds which were rendering them a semi-speculative investment, and therefore unsuited to the purposes of banks seeking an outlet for their surplus reserves. In such circumstances it is not altogether surprising that even when,, in the summer of 1931, the return on many government securities fell to the neighbourhood of 3 per cent, the unattractiveness of the rate was insufficient to drive an effective number of investors into lower-grade bonds. The latter continued on their irregularly

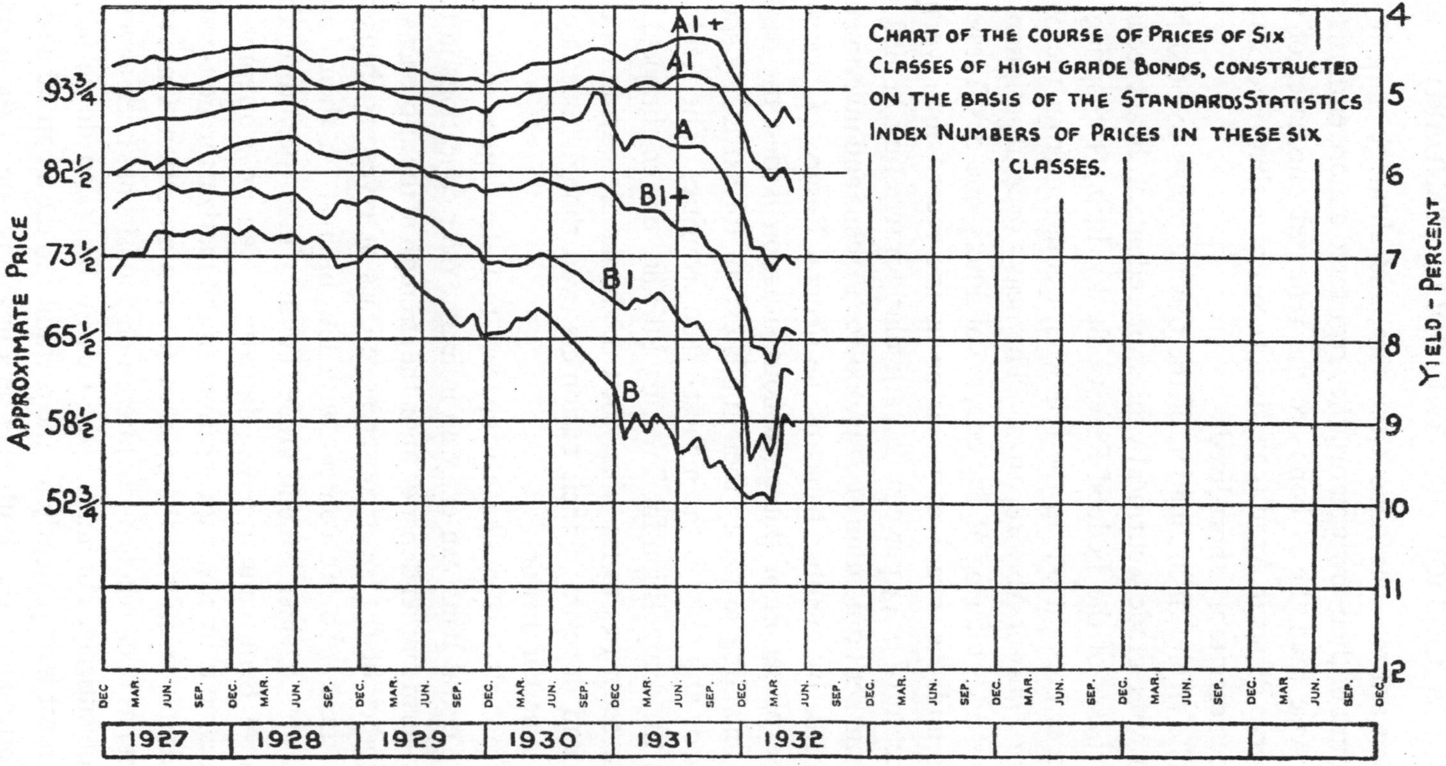
Chart of the course of Prices of Six
Classes of high grade Bonds, constructed
on the basis of the Standards Statistics
Index Numbers of Prices in these six
classes.
A1+
A1
A
B1+
B1
B
Approximate Price
93¾
82½
73½
65½
58½
52¾
Yield - Percent
4
5
6
7
8
9
10
11
12
DEC
MAR.
JUN.
SEP.
1927
1928
1929
1930
1931
1932

CHART IX

downward way throughout the year, and although, largely on account of their lowly status, they registered a more enthusiastic response than the A bonds to the renewed purchases of the Reserve Banks in April 1932, their recovery at that time proved to be regrettably short-lived.

The strong disinclination of the private banks to be driven into lower-grade securities by the unprecedentedly heavy security purchases of the Federal Reserve Banks during the spring of 1932 is brought out in the following quotation from the *New York Times* of May 18, 1932. "The heavy oversubscription to this week's offering of $75,000,000 of ninety-one-day Treasury bills and the award of the issue at the record low average discount of 0·43 per cent is particularly interesting in view of the further liquidation of $137,000,000 in loans and investments reported by member banks of the Federal Reserve. Obviously the explanation of this anomalous situation is that the banks are unwilling to tie up their funds except for extremely short periods and only in the highest-grade securities. The result is that the competition for Treasury bills has driven the yield on these securities to less than what the banks are paying on the demand deposits of their customers even though that rate is the lowest in history."

From all this evidence it appears that the degree to which the Central Bank can exert an influence over conditions in the long-term market depends upon the strength of the apprehensive prejudice of the most conservative class of investors, bankers and those who are content with low interest on their bank deposits, against second-grade bonds. This prejudice the Central Bank cannot touch directly; it can only attempt to overcome it by making conditions in the market for first-grade bonds unattractive to the point of non-remuneration. Once this point has been reached and interest on deposits has been almost, if not entirely, eliminated, the Central Bank can do no more and must wait patiently for the prejudice to die a natural death. Unfortunately, the death may be a lingering one, if the period is one of unusual depression, for then the bond market itself may become contaminated with the general decline in prices and threaten those who venture into it with such depreciation of their investments that they will be encouraged to prefer low-yield government securities or even bank deposits which yield little or no interest, but which at least do not depreciate in value. Chart VIII, however, shows that a period of such uncertainty in the bond market as supervened in 1931 is a rare occurrence, so that in less abnormal times the Central Bank may with some justification hope to be able, by means of consistent purchases of government securities, to chase a number of more adventurous investors into lower-grade bonds, thereby giving the necessary fillip to the long-term market.

§ 4. Apart from the ability of the Federal Reserve Banks to influence interest rates, however, the question also arises whether the volume of loans outstanding shows any considerable sign of responding to changes in the various interest rates. Here Chart III is again illuminating. Up to the end of 1927, this chart shows a fair inverse correspondence between the total volume of bankers' acceptances outstanding, allowance being made for the seasonal declines during the summer and increases during the autumn, and the open-market rate, the increases in volume in 1924 and 1927 synchronizing with an easing of rates in both those years, while the gentle annual declines during 1925 and 1926 coincided with firming interest rates. There, however, the correspondence ends; the years 1928 and 1929 saw an unprecedented increase in the volume of acceptances issued despite a vigorous stiffening of rates, the declines in the spring of both years being considerably less, and the rises in the autumn considerably more, than seasonal. The sweeping relaxation of rates during 1930, on the other hand, evinced no other response than a marked decline in the volume of acceptances, a decline which was rapidly accelerated during 1931 and the early part of 1932 despite the lowering of rates to a low record of seven-eighths of 1 per cent during the summer of the former, and the spring of the latter, year.

Chart V bears very similar testimony. Here allowance must be made for a "secular trend" in graph 3, the curve of the total loans of reporting member banks of the Federal Reserve System. (Monthly figures are unfortunately not available for total loans of all banks in the United States, but the figures for the reporting member banks may be taken as symptomatic.) On the supposition that production in normal times increases at the rate of 3 per cent per annum, it is reasonable to expect loans to increase at an equally steady rate. Allowing for this fact, however, it will be seen that a more than secular increase set in in the total volume of loans in May 1924 simultaneous with a noticeable fall in customers' rates. This "unsecular" increase continued throughout 1925, although rates firmed mildly during the year. Early in 1926 the rate of increase slowed down to normal and continued so until the spring of 1927, when, contemporary with a slackening of interest rates, a further marked rise occurred.

After the close of 1927, however, the inverse correspondence between the two sets of curves disappears, as in the case of the curves of Chart III. Total loans continued to increase at an unsecular rate up to the autumn of 1929 despite a very considerable rise in interest rates, while, during the remainder of the period covered, there is no visible connection between the movements of curve 3 and of the other curves.

The unavoidable conclusion is that, during the years 1928–31 inclusive, considerations other than that of the height of interest rates predominated in the minds of borrowers. The first half of this period was one of almost unprecedented prosperity when the employment of funds, whether for production or for speculation, offered promise of high and speedy returns. Such slight increases as actually occurred in rates charged for advances, even when reinforced by the bankers by such devices as the raising of the minimum sum which the borrower must always leave on deposit at the bank, were totally inadequate to deter the lenders who saw their opportunity to partake in the bountiful profits which the season afforded. We have seen how slightly the influence of the Reserve System towards raising rates was reflected in the charges for advances to customers. It is hard to imagine that the maximum rise of three-quarters of 1 per cent which occurred in rates in the twenty-seven southern and western cities between the spring of 1928 and the autumn of 1929, or of $1\frac{1}{2}$ and $1\frac{3}{4}$ per cent which occurred in the same interval in the other two classes of customers' rates, can have exercised much influence over the decisions of entrepreneurs or speculators as to whether or not to increase their borrowings if opportunities for the profitable employment of funds seemed to have presented themselves.

Similarly, during the latter half of the period, the failure of the volume of loans, except for a short seasonal upturn during the spring of 1930, to respond to the encouragement of steadily declining rates indicates that here also interest rates were playing but a minor part in the minds of borrowers. The solution, of course, is to be found in the fact that this was a period of acute depression when prices both of commodities and of securities were declining rapidly.[1] Not only was there no longer a prospect of realizing a profit through the conversion of borrowed cash into goods and securities, but losses were much more likely to ensue than not from such a process.

Thus it appears that the rate of interest, so far from being the determining factor in the volume of deposit currency outstanding, is merely one among the many factors for which borrowers allow in deciding the amount of money that they

[1] Cf. the testimony of George L. Harrison, Governor of the Federal Reserve Bank of New York, before a sub-committee of the House of Representatives Committee on Banking and Currency on April 13, 1932, that during the easy-money period of 1930–31 in the United States "we imported $600 million in gold and reduced the rediscount rate to $1\frac{1}{2}$ per cent, the lowest it has ever been, but despite all this we could not stop the force of the depression."

wish to raise. As such it is easily subordinated to other considerations. In proportion as these other considerations weigh more heavily with prospective borrowers than the question of the height of the rate of interest, the control of the Central Bank over the volume of deposit currency outstanding will be diminished.

§ 5. Chart X has been constructed to show the curves for bank deposits and prices in the United States over the period of nine years. Monthly figures for net demand deposits are available for the reporting member banks of the Federal Reserve System only, but a comparison of graphs 1 and 2 will show that these deposits move in fairly close harmony with the total volume of bank deposits in the country as the latter are revealed in the figures for the quarterly call dates. For present purposes it will therefore be more accurate to compare graph 3 with graph 1 rather than with graph 2, since the latter confuses the issue by giving no indication of the course of events between the quarterly call dates, and by failing to separate demand from time deposits.

In interpreting this chart also allowance must be made for a secular increase in the volume of deposits to correspond with the natural increase in production. When such allowance is made, there is a striking degree of correspondence between the two curves up to the year 1926. From the spring of 1923 to the spring of 1924 deposits fluctuated around the same mean level, and prices fluctuated around a 3 per cent per annum decline. The vigorous rise in deposits during the latter half of 1924 synchronized with a pronounced recovery in the price-index, which was fairly well maintained throughout 1925 under a normal increase in bank deposits. During the next eighteen months, however, the volume of bank deposits was barely maintained without a secular increase and prices steadily declined. On the question of the correctness of the orthodox theory, it is worth while to notice that in this interval a decline

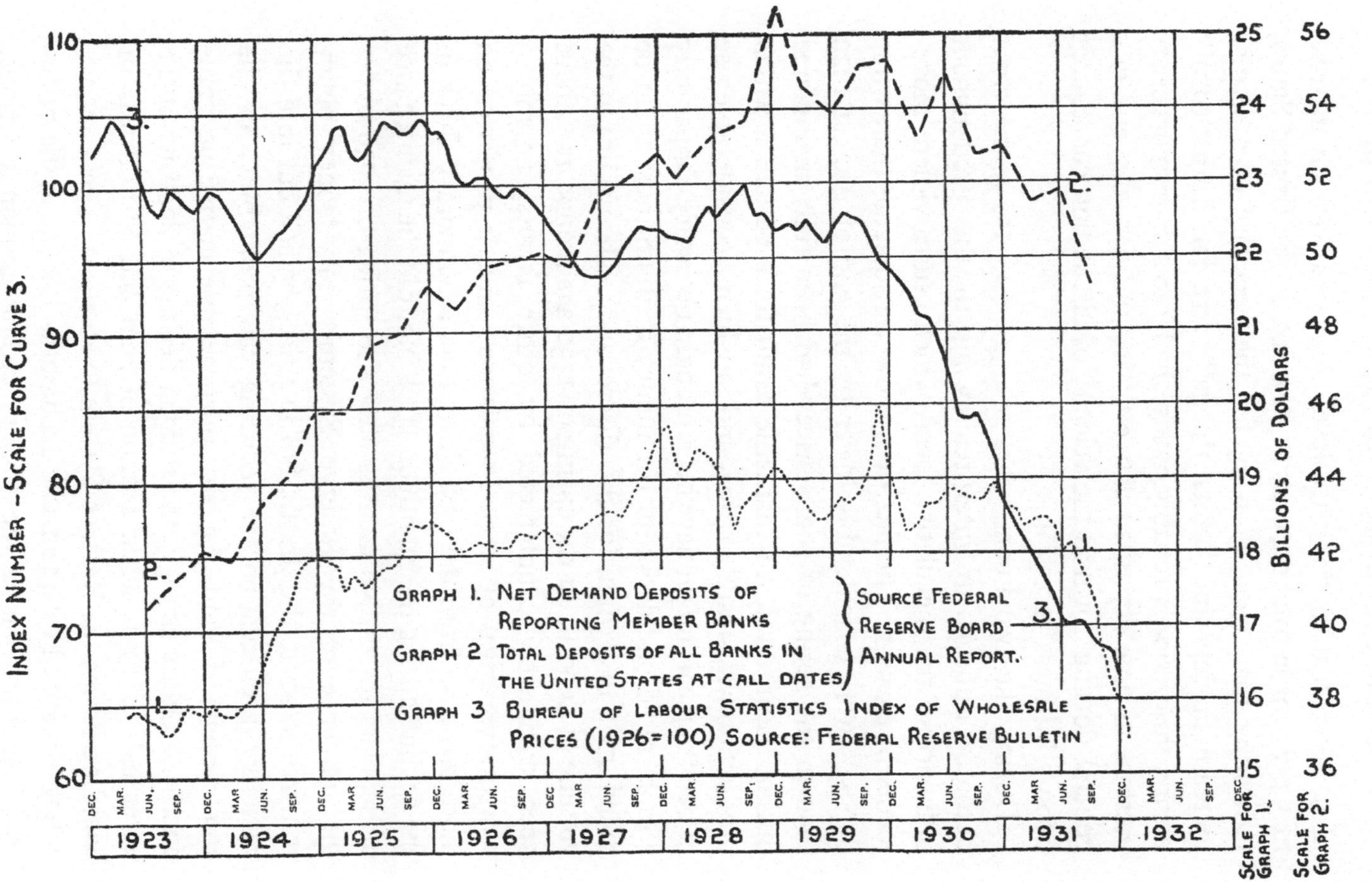

Index Number - Scale for Curve 3.
Billions of Dollars
Scale for Graph 1.
Scale for Graph 2.
Graph 1. Net Demand Deposits of Reporting Member Banks
Graph 2 Total Deposits of all Banks in the United States at call dates
Source Federal Reserve Board Annual Report.
Graph 3 Bureau of Labour Statistics Index of Wholesale Prices (1926=100) Source: Federal Reserve Bulletin
1923
1924
1925
1926
1927
1928
1929
1930
1931
1932

of 9·5 per cent in the price-level coincided with an increase of 5 per cent in total deposits of all banks in the United States, indicating that, even allowing for the necessity of a secular increase in deposits, "other things" were far from "equal" during this period, probably owing chiefly to a disproportionate increase in time deposits relative to demand deposits, and to a general slowing down in the velocity of circulation consequent upon a business recession.

During the two boom years of 1928 and 1929, the chart becomes difficult to interpret owing to the predominant influence of the speculative fever, which causes violent movements in curve 1. The fact does, however, emerge that, while deposits were considerably lower by the end of August 1929 than in the spring of 1928, prices had been fully maintained during the interval, a remarkable result for a period in which production was steadily rising, and in which a considerable rise in bank deposits might have been thought necessary. Apparently a more rapid circulation of the money medium must again be relied upon to account for this discrepancy. The upturn in the volume of deposits in the spring of 1930 again appears to have been completely counteracted by other factors, notably a temporary revival of stock speculation, since it produced no more response from the price-level than a temporary check in the decline during the month of April. Nor did the maintenance of deposits for twelve months after the spring of 1930 under the influence of the Reserve System's easy-money policy contrive to abate the drastic fall in prices, which cut into the velocity of circulation by reducing the profitability of the employment of funds for any purpose, speculative or "productive." Oddly enough, the sudden decline in deposits in the latter half of 1931, when a drain of gold and an outbreak of hoarding forced the Reserve System to abandon its easy-money policy, coincided with a smaller six months' decline in the price-level than during any of the three preceding six-month periods.

Unfortunately the chart cannot throw any light upon the

chronological order in which an increase or decrease in prices and an *ad hoc* increase or decrease in deposits take place.[1] Even if the former preceded the latter, the interval between the two would be too short for the phenomenon to show itself even in a graph constructed on the basis of monthly figures. Contracts entered into at a price above the existing price-level bring into existence the requisite volume of new currency at the time of their settlement, and, when business is good, settlements are likely to follow contracts by a comparatively short interval.

Perhaps the only safe moral to be drawn from the evidence of the chart is that, while over long periods movements in the price-level tend to correspond with movements in the total volume of deposit currency[2] outstanding, allowance being made for a secular increase to take care of increased production, over short periods other factors are capable of completely upsetting the relationship; and that in all cases it is unsafe to dogmatize as to which of the two movements precedes or causes the other.

It should be noted that the index from which curve 3 was constructed is, like the majority of usable index-numbers, computed from the prices of certain selected commodities at wholesale. Apart from the impossibility of ascertaining what is the course of retail prices in various parts of the country at any one time, such an index also omits the prices of stock market securities. Yet movements in stock prices are apt both to cause and to absorb increases or decreases in the volume of net demand deposits. To the extent to which they do so, movements will occur in the latter which naturally have no counterpart in the price-level of commodities at wholesale.

[1] Cf. chapter ii, § 3.

[2] In countries where the banking system is less developed greater emphasis must, of course, be placed upon the volume of notes and coin in circulation than in the case of the United States or Great Britain where deposit currency constitutes an easy preponderance of the total supply of "cash."

§ 6. The foregoing statistical examination of the experience of the United States in their attempt at currency management during the last decade would appear to justify the conclusion stated in chapter vi that the ability of the Central Bank to govern the domestic value of its own currency unit is limited. It may, of course, be objected that the technique of monetary management was only in an experimental stage during this period. Both in this appendix and in chapter vi, however, we have seen reasons why the power of even an experienced managing authority to attain internal stability is bound to be incomplete. The rigidity of customers' interest rates, the unwillingness of investors to enter the lower-grade bond market in times of business uncertainty (or to leave it when prospects are good), the reluctance of entrepreneurs and speculators to increase their borrowings when prices are falling (or to decrease them in periods of inflation), and the interference of other forces with the relationship between the volume of currency outstanding and the price-level, all these are factors over which the central institution can, with the ripest experience and the fullest information possible, at best only exercise a somewhat mild influence. Until means of combating these factors are added to the armoury of Central Banks, internal stability must represent an ideal to be aimed at rather than an attainable goal.

Index

A B C of the Federal Reserve System, E. W. Kemmerer's, quoted 41 *n.*
acceptance rate, bankers' 87, 237
America Weighs her Gold, J. H. Rogers', quoted 65, 75 *n.*, 105, 106, 107, 110, 120, 121
Argentina 99, 130
"aureal," the 219, 220, 227–8, 233
Austria 87, 88, 130, 131, 169
Austrian Reconstruction Loan 230
automatic self-regulation in the distribution of gold 19, 23, 29, 30, 45, 52, 54, 63, 65, 66, 70, 136, 184, 189

balance of trade (1923–29), International Classification of 115, 117, 119
balance sheets, principle of national 120
bank credit 18, 20, 34, 37, 44, 56, 57, 155, 156, 158
bank deposits 20, 34, 35, 37 *et seq.*, 48, 54, 153, 173, 198, 262–5
bank failures 91–3
Bank for International Settlements 168, 169, 171, 215, 221, 230
Bank for International Settlements, P. Einzig's 215
Bank of England 20 *n.*, 60 *n.*, 76, 96, 99, 181, 182
Bank of France 95, 97, 100, 101, 102, 179, 182, 228
Bank of the Netherlands 102
Bank rate 20–3, 59, 60, 61, 62, 70, 75, 76, 82, 90, 143, 144, 147, 185, 189
banking system and currency-control 189
banks, English 37, 38
banks of issue, task of the 157
barter 13, 16, 209
Belgium 101, 102, 129, 133, 183, 206
bimetallism 13
Bolivia 130, 131
bond market, private banks and the 248–50
bond market, the 249, 250, 254, 256, 258, 259, 266
borrowers, classes of 151
Bradbury, Lord 125 *n.*
Brazil 99, 126, 130
British imports and exports of gold, 1904–13 77, 78
Bulgaria 130

call-loan rate 237
Cannon, William C. 88
capital, definition of 73
capital, international movement of 78, 82
capital, short-term and long-term, distinction between 83
Central Banks 20–3, 31, 33, 37, 49–52, 54 *et seq.*, 74, 82, 95, 97, 98, 100–3, 125, 136, 137–40, 142 *et seq.*, 151 *et seq.*, 157, 159, 163, 165, 166, 169 *et seq.*, 176, 180, 181–4, 189, 198 *et seq.*, 213 *et seq.*, 235, 243, 258, 266
Chamberlain, Mr. Neville, quoted 97
Cheques 22, 34, 40, 55, 59, 173

Chile 130
Columbia 130
commercial bills 155 *n.*
commercial paper rate 237, 241
Commission on Finance and Industry, British 53
commodity trade balance 121, 122, 125, 126, 128, 133
confidence, international lack of 82, 86, 91, 128
Costa Rica 130
credit cycles 157, 158, 224, 226
credit of governments 109
credit policy 58, 161, 185, 223
currency 16, 17, 54, 66, 70, 123, 136, 137, 156, 163, 183
currency, "flights from" 176, 195
currency, hoarding of 31 *n.*, 33, 91, 92–5, 97, 152, 153
currency, non-metallic 164, 165
currency notes 31, 33, 53, 55, 56, 70, 178
currency, ratio of to gold holdings 15, 31, 36
currency, regulation of, 23, 54, 66, 68, 141, 143, 161, 164
customers' loans 241–6, 261
customers' loan rate 145
Czechslovakia 130

debtor nations, ways of meeting their liabilities 121–4, 133–5
default 109, 112, 122, 137
defaults, international 82
deflation 23, 24, 25, 64, 65, 138, 163, 186
Denmark 130
Dennis, Mr. Lawrence 111
deposit currency 34, 35, 38, 41, 44, 45, 46, 47, 48, 49, 53, 59, 60, 61, 70, 151, 152, 173, 265
deposit currency, relation of to money in circulation 35, 152
deposits *ex nihilo* 44, 45, 48, 49
disequilibrium in bank balances 63, 64, 72, 199
dollar, the 14, 102, 201
dumping 127
Dutch East Indies 130

Economic Committee of the League of Nations 127
Economics of the Gold Standard, D. T. Jacks, quoted 17 *n.*
economics, the task of 29
England and the New Gold Standard, W. A. Brown's 199
Esthonia 130
exchange, stabilization of rates of 14
exchange values 13, 24 *n.*
export trade balances (1923–30)—
  France 118–19
  Great Britain 116–18
  United States 113–16

Fall of Prices, The, J. A. Todd's, quoted 74 *n.*, 96 *n.*
Federal Reserve Bulletin 243, 245
Federal Reserve System, the 22 *n.*, 38, 39, 41, 58, 90, 98, 102, 142, 161, 178, 186–8, 235 *et seq.*, 252, 254, 256, 261, 264
flotations 250
foodstuffs exports, American 113, 114, 115
foreign bonds 109, 121
foreign exchange 57, 58, 70, 72, 85, 123, 126, 141, 184, 209
foreign exchanges, governmental control of 128, 129, 130–2
foreign tourists as an aid to debtor countries 121 *n.*
forward exchange quotations 160

France 84, 85, 95, 97, 99, 100, 101, 112, 118–19, 122, 123, 124, 129, 153, 157, 174, 177, 179, 206
franc, the 14, 201
"free reserves" of banks 41, 43, 44
free-trade 112, 122, 207, 208

Germany 86, 87, 88, 106, 108, 130, 209
Glass-Steagall Act, The 175
gold as a balancing factor 121, 125
gold, bankers' hold of 18
gold bullion standard 180, 182
gold coin and certificates in circulation in U.S.A and France 178, 179, 180
Gold, Credit, and Employment, G. D. H. Cole's, quoted 28 *n.*, 74 *n.*, 138
Gold Delegation of the Financial Committee of the League of Nations 62
gold, demand and supply of 33, 48
gold, disappearance of from circulation 30, 53, 57
gold, distribution of 16, 17, 19, 24, 30, 52, 124
gold, economizing of 178, 181, 182, 183, 216
gold, efflux of 50, 52, 54, 57, 63, 69, 70, 75, 96, 142, 156
gold exchange standard 100, 103, 182, 183
gold, export of 123–4
gold holdings, national 16, 77, 124, 173
gold, influx of 49, 50, 52, 53, 54, 63, 64, 65, 67, 70, 75, 156, 179
gold, maldistribution of 24, 30, 72, 80, 125, 137, 138, 140, 172, 183, 189
gold movements, policy of stabilizing 63, 64, 72, 74, 80
gold production 15, 139, 172, 183
gold reserves 20, 21, 23, 24, 26–7, 30, 31, 173, 174, 175–9, 216–17
gold, "rise in the value " of 17
gold, shipment of 199, 200
gold standard—
  and the Bank rate 21
  as an agent of international price-stability 17, 103, 164, 180 *n.*, 201
  basis of 74 *n.*
  changes in its working 12, 31, 166
  essence of an international 129, 185
  historic reasons for 13, 99
  maintenance of a nominal 126
  objects and advantages of 15, 23, 73, 140, 165, 201
  revolution against 137, 140, 141, 159, 164
  suspension of in Great Britain and in the United States 24, 78, 82, 90, 91, 96, 102, 126, 182, 206
gold standard, international 14, 66, 69
gold, sterilization of 139, 179, 186
gold stocks of the United States 1923–32 26, 78
gold, true use of 180 *n.*
gold-losing countries 64, 65, 67, 99, 126
"gold-points" 199–204, 217, 218
Gold Points and Central Banks, P. Einzig's 200

Gold Production and Future Prices, H. H. Brace's, quoted 33 *n.*
gold-receiving countries 63, 65, 99
Gold Standard and its Future, The, T. E. Gregory's, quoted 14 *n.*, 69–70
gold-standard countries 14, 30, 33, 73
Gold Standard in Theory and Practice, The, R. G. Hawtrey's, quoted 33 *n.*, 54 *n.*, 143, 184
Goldsborough bill 186
government and private enterprice, the 190
Great Britain 24, 32, 34, 35, 37, 53, 75–8, 84, 107, 112, 116–18, 122, 123, 126, 159, 174, 180, 206
Great War, fluctuations in balance of payments during the 76
Greece 130, 131
Guatemala 129, 130

Hall, Dr. Ray O. 121
Hawtrey, R. G. 149, quoted 150 *n.*, 151–2
hoarding 31 *n.*, 33, 78, 80, 91–5, 97, 142, 153, 180 *n.*, 181
Holland 101, 102, 129, 133, 183, 206
Hungary 130

import balance of the United States 114
imports, British 118
index number of world prices 221
inflation 23, 25, 64, 68, 126, 138, 157, 186, 187, 224
Influence of Gold Supply on Prices and Profits, Sir D. Barbour's, quoted 18 *n.*
interest rates 143 *et seq.*, 184, 185, 237–41
Interest Rates and the Business Cycle, Carl Snyder's, quoted 241
International Commodity Clearing Company 209
international co-operation in finance 169–71, 176, 183–5, 188, 195, 208
International Gold Movements, P. Einzig's, quoted 98 *n.*, 100 *n.*
International Gold Problem, The, R. G. Hawtrey's, quoted 227
international lending, disequilibrium in 79, 80, 229
international post-War indebtedness 104 *et seq.*, 134
International Price-Level Adjustments, L. J. A. Trip's, quoted 67

Japan 132
Jones, Mr. Grosvenor 129

Keynes, J. M. 72, 79 *n.*
Kitchin, Mr. 172

Latvia 130
League of Nations 127, 168
legal minima of gold reserves 176–8, 198
legal tender money 56
Lithuania 130
loans, bank 241 *et seq.*
London money market, pre-War conditions of operation 76
long-term and short-term capital 83 *et seq.*, 94, 96
long-term and short-term loans 148–9
long-term foreign investments, America's 105, 106

McGarrah, Mr. Gates 169
McKenna, Rt. Hon. R., quoted 76
Macmillan Report 53, 56 *n.*, 84, 85 *n.*, 125 *n.*, 169, 174, 197, 222
mark, the 14
merchants 149, 150
Mexico 130
monetary policy during the War 66
Money and Banking, W.A. Scott's, quoted 33 *n.*, 46 *n.*
money markets 19, 21, 73
money, price of 73
money, territorial distribution of 18 *n.*
money, the velocity of circulation of 152, 153, 154, 156
Money, Trade and Industry, F. A. Walker's, quoted 18 *n.*

National Industrial Conference Board of the United States 133
Nicaragua 130
non-commercial international transactions 98–9, 100–3
non-economic phenomena in international finance 78, 79
Norway 130
note issues 30, 31, 33, 56, 173, 174, 196
open-market, Central Bank dealings in the 21, 22, 52, 59, 60, 61, 62, 63, 64, 70, 75, 136, 143, 155, 191, 239
open-market rates 21, 237, 239, 241

paper-money 30, 178
paper standard, advantage of a 201
parity of foreign exchanges 14 *n.*
Peru 111–12, 129, 130, 131
Poland 99, 129
Portugal 130
Post-War Monetary Stabilization, Gustav Cassel's, quoted 66, 162, 170
post-War reconstruction 81, 107
pound sterling, the 14, 90
pre-War and post-War loans compared 105, 108, 112, 134
price-rise, causes of 68
private banks 21, 22, 45, 49, 50, 51, 52, 55, 56, 59, 61, 181, 196–8
protection 112, 122, 124
"prudence figure" 49, 50, 60
Purchasing Power of Money, Irving Fisher's, quoted 15 *n.*, 46*n.*
price-index number 161–3
price-level, the 34, 45, 46, 47, 55, 62, 67, 68, 69, 71, 154, 156, 157, 158, 162
price changes 159
Problem of Maintaining Purchasing Power, P. W. Martin's, quoted 191
public works 190 *et seq.*

rediscounting, 39, 40, 41, 44, 59, 94
"reflation" 186, 187
Reichsbank, the 89 *n.*, 228, 229
reparations 205, 210–12, 215
repatriation of balances 102
reserve balances of private banks 49, 55, 59, 61, 70, 91, 94, 181, 196–7, 213–14
Reserve Banks 39–43, 59, 92–4, 142, 186, 235 *et seq.*
"reserve ratio," banking 37, 38, 39 *et seq.*, 48, 51, 57, 60, 61, 64, 196, 198
Ricardo 16
Rist, Charles 157
Rogers, Prof. J. H. 5

Roosevelt, President 179 *n.*
Roumania 130
Rueff, M. Jacques 62, quoted 153 *n.*, 154 *n.*
Russia 87 *n.*

"sheltered" commodities 67, 68
short-term credits 120–1, 247
silver 14, 16
Snyder, Mr. Carl 243
Some Problems of International Banking Policy, Dr. M. Palyi's, quoted 74 *n.*, 75 *n.*
South Africa, Union of 129, 130
South American republics, reckless finance by, 110–11
Spain 130
special transactions in gold-movement 99, 100
speculation, money market 78
speculation of 1928–29, American Stock Market 79
Sprague, O. M. W., quoted 161 *n.*, 162 *n.*
stability, price 62, 63, 64
state control of foreign trade 209
Strakosch, Sir Henry 139
Strong, Governor 58
Sweden 130, 133
Switzerland 27, 129, 133, 183, 206

tariffs 108, 123, 124, 125, 127, 129, 137, 184, 189, 205–8, 212
till-money 181, 182, 196, 198
trade unionism 69
transfer problem 81, 84
Treatise on Money, J. M. Keynes', quoted 47 *n.*, 176 *n.*
Trip, L. J. A., quoted 141, 157
Turkey 132

United States 24, 34, 35, 36, 38, 53, 58, 62, 78, 79, 90, 91, 105–7, 112, 113 *et seq.*, 122, 129, 133, 141, 164, 174, 178, 179, 183, 187, 206, 230, 235, 266
unproductive intergovernmental debts 106
"unsheltered" industries 67, 68, 69
Uruguay 130

Wages 69
War debts 104 *et seq.*, 205, 210–12
Whitaker, A. C. 61 *n.*
Who Buys Foreign Bonds? D. W. Morrow's 109
Wiggin, A. H., quoted 125
Working of the Gold Standard under Present Conditions, O. M. W. Sprague's, quoted 165–6
World Central Bank 213 *et seq.*
World Central Bank, Summary of the advantages of a 232
World Economic Conference of 1933 170, 208
world trade, fall in value of 132–3
World-unemployment and its Problems, Karl Pribram's, quoted 86

Yugo-Slavia 130